Vector

Rob Swigart

ST. MARTIN'S PRESS/NEW YORK

VECTOR

Published by arrangement with Bluejay Books

ISBN: 0-312-90453-3 Can. ISBN: 0-312-90454-1

Printed in the United States of America

First St. Martin's Press mass market edition/January 1988

10 9 8 7 6 5 4 3 2 1

RED BLOOD IN BLUE HAWAII

Renfrew pulled back and waited. It was only a matter of time. He watched the cloud formations moving in the sky. He could hear the white water of the rapids downstream, the faint hiss of moisture moving on the stems and leaves of the grasses beside him. He was listening for something else. Finally he heard it. The girl was screaming. Very leisurely Renfrew moved down the trail until he could see the couple.

The male subject was sprawled in the rapids. His feet and arms were twitching randomly on the rocks; blood began to stain the water as the rock cut his ankles and feet. The girl was still screaming, her hands over the mouth. Renfrew could barely make out her words above the white water whipping over the boy's body.

"What is it?" she was screaming. "What is it? What is It?"

The boy's eyes had rolled back into his head, his mouth had fallen open, and he appeared to be trying to swallow. It was just like the old woman. Renfrew made a note of that in his pocket recorder. The girl had carried the poison or whatever it was. The pair had made love. The boy had died.

Mission accomplished.

Other books by Rob Swigart

LITTLE AMERICA
STILL LIVES (poems)
A.K.A./A Cosmic Fable
THE TIME TRIP
THE BOOK OF REVELATIONS

To Patrick Bavoil and Wayne Johnson—thanks...

The bell of the Gion Temple tolls into every man's heart to warn him that all is vanity and evanescence. The faded flowers of the sala trees by the Buddha's deathbed bear witness to the truth that all who flourish are destined to decay. Yes, pride must have its fall, for it is as unsubstantial as a dream on a spring night. The brave and violent man—he too must die away in the end, like a whirl of dust in the wind.

—TALES OF THE HEIKE

Part I

PARADISE

1

Cobb Takamura ignored the light rain-hiss on the sagging metal roof of the porch. The drops sliding down the corrugated grooves were dark with rust when they fell on his porkpie hat. He absently wiped the brim with a delicate forefinger, then looked at the red stain with a bemused smile. The falling drops obscured his view of the body seated in the doorway.

It might have been the cheerful smile on the body's face that kept anyone from noticing that rigor had set in long before. A greeting hello-how-are-you smile, nice-day-today-eh?

Now, though, with the steady dripping from the rusted roof, the low gray clouds overhead trailing veils of light rain, with the sibilance of moisture caressing banana leaves, the flat green light of early afternoon, the slick mud of the road that twisted through these urgent volcanic foothills and with the swift gurgle of the river nearby, the smile seemed less authentic.

In fact, Takamura observed, it was not a smile at all, but death rictus, and it spoke not how-are-you? but good-bye agony. He sighed heavily. This was a quiet island. He hoped this wasn't a homicide. It was only February; a homicide would double his statistical averages for this time of year.

The wooden porch creaked under his weight. Takamura was not a big man, but the porch was rotten, the shack a one-room affair with gaps in the boards. An abandoned kitchen sink was tilted in the red dirt under a drain spout beside the porch; a ragged hole had apparently been kicked through the wall to give the inhabitant access to the water in the sink, water which at the moment quivered darkly with mosquito larvae. He crouched down to look through the hole in the wall at the interior, but the light was dim and the chaos within total. He turned back to the body.

Male. Age unknown. Ethnic origins unknown, though apparently mixed. Like the house, the grin had several gaps. Cause of death: unknown.

"Sammy!"

Sammy Akeakamai, leaning against the faded yellow Toyota skewed at the end of the dirt road, took the toothpick from his mouth and looked up. "Yeh?"

Takamura gestured for him to come up. Sammy threw his toothpick into the wild lantanas and threw himself into his half-speed waddle. He was overweight. Too much poi in his diet; he liked to claim he was on a high-starch, low-protein diet designed by his ancient kahuna ancestors to promote mystical powers. For this reason, among others, Takamura often referred to him as The Kukui Nut.

"Whadda you think?" Takamura asked, pointing at the body.

The body's face had a coppery color that gave it the tanned look of robust good health. From a distance. One skinny arm was draped across the casually crossed knees, palm up, exposing the inside of the elbow.

"Tracks," Sammy grunted. He hunkered down on his heels. His pudgy forefinger touched the needle marks. The flesh was like wood.

"Mmm," Takamura murmured. "Know him?"

Sammy shook his head; his jowls rolled back and forth. "Lotta boys up here in the woods. Don't see 'em downtown much. Some of them never, maybe. Think you know everyone, then somebody's relative turns up somewhere, down from the mountain where they been living on taro and bananas and mangoes." He shrugged, a lugubrious gesture. "Or tourist, maybe."

"Maybe." Takamura looked doubtful. He uncoiled to his feet and stepped inside over the body.

The odor rocked him for a moment. It shouldn't smell this bad, not with all those gaps in the walls, the hole for the sink, the rain. This was the wettest February in years. Hot, too. He leaned back to breathe, then plunged in.

The hut said bare survival. It said below the poverty line. It said indifference and (he was quite sure from the smell) terminal despair. He glanced back down at the Toyota. The end of the road. The body had quite possibly put this place together itself. Very little skill was in evidence.

"Starvation. Disease. Overdose." Takamura ticked off items on his list in a quiet voice. "Homicide. Maybe." The body had lived here for some time. If you could call it living. There were no toilet facilities per se. "Per se," Takamura said aloud. "Per se."

"What's that?" Sammy called, still hunkered by the body. He was watching the grin. A fly explored it, moving from the teeth to the upper lip when it came to a gap. The fly moved away from the grin, crossed the fleshy part of the nose and cautiously approached the corner of one open eye. Wrinkles of good humor radiated away from the eye, and the fly paused there to probe some gummy fluid.

"Per se," Takamura said, a little louder. "No toilet per se. He used the floor."

"Oh." The fly was cleaning its legs.

Takamura appeared in the door again, trim in his flower-printed shirt and tightly creased tan slacks. His watch had a black plastic strap, his smoke-tinted glasses had a black nylon cord that looped around his neck. He shrugged eloquently. "No help," he said. "No I.D., nothing." His mouth twitched in disgust. "No paper at all in there." He flicked his hand at the body. "Nothing on him either, uh?"

The Kukui Nut shook his head and grinned. "Paper no last long in tropics, bwana sahib."

Takamura smiled. "Give 'em a call, Gunga Din. Tell Kim to bring the pickup. I don't think this stiff is going to ride into town lying down. To quote the great detective—"

"Charlie Chan," Akeakamai interrupted.

"Charlie Chan," Takamura agreed. "'Man who flirt with dynamite sometimes fly with angels.'"

"What the hell is that supposed to mean?" Sammy wanted to know.

Takamura made a gesture with his hand, and the fly buzzed off. The rain had stopped. A mourning gecko the color and texture of bark crouched beside the tilted sink; it casually flicked its tongue and the fly was gone. The lizard winked slowly at him.

Takamura winked back.

2

The rain clouds had blown away by the time Rake Wyman finished loading his gear. He scratched the gray stubble on his chin and squinted into the sun for a moment. Pete Williams tossed the mesh bag containing Rake's speargun and knife into the boat.

"Bring back a big one," Pete said without conviction. Rake never brought anything back. He was a nut who liked to dive alone, and someday he wouldn't come back at all.

Rake answered with a grunt. The exchange was a long habit to which he paid no attention. "Gonna be hot," he said. He always said that too. The temperature never varied more than ten degrees from winter to summer. Not here in the Waiakale harbor on the south side of the island. And the water temperature never varied anywhere.

"Yeah," Pete agreed. "Hot."

Rake started the outboard with a roar and carved a wake around the breakwater of Hanalolo to the west. He was right about one thing: it was going to be hotter on the west side where it almost never rained and the sun glared off the water. In half an hour Rake was opposite the Navy's Pacific Missile Approach Network Facility. The waters were restricted here, but Rake had never paid much attention to arbitrary boundaries. He gave PACMAN (some wag in Naval Operations had thought that one up) the finger, certain that although no one was visible on shore, he was well registered on radar or sonar or infrared or some such. Maybe satellites, for that matter.

He was right, of course. Lt. J.G. Spencer Collins was watching Rake's boat through his binoculars, momentarily undecided whether to send out the patrol boat to wave Rake Wyman away, or merely to log the passage. There were no tests scheduled today, so he decided to log the incident. It was roughly the twentieth time in the past three months that Rake had challenged him with his middle finger. Lt. J.G. Spencer Collins knew who Rake Wyman was. His predecessor had warned him of Rake's habit—the other dive boats always observed the restricted limit.

Rake laughed as his boat moved north of the boundary and he picked up speed toward The Slip. It was almost noon.

Lieutenant Collins entered Rake's passage in the computer log, noting only that nothing was happening aside from a research dive that had left several hours before. Lieutenant Collins went back to his missile-attack simulation. At the moment a massive flight of Soviet Backfire bombers was sweeping across the Bering Sea and he was monitoring a three-pronged response of Bl-fired Cruise air-to-air missiles the computer had provided him along with satellite-tracking cluster-spray mobile-launched SAMs from a remote army base north of Anchorage, and his own sub-launched radar-frequency seek-and-destroy anti-intruder Ferret missiles. Most of this defensive hardware existed only in the computer's memory and the imagination of Naval programmers in San Diego, not in the real world. It was considered good training, though, and Collins was going for a Facility record score, so it was with considerable dismay that he watched the Soviet Backfires destroy his Alaskan base, electronically derange the Ferrets and dodge most of the Cruise missiles, which were, of course, very slow.

Lieutenant Collins was watching most of the Pacific Northwest vanish under a nuclear barrage when Rake dropped anchor over The Slip, a ragged tumble of rock and coral left over from the eruption of Wai'ale'ale some four million years before.

Despite the gentle swaying of his Zodiac as it rode the swells, Rake managed a sizable toot for clear-headed appreciation of the deep aquamarine, wiped the white powder from his nose with the back of his hand and licked it off. His tongue flashed numb as his nose and he was ready.

He screwed down the regulator, opened the valve and sucked once. It worked fine. Habit told him just the right amount of air to let into his buoyancy compensator. He spit in his mask, swirled it in the ocean and slipped it on. He stuck the second stage in his mouth and tipped himself overboard.

He drifted casually along the rock wall. He'd been out here too many times. The Slip was a favored dive location, and he expected to find half a dozen groups of tourists poking through the reef, gawking at the fish, but there was no one around. No one.

He floated to a halt before a hole in the rock wall. A moray pulled back slightly, wicked mouth agape. Rake poked his spear at the eel and shook his head. He could almost imagine the ugly creature hissing at him.

He checked his depth gauge. Sixty-five feet. Plenty of time.

He *knew* the *Valiant* was down here. He felt it in his bones, his gut. The Navy wouldn't admit it, or it didn't know, but he had traced the ship to this location years before, yet no one had ever found it. Perhaps only Rake Wyman knew it was here. Perhaps.

This was why he preferred to dive alone. The *Valiant* had been carrying platinum bars when the kamikaze got it off Kauai in 1943. Rake wanted that cargo. He'd been looking for it for almost twenty years, and he believed fervently that it was just within his grasp now.

Clouds of sergeant majors scattered around him. A silver school of bonitas paralleled his course for a time, then vanished over a ridge.

He could no longer see the bottom, for the relatively level area on the north side of The Slip dropped in vast steps to an abyss nearly three miles deep. Rake prayed the ship had not gone down much farther north where it would be out of his reach, but three weeks before he'd found the propeller. It was heavily calcified, and a bitch to get up and into the boat. Now, though, it sat in the garage behind his shack in Wailanai covered with burlap.

He had found it at 134 feet.

He raised his auto-inflation hose and vented some air out of his BC. As he began to drift downward, he flipped over and swam toward the dark. The rock and coral wall shimmered beside him. He ignored it. What he wanted was down below somewhere. He entered a narrow sloping defile; at the end he looked down. A long, vaguely regular shape was outlined in the silt below, and elation rose in him. The *Valiant*! It had to be.

He hovered for a moment, wondering whether he was imagining the shape; whether this really was a regular shape. It could be just a ridge of volcanic rock softened by currents. He checked his depth gauge, noted he was at 145 feet, and was about to tip down to the ship when he sensed a presence behind him. As he twisted a half-turn in the narrow defile to look, his air stopped flowing. He sucked hard on the regulator, certain at first he had merely run out of his main tank and needed to pull reserve. He reached behind him as soon as it hit him that, pull as he might, no air was coming through. The reserve valve moved easily, but still the air did not come. Then he felt a touch on his shoulder.

Rake's eyes were wide behind his mask when he saw a muscular Navy diver beside him. For a moment he thought the frogman was going to kill him for crossing the restricted zone, but then he saw with a flood of relief that the man was offering him a regulator from his second tank.

Rake dropped his own regulator, seized the proffered one, purged and breathed. Air flooded into his lungs. Gratitude flowed into him with the air and he nodded his thanks.

The diver circled thumb and forefinger and pointed at him. You okay?

Rake gave his okay sign. The other diver reached over

and took Rake's dangling regulator, unkinked the line and purged it. Bubbles burst from it.

Rake nodded. His line had gotten twisted. He didn't notice the second diver drifting away around the edge of a sharp scarf of the rock wall, a pair of heavy-duty clamps in his hand.

The first diver, who looked like a body-builder, nodded. He handed Rake's regulator back and swam off with easy, powerful kicks. Rake went back onto his own air and backed out of the shallow crevasse. It wasn't until he had come to a halt above the boat shape on the bottom that the funny feeling hit and suspicion flooded him.

A wave of black light washed across his vision; for just a moment he thought it was nitrogen narcosis. But Rake was experienced in narcosis, and this was something else.

As a whirlpool opened beneath him, he started to gasp for air. He realized as he was dying that the Navy did know about the *Valiant*.

With his last strength he yanked the emergency cord on the CO_2 cartridge; his buoyancy compensator exploded full, and heedless of bends or decompression he shot toward the surface. By then it was too late anyway. The pit had opened inside him, and although his body went up, all the rest swirled away in fragments.

3

Charles Koenig stood beside a stainless steel sink, frowning at his white lab coat thrown casually over the back of a metal chair. In his hand he held a small vial marked Radioactive. In his other hand he held another vial.

He was about to tag the proteins with radioactive iodine.

A young man with a fuzz of down on his cheeks came in holding an infant.

"Hi," he said. Chazz nodded, then saw he was talking to someone else at the other end of the lab. The other, a stocky girl in a lab coat, cooed over the baby. Chazz shook his head and pipetted the ^{125}I into the second vial. It was not his baby. He had no children. Babies, Patria said, got in the way; they were responsibility, a burden; they interfered with the important things—career, for example. Instead, Charles Koenig was in this Hawaiian laboratory pouring minute quantities of radioactive iodine from one jar to another. Career. His . . . and hers. Patria definitely did not want babies. Patria was in the jungles of Yucatan, doing her science.

"Science," he said to himself, as no one was nearby. "Science favors the unprepared mind." His mind was much too well prepared.

He scratched his cheek with a blunt finger. Graying hair fluffed out of his open shirt. He heard the hum of refrigeration units, the hum of fluorescent lights, the faint whine of a centrifuge. Once all these sounds had been comforting and familiar, the ambience of his professional life—these sounds and the touch of plastic containers, of pipettes and microscope controls, cool controlled air. Out the window stretched green lawns; broad palms swayed in a breeze he could neither hear nor feel. He could see the red splash of poinsettias against the far wall where his office was. He could hear the baby cry out, a soft, gurgled bark.

Suddenly he put the vials into the fridge, hung his lab coat in a locker and went out to his van.

The desert was empty. He preferred the emptiness. Boredom grew distant there, the restlessness faded, the tender spot around the heart grew tough again. He got out and hiked until he sweated and the dust blew around his boots in small familiar dragons.

Sand was blowing over the southern highway as he started back. He crossed the Waimea River at the mouth of the canyon where it flowed through the village of Hanapepe. An ancient truck with a bed full of automobile wheels rattled along in the opposite direction, load swaying in the rising wind. A haphazard network of carelessly looped rope lashed the tires.

The road wound in a broad rising S-turn along the hills that marched eastward from a promontory called Sinner's Head. The highway then flew straight for six or seven miles.

As he swung out of the final S-turn, he came up behind a yellow Datsun sedan moving steadily at 35 m.p.h. It was some time before he began thinking there was something odd about the Datsun; from his height in the rented VW van he could not see in, of course, but the car seemed to be moving too rigidly. The driver ought to be adjusting to the minor variations in the roadway.

He wasn't. He was going absolutely straight despite a series of gentle turns. Koenig honked to get his attention. He must be dreaming. If he kept driving like this there would be an accident.

There nearly was an accident. A silver BMW sedan approached from the east. Chazz could see the driver, an elderly woman, lean on her horn, a look of horror on her face as the Datsun bore down on her. She swerved onto the shoulder, passed and was gone. In his rearview mirror Chazz saw her come to a stop. Then he topped a small rise and she dropped from sight. The Datsun bore on, relentless as a wave.

They passed a road sign indicating that Pua'ahala was four kilometers ahead, where the Koloa Road branched off to the right. Chazz dropped back to give the driver of the Datsun room. He was probably drunk.

Sugar fields crowded the road edge. From time to time the red gash of a sugar cane road cut into the tall stalks. A truck hauling a sagging open iron bed that resembled a pregnant metal dinosaur bearing a forty-ton fetus of cut cane rattled across the highway fifty meters ahead. The Datsun neither slowed nor swerved, and for a moment Chazz thought there would be a collision; but the cane truck made it and had vanished into the green stalks to the south by the time the Datsun got there.

As the hill descended, the Datsun picked up speed, kicking dirt from the shoulder of the road one moment, crossing the yellow line the next, until finally, at a gentle right turn, it crossed the highway and plowed several meters into the sugar cane, crushing the thick stalks before it came to a halt. Steam spouted from the radiator, clouding the car. Chazz could not see the driver as he pulled to a halt on the shoulder and walked across the highway.

It wasn't a particularly serious accident. The Datsun hadn't been going very fast and the sugar cane had cushioned the impact. Certainly the hood was sprung, and the radiator was obviously ruptured, but the driver ought to be all right. Drunk, but alive.

He was quite close by the time he saw what had happened. There was no way to soften the horror.

The Datsun's windshield was gone, a ragged mouth with shards of glass teeth. Wedged through the windshield on the driver's side was an automobile wheel; a bald tire formed a small arc over the steering wheel. As Chazz looked in through the window, he saw that the driver was still there, and that his head was pulp smeared across the tire that bristled with spines of broken glass.

Chazz noticed that the air was thick with the over-sweet smell of crushed cane.

4

As he emerged from the cane, a Toyota pulled up behind the van.

"There's been an accident," Chazz told the driver. "We've got to call the police."

Cobb Takamura climbed out of the Toyota. He took off his porkpie hat and brushed the beads of sweat under his receding hairline with the back of his hand and tossed the drops away. "Is it so? An accident?"

Chazz nodded. "We've got to call the police. The driver's dead. His head—"

"They're here," Takamura said, distracted. "Sammy. Another problem. This is not my favorite day," he told Chazz.

"What do you mean, they're here?"

"Oh, sorry. Cobb Takamura. Lieutenant. Sergeant Akeakamai. We are police. Anyone injured? A passenger? We'll need an ambulance?"

Chazz shook his head. "There was only one person in the car." He led the way to the Datsun, tipped into a shallow furrow inside the cane.

"Yes," Takamura said. "He is most assuredly dead. This seems to be a day for dead ones. A rental." There was a Hertz sticker on the back window.

"I saw the truck. Carrying a load of wheels. Back in Hanapepe. I came up behind him . . . this one, I mean, not the truck." Chazz was talking too fast. He took a breath. "He went on a few miles, never swerved. It was weird, thirty-five miles an hour. His foot must be wedged in there. The wheels were spinning in the mud." He looked down at his slacks, red to the knees. "I turned off the engine."

"Sit down for a moment," Takamura suggested, taking Chazz's arm. There was nothing to be done for the driver of the Datsun.

"Yes."

Sammy was on the radio when they got back to the Toyota. "Yeah," he said and re-mounted the microphone under the dash. "Traffic is on the way," he said. "Meanwhile we have another one."

"Another accident?" Takamura asked.

Sammy shook his head. "Body. A diver over The Slip. B.C. full, but he was dead. Still is."

Takamura shook his head. "The Kukui Nut," he told Chazz. "Still is. Ha ha. 'Trouble rain over many already wet.' A floater?"

"Looks that way. A couple of Navy divers found him."

"Shouldn't be our problem, should it," Takamura said. "They take him to the morgue, hah. Dr. Shih will be busy tonight. Three autopsies. Hasn't been this much work for the medical examiner since the Kapa'a pileup last fall."

"Excuse me," Chazz interrupted. "Do you need me? I'd like to get—"

"Ah, so sorry. I'll take your name and address, please. In case we need you again. For the statement, you understand."

"Yes, of course. Charles Koenig. Chazz. I'm staying in Koloa, Kapuna Road. Number forty-seven."

Takamura nodded, writing it down. "What is it you're doing in Kauai, Mr. Koenig?"

"Research. I'm a biologist."

"A biologist?" Takamura was unfailingly polite. "You are a doctor, then."

"I'm a research fellow at the Douglass Research Center. I just got here a few days ago. This . . ." He gestured at the patch of yellow in the cane.

Takamura smiled. "Not a good welcome to our island, Dr. Koenig."

"No." Chazz smiled back.

"I understand Douglass Research is a botanical garden, Dr. Koenig. You are a botanist, perhaps?"

Chazz shook his head. "Microbiology, viruses, though now I concentrate mainly on molecular biology. Genetics. Douglass Research is no longer exclusively botanical. Why do you ask?"

"I don't know. A hunch, perhaps. Are you interested in diseases?"

Chazz shrugged. "It's part of microbiology. Human pathogens used to interest me."

"Used to?"

"I've been looking for a change. Professional burnout, I think it is. Bored with routine lab work, that sort of thing. I was invited here, so I came. I thought it might refresh my interests. I'm also on the research ethics committee for Triple-A-S."

"Excuse, please, but I am not familiar with Triple-A-S."

"My fault. American Association for the Advancement of Science." He shrugged. "A professional association."

"Ah, I see." The radio crackled for Lieutenant Takamura. "Excuse me," he said, moving to answer.

Chazz asked the sergeant what Takamura meant. "He said something about trouble raining on people already wet or something."

Sergeant Akeakamai chuckled. "When you get to know the boss, you know he quotes an old movie detective named Charlie Chan all the time."

"I see."

Takamura returned. "Routine." He shrugged. "I see you enjoy hiking in the desert, too." Takamura indicated Chazz's dusty hiking boots.

Chazz nodded.

Takamura laughed softly. "Ah. I also like to hike, Dr. Koenig. Perhaps we could go together sometime. I do know some interesting trails hereabouts."

"I'd like that."

"Wonderful. We needn't detain you anymore. Here is my card in case you think of anything more regarding this unfortunate accident. But I may well take the liberty of calling you first. I've a hunch, Dr. Koenig, that this meeting was not entirely accidental, if you understand what I mean. Fair warning."

5

Chazz, isolated amid the buzz of the party, contemplated Douglass' portrait over the carved pecan mantel, subtly lit by an inconspicuous fixture set into the ceiling. Frederick McCobbell Douglass—stated a small framed plaque near the portrait—had been stranded one year by a hurricane, long enough for him to think he would like to stay. It was considerably warmer in Hawaii than in Chicago, and his blood was thinning. Varieties of hibiscus diverted him in his declining years.

Mr. Douglass was very old and very pale in the portrait. From beneath lowered lids he contemplated a bloom held just below the bottom of the picture frame. Possibly he was inhaling hibiscus fragrance, although plumeria was a more likely candidate. Mr. Douglass had lived well, but it had not prevented his passing.

"The old man," someone said behind him.

"Mm? Oh, yes."

"A wonderful man." It was the director of the Douglass Research Center. "Vigorous old age. What I would hope for." The director was in his early sixties. "I came here as a young man just out of graduate school: horticulture." He shook his head. An overlapping series of wattles undulated beneath his chin. "Mr. Douglass took me under his wing, son. Under his wing. Always planning, he was. Formal English gardens, Italian gardens, Chinese gardens . . . and Japanese, of course. Gathering tropical plants, Mr. Douglass was, from all over the world. Of course you know all this."

"Yes," Chazz agreed. "I had the tour Monday."

"Right. Right." The director nodded and his wattles collapsed and expanded. His name was Morgan. "You'd be Koenig. Microbiology, isn't it?"

Chazz nodded. "What about your line of research, Dr. Morgan?" Chazz hid his face in his virgin piña colada.

The director surprised him. "I'm just a gardener, Dr. Koenig. This is not false modesty, I assure you. I am very good at growing plants. But I have very little aptitude for research. I am a fair administrator, and that is what Mr. Douglass bequeathed me, an administrative job at this well-endowed and well-equipped research center. Some good work gets done here, Koenig. We have patents for improved agricultural strains with increased disease resistance. The tropics are rich in diseases, you know. Fungi, rots, viruses. In the past fifteen years we have moved into your area more and more. You've seen the equipment? The latest technology, scanning electron microscopes, sequencers, computers, access to advanced data bases, all of that, electrophoresis, anything you need for recombinant DNA. I seem to recall you were interested in recombinant DNA? Of course. I know very little about such things, but I can administrate, Dr. Koenig. Frankly, though, I like plants best. Now let me introduce you to some of the others. A center like this provides opportunities for the cross-fertilization of ideas to produce new hybrids, more vigorous knowledge."

He took Chazz's arm.

"You know Dr. Silver, of course."

"Of course."

The director addressed a stork of a man. "Perhaps you could introduce Dr. Koenig around, Ben. I see our three new graduate students are at the door." Dr. Morgan excused himself.

"Yes." Dr. Silver peered fondly at Chazz from under very bushy brows. "You'll like it here, Chazz. Amazin' freedom.

No academic committees, no department meetings, no student papers. Wonderful facilities."

"It was always the meetings I liked, Ben. The give and take, the hammering out of issues."

"Ah, yes, of course. Asilomar. You were very vocal at Asilomar, weren't you?"

"Ethics, Ben. They were important issues, what kind of controls to put on recombinant DNA research. Human problems with human answers."

"Yes, yes. But that was more than ten years ago now, Chazz. Water under the bridge. None of those terrible scenarios developed. The research poses no threat."

"Because we limited ourselves, Ben. Scientists made a choice. The right one, I believe."

"I'm old-fashioned, Chazz. I believe scientific inquiry should be unfettered."

"Of course." Chazz smiled. "I remember your position at Asilomar, Ben. We were on opposite sides of that aisle."

"Well," Dr. Silver said negligently, waving away their differences, "I've learned to live with your rules, Chazz. But you were an arrogant young graduate student even before Asilomar."

"Yes, sir, I guess I was," Chazz agreed.

"I still say you are going to like it here. This is paradise. Lovely weather, beautiful beaches, exotic plants. For instance, you may find a few bugs of interest up in the crater, and in the swamp. But be careful," he hissed suddenly, winking. "Kahunas are still at work up there. Ha!"

"Kahunas?" Chazz was used to Silver's conversational swerves.

"Witch doctors, that sort of thing. You'll run into them some time or other. I believe young Dewilliter has been consulting one. Knowledge of local botany is said to be quite remarkable. Healing or killing. Very interestin'. It's been said they can pray a man to death. One of these overweight Hawaiian kings died of it, they say. In a hotel in San Francisco. Rubbish, of course." He grinned engagingly. "It was probably the water."

"I always liked your sense of humor."

"And I," Dr. Silver said, leading the way to a small group gathered around the punch bowl, "always liked men who like my sense of humor. I'd better discharge Dr. Morgan's commission for me and introduce you around, though. This is Dr. Thomas."

Before Dr. Thomas could do more than nod, Dr. Silver was on to the next. "Dr. Bradlow, genetic evolution of the arborescence of the koa forests. Dr. Dewilliter, viruses which prey on the lobelioids. Dr. Cutter, entomologist. Bugs, hah! Little bugs among our lovely leaves."

Cutter nodded, smiling. "Hawaiian bugs grow to enormous size. Dragonflies, grasshoppers. Very important for all those lovely leaves, Ben."

Silver slapped him in the upper arm. "Oh yes, oh yes. Very important. And you remember Andrea Silver, perhaps? My wife. Sedge tussocks. Very humble, the sedge tussock, but its molecular structures show extraordinarily subtle variations. Difficult as hell to analyze, but oh so vital."

She was short and sturdy. "Ben is an idiot, Chazz. Sedge tussocks are not vital at all. To me they are moderately interesting and not particularly difficult to analyze. If he bothers you, tell him to fuck off. As I do. Fuck off, Ben. I'll let you in on a secret, Koenig. He snores!"

Silver laughed. "A sign of intelligence. More awesome than the sedge. As for this woman, I can point out, as in remark, that she is a bit competitive. It keeps us on our toes, and that's a fact."

The jocular malice of this couple reminded Chazz of Patria, now off scrounging the forests of Yucatan, learning tribal medicine among the Lacandon Maya; she had some of Andrea's spice. Perhaps they would like each other.

"Did you hear about the diver?" It was Dewilliter, viruses of the lobelioids.

He was youngish. Not young. Not old. More young than old. Youngish. Chronologically mid-thirties, but with a broad, open face. Full of trust and innocence. Chazz found himself disliking Dewilliter. Something about that trusting face seemed dishonest.

Chazz knew what Dewilliter was talking about. But he asked, "What diver?"

"The dead one. Off the west side. He was just bobbing around on the surface, dead."

"Drowned?"

Dewilliter shook his head. Sparkles of chandelier light flashed off his rimless glasses. "Doesn't look that way."

"Oh. Shark attack?"

"Not a mark on him. Funny look on his face, I heard."

"Where'd you hear? I mean, where does one get news like that."

"Oh," Dewilliter laughed, "this is a small island. Hell, the whole place is no bigger than a small town on the mainland. Thirty, forty thousand people. News travels fast in a small town. February is a slack time for tourists, too. You'll see, when you've been here a few weeks. Personally, I think he saw something down there. Scared him to death."

"Monsters from the deep? Atomic testing in the nineteen-fifties? Mutants patrolling our waters? Come on." Chazz did not want to be intrigued by Dewilliter's morbid pursuits. "Or witch doctors, perhaps?" he asked.

Dewilliter took him seriously. "Perhaps. They can do that, you know, from a distance. Scare a man to death."

"Is that so?" Chazz asked with exaggerated politeness, knowing he was being unpleasant. To make up, he said, "Actually, I saw something weird today myself. An accident, a real freak."

Dewilliter nodded vigorously and his drink spilled a little. He scuffed the drops into the carpet with the ball of his foot. His shoes were formal, with little leather bells. "That's what I'm talking about, weird things. For instance, you saw the guy with the tire through his windshield, right? Believe me, there's more to this than meets the eye. Wait'll you meet Paul Ulana, hm? Reads your mind, he does."

Chazz knew why Dewilliter annoyed him: a conspiracy nut. "I bet you know who killed Kennedy," Chazz said.

Dewilliter looked at him. "No," he said shortly and turned away.

6

Renfrew was running.

The trail wound along the red dirt ridges, slick mud sucking at the rubber soles of his lightweight camouflaged guide boots. His breath was harsh and tasted of rust.

Renfrew loved running. He loved mission, the slap of the quiver against his back, the sharp line of bowstring, the splat and suck of mud.

He loved the solitude of the hunt. It was other people Renfrew disliked.

A mile back he had seen the pig-sign, the trampled and eaten fern, trotter prints in the mud—a hefty boar, by the size of them. This trail, a barely discernible track along Ki'ikolu Ridge, was a favorite of the feral pigs.

He slowed as he came around a bend into a thick cluster of koloa lau nui, kukui, breadfruit and the delicate bare stems of ti plants. He felt the presence of pig here. He suspended his breath a moment, listening. It was there, the heavy huffing of the boar. Slowly he let his own breath out as he slipped the recurve Bear bow off his back and notched one of his Game Getter plastic-fletched Easton aluminum arrows. The steel Wasp barb glittered in the greenish light of the rain forest. Trails of low cloud like steam drifted among the trees, as close to mist or drizzle as cloud could be. Muscles between Renfrew's ribs ached with the pressure of holding still after the exertion of running.

He crouched on the trail, the knees of his camouflage fatigues pressed into the mud. Off to the left, maybe ten meters, the boar, still not sure he was there, snuffled in the underbrush. Renfrew cocked his head, turned his right ear toward the boar. It was there. Definitely. Renfrew could sense its posture, facing him, legs braced, head lowered, tusks curled yellow in the damp dimness. He was there. All Renfrew had to do was wait.

He told himself that silently, still controlling his breath.

Renfrew, all you have to do is wait. He'll come back to the trail where the going is easier and quiet. He won't take to the brush. He won't. He can't. He'll break this way. Just wait.

Renfrew pushed his hair back behind his ear and tugged his cap tight to keep it from drifting back in front of his eyes. He settled himself onto one knee and sighted toward the brush. Slowly he pulled back on the string. The arrow's polished shaft slid back along the web of his left hand, callused from constant practice. He pulled all the way back to the head, then eased off. The nock was green plastic below his right eye, the fletching stiff crimson. He waited.

Silence settled like mist around them. The silence became the glue binding Renfrew and the pig. The connection between them grew, a psychic bond tightening by the minute, like a rubber band winding around a propeller shaft. Soon the pig would break. The silence deepened. Very slowly other sounds seemed to drift by—birdcalls, moisture condensing and dripping from the tips of banana leaves, a distant swirl of water gathering into a rivulet at the bottom of the ravine to his left, below where the pig was standing, his trotters braced against the dirt. Pig breath came shorter, inbreath pulling for Renfrew's scent amid the thick odors of damp earth, of rotted leaf and snail and death all around, of pollen burst and swelling life, of endless efflorescence and death, sex and decay.

The air thickened. Renfrew felt it was more rain swelling the clouds this close under the lee of Wai'ale'ale. Pregnant clouds, fat, fatter, fattest, ready to burst again, send torrents down the ravines, sweep away the brush, tumble the rock, churn to chaos the placid river below. Muscles jumped in

Renfrew's jaw, in his shoulder. The barbed tip twitched in front of him.

Then it happened. The sharp crack of underbrush, and the dark striped body broke from cover, headed up the trail, almost out of sight, swerved suddenly and, kicking sprays of watery red mud, homed on Renfrew crouched. The tusks were curved, age-yellowed but still sharp, and the heavy jowl muscles writhed. Renfrew felt the exultation rise as he pulled the arrow fully back and sighted without thinking and loosed the string, heard the sharp whoosh of the arrow springing away, the twang of the string vibrating familiar music and the almost simultaneous padded thunk of the tip burying itself in the thick brisket.

The boar kept coming, though, pumping blood around the shaft protruding from his chest. A horrible gurgling snort drooled from his snout as he slid, legs splayed, splashing mud, legs churning the air. Oddly, he regained his feet somehow in those terrible fractions of seconds and staggered again toward Renfrew reaching for another arrow, too late. The boar collided with him, hooked back the vicious tusk across Renfrew's side, still crouched, struggling with the arrow; and Renfrew's own blood joined the boar's to mingle invisibly with the red mud now washed by falling rain.

Renfrew's breath was a whisper under the steady white noise of the rain. The boar was dead, half on top, pinning Renfrew on his bow. He tried to shift sideways from under the carcass, and fire shot up his side, down his leg to the very waffled sole of his guide boot.

He reached across with his right arm and pushed against the heavy boar's head. By centimeters it moved; at last it fell with a splat into the wet trail beside him.

Then Renfrew went to sleep. In his dreams he was running.

7

Chazz sat in Zen meditation, but there was no peace. His leg ached. His breath was shallow and ragged. He saw the yellow Datsun grinning into the sugar cane. Outside, occasional traffic swished by on the rain-wet pavement, and his mind leaped. There were bodies in the rain, bodies in the forest and the desert and bobbing in the ocean surge. Chazz saw them all in the blurred and swirling white wall before his eyes.

He sat relentlessly, though. He put his mind into the pain in his leg. He sat on the pain, and the pain squirmed. It squirted down his calf. He moved his mind there, and the pain shot to his abdomen.

Dewilliter, he thought. He tried looking at the name *Dewilliter*, and the name drifted away. Ben Silver arose, leviathan from dark mental waters, streaming sardonic goodwill and wry humor.

What were Dr. Silver's current research interests? When he directed Chazz's dissertation research, he'd been working on molecular genetics of simian virus SV-40, a type of cloning later prohibited for a time by the guidelines developed at Asilomar. The clones had been destroyed, Chazz was sure of that. What was he doing now, here?

At some point in the course of the evening Chazz had asked him, wondering why Silver had invited him to DRC, and Dr. Silver had waved his thin aristocratic hand vaguely, indicating some inconsequential item beyond the French doors. Dr. Silver talked instead about kahunas, medicine men, shamans, witch doctors. Silver wouldn't know that was Patria's province. Chazz and Patria got married later. Silver had never met her.

Chazz shook himself, his shoulders. He leaned forward, his wrists bent against his knees, stretching. He should go to bed, but the party still swirled in his brain—and the Datsun engine whining in the crushed sugar cane, and Dewilliter's conspiracies, and lobelioids, and a drowned body bobbing on the ocean surface with a strange expression on its face.

"It's not my problem," he said, standing. The white walls surrounded a great deal of glass, which in turn revealed pool and palms, a huge ficus in the courtyard and, in the other direction, a scrubby desolation where cattle once foraged.

It wasn't his problem. He went for a walk.

There was a moon of sorts whipping merrily along behind dark scraps of cloud. "'The moon,'" he quoted to the the scrub. "'A ghostly galleon. Tossed upon cloudy seas.' Or something like that."

A dirt road led off into the scrub. The deep tire marks of four-wheel drives gathered pools of silvered water in the oval depressions. Dark splotches dotted the track. It was a long time walking along the road staring at the splotches before he knew what they were.

They were toads, legs splayed out. Toads, pancake-thin, flattened amazingly by truck tires, dried by sun. The farther he walked, the more toads there were on the road, not just the random blotch of dead toad here and there, but a carpet of dead toads, toads toe to toe, side by side, thousands of toads, all dead, all flat, some long-gone and leathery, some still moist with spilled guts and protruding tongues squeezed from their innards, brainless toads hopped onto the dirt from the surrounding scrub to seek mates in the dusk and stupidly run over by beer-drinkers from town.

He tried not to step on them as he walked, but it was impossible to avoid them all. Finally he shrugged and stopped watching where his feet fell. It was Patria, of course. His fault. Her fault. His fault. Hers. He took long walks in the Berkeley hills like this after she left for Yucatan, leaving him in the house with the Bay and San Francisco view and a garden full of dead vegetables. They'd been fighting a lot, and when the field trip came up, she went to Yucatan while Chazz sat in the library or walked in the hills or taught his aikido class.

The phone was ringing when he got back.

"It's three o'clock in the morning," Chazz was going to say, but Takamura spoke first.

"It's three o'clock in the morning, Dr. Koenig," he said. "You've been out, I know. I called Dr. Morgan at the DRC. He said you had left. That was some time ago, so sorry, but something has occurred to me and I couldn't sleep. So I've been trying to reach you." He sounded genuinely apologetic.

"It's all right," Chazz said. "I couldn't sleep either."

"So. You know something of poisons, perhaps?"

"In a way, I suppose. A number of microorganisms produce toxins of one kind or another. Why?"

"We may have a homicide, Dr. Koenig. Perhaps you could come in as a consultant. I'm afraid the biological expertise of myself and staff is not great. Dr. Shih was unable to identify the substance."

"Substance?" The moon was tipping down the lanai, almost gone behind the enormous ficus decorating the central plaza of the complex.

"A small puncture wound, Dr. Koenig, on the victim's left thigh. A powdery substance around a very small wound. Almost too small to notice, that wound, especially considering that the victim was addicted to drugs and was, well, peppered with puncture wounds. 'Useless,' as Charlie Chan says, 'to sprinkle salt on tail of time,' though. He is dead. We don't have many addicts in this island, Dr. Koenig, but here is something we do not understand. A powdery substance Dr. Shih thinks resembles pollen. Or spores."

Chazz could almost hear the shrug over the phone. "Perhaps you could help? I'm sure it would take only a few minutes of your time, and I think I can promise you that as a reward I might persuade Mrs. Takamura to prepare her famous *ebi no tempura* for you."

"I could stop by tomorrow. I'm not sure I can help much,

but I haven't really started on my own research yet, and I'll take any excuse to put it off."

"Thank you, Dr. Koenig. I feel, like Charlie Chan, that my day's work has been 'useless as life preserver for fish.'"

8

Renfrew opened his eyes: Nam again, left for dead, but the smells were different, the sounds too, and gradually he saw the light, and that was different.

Bamboo slats were the same, but the light was yellow and the heat was thicker and his side ached. But most different of all was the man bending over him.

Not the gray hair, long and combed straight back in one huge wave, nor the thick white mustache. Not the faded clothing. Not even the wrinkles under the jaw, along the faintly oriental eyes. None of those. It was the eyes themselves.

They were red, a flaring crimson that glowed in the aqueous light filtered and barred. They were staring into Renfrew. Renfrew closed his eyes, and the red embers winked out to darkness again.

When he awoke next, it was a perfectly ordinary old man sitting by his bed, holding a plaster made of leaves to Renfrew's side. Renfrew noticed his own stink for the first time in years, cutting through the leaf fragrance. He made a sound. The old man's eyes flashed crimson momentarily as they swiveled to look at him, then dulled to brown. A trick of the light, Renfrew decided.

The old man was doing something, pulling the leaf away

from his side. Suddenly the pain was fire in his side, and Renfrew's back arched.

"Easy," the old man said. Tears blurred Renfrew's vision, but he saw the old man was squeezing something onto his wound. "The fruit of the *noni*, the Indian mulberry," the old man said softly. "Though painful, it will help the healing." Renfrew could feel the flesh pucker together as the old man replaced the leaves. "Plantain," he said, pressing the broad flat leaves to the wound.

"Who are you?" Renfrew asked. His voice was barely a whisper.

The old man bent low. "Just an old man," he whispered back.

Later Renfrew asked how he'd found him. "No one uses that trail," he said.

"Oh." The old man smiled, showing his teeth. "I've seen you before. Your name is Renfrew. And I knew that boar, *O'o-a-moa* he was called, 'Death Rattle.' You were lucky."

It was a long time later he realized that his question had not really been answered. He was sitting up, back to the thin wall, eating poi with his fingers. It was raining steadily outside, the sound of it so loud and continuous he didn't notice it until he tried to speak.

"Where are we?"

The old man shrugged. His heavy shoulders shuddered like vulture wings. "Puu Ki. Not far from your trail on Ki'ikolu Ridge. Power lines that way. I suspend time up here. It is a good place, much mango, ti, kukui, plantain. Some old taro terraces beside the stream. Water. Pig, of course. One can live. One can live. You will have a visitor soon."

"What're you talking about?" Renfrew asked, though he didn't care.

"You may call me Kalaipahoa." He smiled again. Renfrew heard, as a whispered rasp, the words, "Kalaipahoa is poison god," but the old man had laid his finger beside his nose, eyes red again, and his lips had not moved.

"Witch doctor," Renfrew said stubbornly. He didn't believe in magic.

"No." The old man laughed. "Not a witch doctor. It's all

right, you don't believe. Not yet. But you would like to know why *O'o-a-moa* attacked you, yes?" Kalaipahoa said softly. He was looking the other way, and Renfrew did not see him speak. The poison god.

"I am just kahuna." The old man nodded. The red winked out again. "Your visitor has work for you. He is filled with purpose, your visitor. Listen, you can hear him."

"I don't hear anything."

"No, no," Kalaipahoa said. "Not with the ears. Never mind, Renfrew. He is here and I must gather some plants. Good-bye." He got up and left.

All Renfrew heard was rain, mud trickle, pain in his side, breath in his nose. But the old man was right. The visitor came through the door without knocking.

"Hello, Renfrew," he said. He stood in the gloom just inside the doorway, looking down at Renfrew, who nodded.

"How are you?" he asked. "On the mend?" The man's voice was hard and humorless despite the joviality of his words.

Renfrew grunted, noncommittal. The rain was loud just behind his head, hissing in the walls. He held the tin of poi close to his mouth and ate slowly, eyes half closed.

"Good," the stranger said shortly, as if satisfied with Renfrew's answer. He was compact and muscular, with a neat dark mustache; about Renfrew's age. He had the look of a diver, the special tan, the indentations where mask fit, the lines around the mouth. There were lots of divers in Kauai. "Not like Vietnam, eh?" He swept his arm at the rain forest outside the window.

"No," Renfrew said shortly. "Not like Nam."

"So, how's the hunting?"

Renfrew shrugged. The pain in his side flared and subsided, a flashbulb of pain.

"Heard you got a boar. Heard the boar got you, too." The man smiled at his little joke.

Renfrew said nothing.

"Huhn," the man grunted at last. "Well, we have more work for you."

"Not interested." The poi was gone; Renfrew set the can aside.

The man nodded. "The old man who saved your life is a kahuna. You know what that is? He's a man with power, Renfrew. A healer."

"I'm not interested, John." Renfrew used the man's name for the first time. "I told you before. I'm just a hunter."

"That power could be yours," John said. "You could study with the kahuna, learn a little magic, eh?"

"I'm not working for you anymore, John. I'm retired."

"No. Of course, you retired, didn't you. Imagine, though. To be able to heal with chants, herbs, native medicine. To read people's minds at a distance. It makes you think, doesn't it?"

"Yeah, it makes me think. How about you?"

"Oh, it makes me think, too. Listen, Renfrew, we need you, your . . . expertise."

"Yeah?"

"Name your price," John said.

"The old man knew you were coming." Renfrew said. "He told me you had work. Was that magic?"

"Oh." John laughed. "Probably not. He told us you were here."

Renfrew nodded again. "What kind of job?" he asked.

9

"'Every bird seeks its own tree—never tree the bird,'" Takamura quoted. "Thanks for coming." He took off his sunglasses and squinted away from the bright sun as he rubbed his eyes, but an imp-grin twitched on his lips. This afternoon there were no clouds.

"The great philosopher Charles Chan?" Chazz smiled back.

"None other," Takamura affirmed. "I'm glad you could come. This won't be pretty, I fear."

Chazz shrugged.

"We have too many bodies today," Takamura went on. "Dr. Shih is busy. She's the medical examiner here – a pathologist, really. It's a part-time job, usually. Shall we?"

The morgue was in the basement of the hospital. Narrow casement windows of one-way glass looked across to the A & P parking lot. Only the tops of the nearest cars caught the sunlight and splashed it back through the window onto a row of glass-fronted cabinets. The glass in turn reflected light back into the white-tiled room and concealed the contents of the cabinets.

There was no one around. Only the thick formaldehyde smell of a morgue.

No one living. Three of the four tables held shrouded forms. Takamura lifted the corner of the sheet that draped the nearest with his thumb and forefinger, and grunted.

Chazz leaned against the second table. He realized it was occupied when his hand touched the body and he jerked away. He laughed nervously.

Takamura sighed, dropping the sheet. "Dr. Koenig, my statistics are shot to hell. It took a traffic accident to bring in this many people last time."

"Excuse me." A small woman stood in the doorway. "Lieutenant Takamura. Nice to see you again."

"Ah," Takamura said. "Dr. Shih."

She was middle-aged, frail and myopic, her head tilted to one side as she considered Chazz through bifocals. Stainless steel instruments, scissors and probes, peeked out of the breast pocket of her white coat. "You would be the biologist, I guess. Good."

She shook his hand, dropped it abruptly and continued to stare quizzically at him until he felt himself wanting to fidget. "You found something?" he said.

"Ah, yes." Dr. Shih seemed delighted, and clapped her hands together. She produced a small plastic box from her pocket and handed it to him. There was a slide in it resting on cotton. A label identified it as John Doe. "This. A . . . substance. Fixed. A powder. Unidentified."

"Could he have snagged his leg on something with thorns? The so-called Apple of Sodom has thorny leaves and is quite toxic."

She leaned back to look up at him. "Well," she said shortly, "perhaps you could look at the slide before offering explanations, please. Evidence before speculation."

"Of course." He looked at Takamura, who was laughing silently.

"'Every Maybe have a wife. Wife called Maybe Not,'" he said.

"Apple of Sodom poisoning causes excitement, tremors, paralysis of the central nervous system, collapse, and ultimately death in deep coma," Dr. Shih said, ignoring the interruption. "While some of these signs are not inconsistent with autopsy results, the gastrointestinal inflammation and hemorrhagic nephritis common in cases of *Solanum sodomeum* poisoning were not present, nor could I find traces of saponin. There was slackness of muscle tone, but no evidence of any sudden and remarkable fall in body temperature prior to death. No, not Apple of Sodom poisoning."

"I apologize, Dr. Shih. I didn't mean to imply you weren't doing your job. I'm not a doctor. Nor," he added, looking at Takamura, "am I a policeman. I was told I might help identify an organic substance you found on the body."

"Perhaps you may do just that. Please. Take the sample. Look at it. Tell me what you think it might be."

"Okay." He put the plastic box in his pocket.

A telephone on the wall chirped quietly. "Excuse me," Dr. Shih said and went to answer. "Lieutenant Takamura?" She held out the phone.

Chazz lowered his voice when he spoke to Dr. Shih. "What were the symptoms? I could be looking for alkaloids, glucosides, even pollens or spores."

"Signs, Dr. Koenig. Symptoms are subjective. The victims are already dead and no longer in a position to report symptoms."

"I stand corrected." Chazz smiled.

"Death resulted, as I suggested, from effects on the nervous system. Flaccid paralysis and extreme weakness, certainly. Some evidence of violent tremors prior to death. A great deal of pain, it would seem. Not pleasant at all. A violent, convulsive death. It could be a neurotropic toxin, or even a new flu virus, but I don't really believe that."

"Why not?"

"The diver indicated some of the same signs, Dr. Koenig, but there were no puncture wounds on him. I did section this, however." She produced another plastic box, identical to the first. The identifying label on this one read Wyman, Rafael Watt.

"Lung tissue. Mr. Wyman's lungs were discolored by hemorrhage. I have worked all morning on him." She nodded toward the white-draped form on table two.

"Oh."

"Unfortunately," Dr. Shih continued, "I could discover no traces of this substance in his lungs. I did find other substances, though. Cocaine, I believe. It appears he too was a user. If you want my opinion, that may be all we have here, substance abuse, possible overdoses or the drugs have been cut with something lethal. Some of the signs are similar to overdose, though not precisely the same. Of course, this is not the most sophisticated laboratory in the world, and the subject"—she nodded toward the table—"was no longer available to describe his symptoms. But Mr. Wyman's lungs hemorrhaged. His face mask was full of blood. Extreme rictus; he looked like he was grinning. Would you like to see? I left his face intact."

"No. No thanks. May I take the samples?"

"Where could you do the best job?"

Chazz shrugged. "DRC would be best. They have a good library, scanning electron microscopes and computer access to medical and biological databases."

"You have another one," Takamura told Dr. Shih, hanging up. "They're bringing her in. I must drive up and look around. Would you like to come along, Chazz?"

"A woman?" Dr. Shih pushed Takamura toward the door. "Another body? Then go. I still have much work to do."

She nodded toward the third occupied table. "The traffic accident," she said, turning away. "And now another on the way."

10

"Hanalei valley," Takamura said as he maneuvered the Toyota into a tight left turn at the end of a one-lane iron bridge. "As you can see, it's a lovely place, ancient taro fields, some of them still maintained. Not developed yet. Even the roads are bad. Still cheap housing up here. A few ex-hippies living on taro and dope. Quite far in, difficult to get to, and not worth the effort. We tolerate them; they don't cause trouble, and no one seems to mind. There are a few old folks, families all gone, who live on patch farming and welfare. Sally was one of them."

Her house was small and very shabby. Chazz stared at it, trying to place this shack around someone's life. It was more like a garage than a home. Siding peeled away from the studs, warped by moisture and neglect. Finally he climbed out of the car.

Takamura was already inside. "Not much," he said, gesturing at the room.

"No," Chazz agreed. "Not much." A narrow iron bed, thin mattress. A sink, a pine table. Two chairs. A curtained-off corner which contained a toilet. Pictures cut from magazines were pinned to the walls—advertisements, mostly, for televisions, Scotch whiskey (a black chemist whose hobby was hang gliding, whose last book read was *The Rise and Fall of the Third Reich*, and whose whiskey was Dewars), Aloha Airlines.

Not much.

"Sally Cameron. No use to anyone. Hawaiian-Russian mother, American father," Takamura muttered. He took off his hat and ran his fingers around the brim.

"Hi." A small voice at the door.

"Hello," Takamura said. The boy was small. His face was as dirty as the shorts he was wearing.

"Sally's gone, yes? Dead?"

"I'm afraid so. When did you see her last?"

"Morning time. She gave me this." He held up a rag doll very much the worse for wear.

"Was she sick?"

"Nope. She was good." He was very definite.

"See anyone around? Since, I mean."

"Nope. Just the car." The boy twitched his head toward the mud road outside.

"Car?" Takamura pretended to be interested in the hang-gliding chemist on the wall. "Mmm."

"Sure. Dark car. Big, old car. Drive up, drive back. Tourist maybe, lost. Not many come up this road, mister, just people who live here, you know? I was up there." He pointed carefully out the door at the hillside. "Bananas up there. I saw the car, though."

"See anybody in the car, son? What they might look like?"

The boy shook his head. Stuffing oozed from the doll's armpit.

"Any idea how long the car was here?"

He shook his head again. "Not here when I went up the hill. Saw him go out, that's all. No one up here. Except *akua*."

"*Akua*?"

"Sure, many *akua*. Eat dead people's brains. Live up high." The boy pointed at the mountain. "Come down at night."

"Oh. Hippies."

"Nope. Hippies are people. *Akua*. Big, long arms. They eat brains." The boy grinned at Takamura.

"Not very tasty, I shouldn't think."

The boy shrugged. "Dunno." He spun on his heel and ran out.

"Well," Takamura said. "Big dark old car. There are only about ten thousand cars on this island. Many of them are big, a number are dark, most are old. But as the great detective would say, 'Never hunt rabbit with dead dog.'"

This was too much for Chazz. "What does that mean?" he asked.

"Beats me," Takamura shrugged. "Let's go."

They stepped into the bright westering sun. "We won't find anything," Takamura said. "Sammy's been here, the ambulance's been here, and the day's been dry. No tracks except in the dust, gone by now. Don't know why I dragged you here. People liked the old lady. Harmless. Every Friday she rode the bus to the welfare office to pick up her check, rode the bus back." He looked at the scraggly patch of garden. The top of the soil was already cracking.

"My grandfather was a farmer," Takamura said, gazing at the dusty garden. "My father's a fine calligrapher as well as a politician. A long way from being a farmer. The Japanese were brought over here in the 1870s to work in the cane fields. They brought, and kept, a little of Japan. It is odd in a way, because calligraphy was a samurai art in Japan. Farmers knew little of such arts. Here is democracy. Now we do Zen, make gardens, calligraphy, ikebana, aikido."

"Aikido, too?"

"You know of aikido?"

"I teach in Berkeley a couple of times a week."

"Then you are *shodan*, of course. You should meet my friend Shinawa. He is the aikido teacher here."

"Shinawa is here?"

"Ah, yes. You know of him?"

"He's a well-known teacher. Do you do aikido?"

Takamura smiled. "I'm afraid I've never had the time. Police academy hurry-ups and immobilizations only. Also shooting. Police are fond of shooting. We go to Honolulu for training. Here I have never done shooting. This is a quiet island. Why did you take up aikido? You are a big person, Dr. Koenig. You should have no need of a martial art."

"I was an angry person, Lieutenant; too violent, sometimes, I thought. I wanted to learn how to not kill people." Chazz was squinting into the sun, not looking at the policeman.

"Ah," Takamura said softly. After a pause he said, "Perhaps you would like to visit Shinawa? He would be happy to see you. Later we will call him."

The radio in the Toyota crackled. Takamura went to get it.

"Drugs?" Chazz asked when he returned.

"You thought of that, eh? No, I'm pretty sure not. We have something else here. She was no drug addict. Maybe it was *akua*, hah?"

"Or a curse, maybe? Someone prayed her to death? Silver says the witch doctors can do that sort of thing."

"Same as *akua*. Why?"

"I don't know. How about natural causes?"

"Well, she had the same expression on her face as the others. Until Dr. Shih gets done with her, we won't really know. But it sounds the same. That was The Kukui Nut on the car radio. Clever police work has uncovered the identity of your traffic accident."

"And?"

"Very curious. He had no identity."

"And?"

"Everybody's somebody. This man was Ronald Smith. From Indianapolis. Sold insurance from his home, curiously without a phone. No family in Indiana or anywhere else. No fingerprint record with the FBI. Never went to school. Was never in the U.S. military service. Does not exist. Curious."

"Driver's license?"

"Address is 1305 Broadway in Indianapolis. Happens to be the address of the Indianapolis Police headquarters. Curious. 'Roots of tree lead in many directions.'"

The small boy was digging in the middle of the empty field. Chazz watched for a moment. "What's he doing out there?"

Takamura shaded his eyes with his porkpie hat. "Digging," he said. "He's digging a grave."

The boy was burying the rag doll.

"What's an *akua*?" Chazz asked. The boy poured dust through his fingers onto the grave.

"Monsters who live in the woods. Come out at night and kill people. Never heard of them eating brains, though."

"Do you think we might be having an epidemic of some kind?" Chazz suggested. He did not like the idea.

But Takamura assented. "Of some kind," he said.

11

Dewilliter stopped Chazz in the hall. "Something's going around," he said.

"What?"

"Disquieting rumors," Dewilliter said.

"Oh?" Where did Dewilliter get phrases like that?

Dewilliter's broad face bobbed. "Some kind of infectious disease. I've heard rumors. A plague in the tropics. A Sense of Foreboding on the Horizon."

Chazz put his hand on the two slide boxes in his jacket pocket. Dewilliter appeared to be waiting, head propped to one side.

He spoke finally. "Aren't you curious, Koenig?"

"My field is microbiology," Chazz said. "And I don't think it's funny."

"No. A new disease, Koenig. Or perhaps a very ancient disease. I think it's the Russians, but Silver says the old Hawaiian witch doctors know a lot about such things." He shrugged. Chazz noticed that Dewilliter had a belly.

"But you said you knew a kahuna yourself."

"Oh, Ulana, of course. Nice old man, but he's not a witch

doctor. He knows a lot about the plants here, though. I've been consulting with him about lobelioids, Koenig. See, there's a spindle virus that plagues the lobelioids, and we needed them for the Lolo Project—"

"Lolo? What's that?"

"Never mind, it's nothing. I was thinking about pakalolo. Marijuana. No, it's the other ones, the bad ones, the *ana'ana*, that're the witch doctors. Sorcerers. They're the ones who kill at a distance. It drives men mad," Dewilliter insisted. "There are strange practices in the mountains. Rituals. Ask Silver, he knows."

"Okay."

As if in answer, Dr. Silver appeared at the end of the corridor, carrying a stack of clear plastic culture dishes. When he saw Chazz and Dewilliter he paused, then came toward them.

"Nitrogen-fixing bacteria for bog plants," he said, nodding at the tray.

"Your current line of research?" Chazz asked.

Dr. Silver gave his benign smile. "Oh, no, I've gotten rather interested in ethnobotany now, to tell you the truth. How people used plants. Or, as some might have it, the other way around?"

"'Day of the Triffids,'" Chazz said.

"What's that?"

"Intelligent plants with an abiding hatred of human beings. They counterattack. An old science-fiction film."

"Oh, yes. You have a fondness for B movies?" Dr. Silver looked distracted. "That wasn't quite what I had in mind." He hurried away with his tray of seedlings.

"I didn't know you knew Silver," Dewilliter said. He seemed aggrieved.

"He invited me here."

"Oh."

In his office, Chazz put the John Doe slide under the microscope and focused. Two hours later he pushed back his chair and stretched.

Wyman's lung tissue meant little. Some cell walls were ruptured, of course, as if invaded. The effect could be viral work, or something corrosive, but on the whole it didn't look like anything life-threatening.

The other slide held cells and cell parts of all kinds—epithelial, plant tissue, bacterial—but few whole cells. He would have to use the scanning electron microscope.

On his way to Electron Microscopy, he ran into Dr. Silver again.

"Say, Chazz, I'll be leaving town in a couple of days. Before I go, I wanted to invite you along on a little field trip we're planning tomorrow. You'd be welcome. There are some interesting primitive plant survivals on these islands. How about it? A hike will do you good. Can't be all work, you know. Lab work is pretty routine; you'll get stale."

"Okay, sure. Where are you going?"

"A swamp above the reservoir. Not up on top, just a few miles up a dirt road. A strenuous hike in, of course, but there are trails of a sort."

"Sure, Ben," Chazz said. "What time?"

"We'll leave here at noon. See you then." Ben loped off down the corridor.

Chazz spent the next hour preparing specimens for the electron microscope. He rubbed his eyes, put the specimens aside and went by Dewilliter's office. "Are there any poisonous lobelioids, Dewilliter?"

The smooth round face took on a glow. He probably did not get many questions about his specialty.

"Poisonous lobelioids?" he repeated. "Oh, yes, certainly. Some quite rare ones, too. For example, there is the *Isotoma longiflora*. Otherwise known as Star of Bethlehem. A broad-leafed weed, rather spiky in appearance. Has a five-petaled flower and a fruiting body. . . . The alkaloid is called lobeline, and is mildly toxic. Why do you ask?"

"Oh, I don't know. Just curious, I guess. People are dying more frequently than usual. Those Disquieting Rumors you mentioned."

"You don't think I'm responsible, do you?" Dewilliter seemed genuinely alarmed.

"No," Chazz assured him. "No, I don't."

"Well, I'm glad to hear that. By the way, there seems to be some kind of cult. Have you heard?"

"No."

"According to Silver, those witch doctors could pray people to death. Some kind of extrasensory projection or something."

"Really?"

Dewilliter was hurt by the irony. "That's what Silver said. The other night, at the party."

"But what about this fellow you know, this Ulana?"

"I told you, he's just an old man with arthritis who knows a lot about local botany, that's all." He turned back to his drawings of a lobelioid, which looked like a lettuce head perched on top of a fishing pole. He was working meticulously on a genetic chart under the drawing.

"Cult," Chazz said to himself. He went to the library and signed on a terminal. He took a number of books with him to the carrel. Sedentary science was dulling him. He realized how much he looked forward to meeting Shinawa later.

The empty screen stared back at him long enough for Chazz to realize that he could see, faintly reflected in its glass, the window behind him and the poinsettia garden outside. The poinsettia was a "shrub with milky sap and lanceolate leaves," one of the books told him. "The milky juice and leaves are poisonous," it said. "The poisonous substance is neither an alkaloid nor a glucoside, and is probably a resin. It causes intense emesis and catharsis, and delirium before death."

The book was *Poisonous Plants of Hawaii*, by Harry L. Arnold, M.D., 1944. Seriously out of date. Besides, the signs were wrong: no emesis and no catharsis. Paradise concealed an enormous amount of violence. The victims were not eating poinsettia, though.

A traffic death, an old woman, a derelict and a diver, Chazz typed. The letters hung before him, phosphorescent green. He backed up and typed:

A SENSE OF FOREBODING ON THE HORIZON

Again he erased it, called up the telecommunications access program, logged on to SCINOTE, an electronic mail and computer conferencing system for scientists, and sent a message to Patria.

->MAIL EX TBM876
->.DA 13 Feb
->SUBJECT: ANTHRO
->ENTER TEXT: Can you do search Hawaiian kahuna. Need soonest for vital research, esp. poisons or killing techniques. Wish you were here. How are you? Love, BCL498.
->.AR-Acknowledgment Requested Soonest
->Quit

The screen went blank.

12

Later that afternoon Chazz sat on his feet, a position called *seiza*, knees apart. Opposite, a few feet away, an older man faced him in the same position. Their hands rested on their thighs, fingers inward. They wore white karate *gis* and black-skirted *hakama*.

Shinawa was small, baldly brown on top, with a fringe of white hair fluffing over his ears. His face was very wrinkled, with deep smile creases at the corners of the eyes. Neither man moved.

The large quonset hut that housed the Hanalolo Aikido Club was empty and dim; the windows on each end were not only very dirty, but obscured by chicken wire as well, and the lights were off. Chazz could hear light rain trickle down the grooves in the round metal roof, and the slight creak of his own breathing as it pushed his belly against the stiff knot of his belt and the cords of his hakama.

Shinawa made no sound; he sat absolutely motionless. Chazz couldn't see him breathe. This was, of course, an illusion. Shinawa was calm, but he was certainly breathing. Chazz hoped his breath was even half as quiet. It was up to him to attack.

He waited. The mat beneath his knees was gray in the dim light. The walls curved overhead. A rack of wooden weapons: wooden staffs, bamboo and wooden swords, hung opposite him. A desk with a telephone and a record player sat near the entrance. The rest of the hut's floor space was taken up by an elevated mat covered with canvas. The two men were seated in the center.

The attack would have a slow start since Chazz was sitting on his feet. Any movement would telegraph his intentions, any preliminary tension. He would have to spring from *seiza*.

He waited.

Suddenly the telephone on the desk rang; the sound was explosive and loud in the hut. Chazz, as if switched on by that sound, sprang to his feet and glided toward the old man, ready to strike.

Shinawa did not appear to move, did not rise to meet the attack. He appeared distracted, as though hesitant whether to answer the telephone or not. Chazz thrust the blade of his hand toward the old man's face in a vicious, totally committed strike.

Shinawa shifted slightly on his left knee, at the same time joining the wrist of Chazz's striking hand with the back of his own left wrist, resting gently there, riding the motion of the strike, lowering and leading Chazz, at the same time almost lovingly placing his own right hand on the back of his neck.

Automatically Chazz bent his knees to keep his center of gravity beneath him, yet propelled past and led down, his strike passing the old man harmlessly. His own left arm shot out and curled as Shinawa pivoted once again, this time taking a small step on his knees as he brought Chazz's attacking arm in a vertical circle, using the leverage of the shoulder itself to send Chazz rolling at a slight angle away from him. It was not a throw, this smooth *kaiten nage*: Chazz felt no pressure or conflict. He rolled swiftly and came, twisting, to his feet, reaching to grab the hand he found in his face.

The movement of his own hand found only empty air to grasp. Shinawa was beside him, leading him down once more, then smoothly reversing his direction so that Chazz found himself first sprawled face toward the mat, and as he started to straighten, flipped back. Shinawa was seated calmly beside him, arms extended, one hand in Chazz's face, the other over his knees. Chazz had drawn himself into a ball and turned slightly away, a motion he continued, twisting away, springing once more to his feet. He turned for a third attack.

Suddenly he stopped and smiled. Shinawa was seated *seiza* still, but his hands were slightly extended toward Chazz, ready, as he knew they would be, for anything Chazz might choose to do. There was no opening for an attack.

Chazz floated to his own knees and bowed as the telephone rang for the second time.

Shinawa returned the bow and rose jointlessly to his feet. His hakama swished as he moved to answer the phone.

Neither man had said a word since they had bowed in to each other. Now Chazz could hear Shinawa's heavily accented English as he spoke. He was giving a training schedule to a new member. A class would begin in half an hour.

Chazz waited. He felt very happy.

So he was surprised when he sensed Shinawa behind him and turned to face the naked steel of a live sword, not the wooden *bokken* he would have expected. It moved toward his throat relentlessly, and Chazz rose, moving backward, as the needle tip advanced. He realized with a sinking sensation that he had never faced a live blade before. The humor was gone from Shinawa's eyes. Chazz backed up, struggling for calm, feeling fear.

The sharp side of the blade, facing down, gleamed dully along the temper line. As Chazz backed, Shinawa advanced, keeping the tip poised at the soft hollow of Chazz's throat. A short thrust could kill him; the tip was inches away. What did this old man have in mind? This was a good way to scare off students.

Chazz did not consider himself a student any longer, not really. It occurred to him that the truism that one is always a beginner, always just starting from wherever one is, was not just words. He was about to learn something.

He was not sure it was something he wanted to learn. He felt the edge of the mat under his heel. He couldn't back any farther. The sword tip jerked slightly, as if Shinawa were going to raise it over his head to strike, and Chazz twitched back.

"Wait calmly," the old man said quietly. "You must be ready to die."

Chazz had heard those words before; he had even spoken them from time to time when teaching. But Shinawa meant to kill him, and he could feel the adrenaline rush of fear sweep through him. He read commitment in his face even as the blade turned sideways and thrust toward his throat.

Yet, as the blade began to move, Chazz stepped toward it, pivoting sideways. He felt the blade glide past his throat as he placed his right hand on the hilt between Shinawa's two hands, and moved in beside the old man, his own hip behind as he extended his left arm, palm up, in front of Shinawa's neck. At the same time he extended outward with his right palm, continuing the motion of the sword in one direction as Shinawa was forced to either fall back or run into Chazz's arm. Chazz pivoted his hips and body toward the old man. Two objects silently separated, Shinawa spiraled backward over Chazz's hip and rolled away as Chazz turned, holding the sword. The roles were reversed. The sword tip hovered before the old man's throat as he rose to his feet.

Shinawa smiled and bowed. Chazz bowed to the sword and returned it. It wasn't until the old man was by the desk sheathing the sword that Chazz felt the weakness in his knees. Five of Shinawa's students were standing by the door, watching.

Shinawa laughed and smacked Chazz on the back. "That was fine," he said. "Your technique is very strong. But the spirit, ah." He shook his head.

"I'm not sure I'd want to do it again," Chazz told him.

"As long as you are ready, you may not have to," Shinawa said. "But there are always dangers. It is agreeable to have choices, is it not? To protect even those who attack you. To know the harmony there is in the universe and to be in harmony with it. We always say these things, but we seldom live them. You have taken up aikido to learn how to not kill, I hear. Very good. You must also not be killed, eh? Spirit. You need spirit. With spirit the sword can stay sheathed. But your teacher was very good."

"I thank you for him," Chazz said. "He would be honored."

There was a pair of curtained alcoves for changing. While Chazz was getting dressed again, one of Shinawa's students said quietly, "That was something."

Chazz nodded, pleased. It was something.

Shinawa walked with Chazz to the door. "Give my greetings to my friend Takamura. He is a man of great spirit; you can learn from him. But tell him for me he watches too many of those terrible old racist Charlie Chan movies."

13

His wound still hurt. The ugly tear in his side ached continuously, though the red-eyed kahuna had told him it was healing well. He could live with pain; it reminded him of Nam, lying wounded in the rain. He'd been in shock then, and after a time had come to love the shock; it was a high, the floating, the absence of pain. He embraced it.

Renfrew liked the work, the sense of mission. Renfrew,

running, or crouched as now in hiding, felt the rush of purpose, the calm effective power of competence and control. And this new one might be more of a challenge than the old woman. At least the target was not old and feeble.

It had begun to drizzle, but Renfrew didn't mind. He watched the girl through his binoculars. She'd been rummaging in the trunk of her car, but now was leaning against the hood with her pack slumped on the yellow metal. When she took out her cigarettes, he could see the brand clearly. His information was correct. He glanced at his watch. Twenty minutes. Plenty of time. He watched as she stamped out a cigarette, then rose in one fluid motion and jogged down the trail to the road below the parking lot.

A few minutes later he reached the road. He slowed before rounding the last bend, noting the litter of flattened toads. He shifted his pack and sauntered into view.

The girl looked up; a smile twitched at her lips, then vanished in disappointment. He was not the one she was expecting.

"Hi," Renfrew said.

"Hi."

The misty rain had settled in her hair so it glistened. Water roared quietly in the distance. The Slide was a mile upriver and the trail would be muddy, a strenuous walk. That was good. It would keep her blood moving.

"I hiked up the road," he said. "Thought I'd go down the river, that way. See the falls." He pointed at the trail away from the Slide. They would be going upriver. "You ever been down that way?"

She shook her head. "I've only been here a week," she said.

Renfrew sighed and leaned against her car for a moment, shaking out a cigarette. Her brand. "Smoke?" he offered.

She started to shake her head; then, to Renfrew's relief, changed her mind and took the cigarette. He lit it for her, lit one for himself.

He glanced at his watch. Eight minutes. They'd be letting her boyfriend through now. She only had to take three or four drags. Of course, the more she took the better.

Renfrew watched as she inhaled deeply. Her breasts, under

her blue work shirt, were small and firm. Like the Vietnamese girls, Renfrew thought. Thin, boyish girls, tight-muscled bodies. Good metabolism.

"Where you from?" Renfrew asked finally.

"Montreal."

"Ah." He nodded. "Canadian, eh?"

"Yeah." She didn't look at him.

Renfrew finished his own cigarette, stepped on it and shifted his pack again.

"Well," he said. "Guess I'll get going."

She was looking at her own watch. Her hair fell across her eyes when she tilted her head down. She nodded. Renfrew waved and started off. She waved back, looking anxiously down the road. Hers was the only car in the lot. Renfrew hiked diligently into the woods. Behind him he could hear tires on the gravel of the car park. He walked two hundred meters and stopped. Give them time.

It was incredible, he thought. They knew so much. She was just a tourist, only been here a week, a drifter with no family, a real loser, yet they had known this couple was coming here. They must have her room bugged or something. A good intelligence network, for sure, whoever they were. This haole girl had gotten herself a native boyfriend. They liked to do that. The boyfriend must have done something to be on the list. *Why* did not interest Renfrew. He didn't much care who he was working for. He'd figured they were either from industry, organized crime or the government. Since Nam, to Renfrew they were all the same.

He moved back toward the car park. The two cars were there, but the couple was gone. He moved swiftly. There was a high chain-link fence across the old trail. A sign indicated that the Slide was closed to tourists, but a visible track led around the fence. Natives ignored the sign.

The trail was even worse than he expected, water standing in it deeper, the rocks slicker. He kept to the sides where tough sedges held the soil together, but his Adidas were soon soaked. It didn't matter. He was hunting, though the quarry was already dead. It just didn't know it yet.

The couple's tracks were clearly visible. They were having

a tougher time than he was, especially the girl, so he slowed down. He didn't want to overtake them.

It took nearly an hour to get to the top of the bluff overlooking the Slide. They were at the very edge of the swamp here. Water collected from all over the high slopes, found the smooth volcanic channel that had formed here and funneled through it, making a series of three chutes in a quarter-circle arc, perfect for sliding down to a small pool. From here the river flowed through a set of small rapids and a mile or so of jogs before it reached the falls below the car park.

Renfrew settled into the muddy trailside and pulled out his glasses.

She was turned slightly away from him, stepping out of her jeans.

The boyfriend appeared from behind a bush. He was naked, with a slight beer gut. His hair was tied in a ponytail halfway to his waist.

He took her hand and led her to the top of the Slide. They were going to do a little recreational sliding. That was fine with Renfrew. He settled back and propped the binoculars on his knee.

He slipped a minirecorder from his pack and spoke into it very quietly. Not that they could hear him at this distance over the noise of the Slide.

"Eleven twenty-five. Female has taken the bait. The subjects are using the Slide. He weighs around eighty-five kilos, heavy build. She took six drags on the cigarette. That was at ten-oh-three. She's armed and ready, a real bomb."

A real bomb. Renfrew's little joke.

14

"What have you got there?" Dr. Silver was behind him. Chazz swiveled in his chair. Silver gestured at the television screen of the electron microscope.

"Look like seed fragments. Microstructures are right. But of course they're much too small. Why?"

"Oh," Silver said. "I'm just curious. A primitive plant disease?"

"No." Chazz frowned. "It looks like murder."

"Murder? You can't be serious."

Chazz lifted a shoulder, a faint shrug. "People are dying, Ben. This stuff was found on the first victim. It could be a new disease, but if so it's pretty odd. Is it a poison carried by a plant, an alkaloid or a resin? A microorganism? I'm looking." He gestured at the video screen of the electron microscope, which glowed with the false-color display of what looked like a mound of slightly flattened spheres. Chazz had electronically colored them red for the moment.

"Really," Silver said. "Seems more like police work than DNA research."

"Unofficially, I suppose it is." Chazz turned back to the controls. The view on the screen moved, as if he were flying swiftly over an exotic terrain.

"Is that so?" Silver said more thoughtfully. "Well, that explains why you asked Dewilliter about poisonous lobelioids, doesn't it. He was quite mystified. Of course, he's quite flattered when anyone expresses interest in his specialty. He had to come tell me you'd asked."

Chazz grunted. The image was puzzling. It didn't *feel* right.

"Look like *Abrus precatorius* seeds," Silver offered, tapping the screen. "Red seeds. Of course, that's false color. And as you say, they're far too small."

"Mm." Chazz leaned back in his chair and stared at the screen. He moved the controls, and the image swept in on one of the spheres, which expanded as he approached. He twisted a switch, and the magnification jumped. The surface of the sphere took on a rough, pocked look. He adjusted the view once more, moving into a hollow in the surface. Again he jumped the magnification, and entered the hollow. Ridges appeared, eroded valleys, lunar ramparts shading to violet, a fractal landscape. "It looks like a topographic map of the island, doesn't it?" Chazz said. Then he sat up. "Look at that," he muttered to himself.

Then he realized Silver was still behind him. Abruptly he flicked off the microscope and turned around again. Silver was watching him.

Chazz shrugged. "I dunno," he said. "It's probably nothing."

"Hm, well, I won't detain you. Have some things to clean up myself before we go tramping in the muck. Hope you're ready for the swamp. Wear old shoes." He waved good-bye and sauntered out the door. Chazz, hands clasped behind his neck, watched him leave. Then he reached for the phone and called Takamura.

Chazz frowned at the empty screen as he waited, tapping the edge of his desk with a fingernail. Finally Takamura came on.

"Cobb, Chazz Koenig here. Listen, I've spotted something. I don't know what it is, but I think you should contact the Centers for Disease Control in Atlanta."

"What should I tell them?" Takamura wanted to know.

Chazz rubbed his forehead. "I don't know yet for sure. Just tell them what's happening, that we have a possible epidemic. And have Dr. Shih look at the brain tissue. I think it's neurological. A lot of plant poisons and bacterial toxins have neurological effects; the tissue samples might show something. There's *some* kind of agent at work here."

"Okay, Chazz. I'll call."

Chazz took a deep breath, suppressing anger.

It was almost noon. He pushed back his chair and stretched. Then he carefully removed the specimens from the vacuum chamber, leaving it open for the next user.

In his office he put the specimens on the shelf above his desk, paused at the door for a moment and then carefully locked it. It was time he logged on to SCINOTE again.

There was an E-MAIL message from Patria. He ran it through the printer.

"Practicing kahuna?" she asked. "Yucatan has similarities. Could there have been contact, cultural dissemination, between the Hawaiian group and the N.A. mainland? Some correlations in plant use, healing and magic. Kahunas fall into a number of different categories, though. I need to be there. Shall I come?"

Hell, yes, he thought, reaching for the keyboard. He paused halfway. No, he thought. He hadn't actually *met* a kahuna. Rumors from Dr. Silver, a contact, through Dewilliter perhaps. Mention of cults. Praying to death. Better be honest. This would disturb her field work, more important to her than family.

He told Patria that there were rumors only. He told Patria that it was warm here, even in February, and the air was clean.

He told her he could use an anthropologist here.

He didn't mention that he thought he wanted children. She did not want children, and she knew he knew she didn't.

So he flipped through the pages of *Poisonous Plants of Hawaii*. It was on Page 25, the plant Silver had mentioned. *Abrus precatorius*. Otherwise known as the Rosary pea, the Crab's eye or the Jequerity bean. The seeds, ground down to a paste with cold water, could be formed into needle-shaped cylinders. If inserted beneath the skin, death resulted in a matter of hours.

The fatal dose was 0.01 milligrams per kilo of weight. The seeds were red and quite small.

The effects were neurological, similar to snake venom. Unfortunately, the plant was a shrub native to India and

Burma, and the seeds were certainly larger than the two micron structures Chazz had examined under the electron microscope. A contemporary kahuna could have learned to use it, since the recipe was right here in this book. Anyone could have learned to use it, to make needles out of these ground seeds, inserted it into John Doe's skin. But clearly that had not happened. He had not been poisoned by *Abrus precatorius*.

It was a dead end.

15

Renfrew was bored.

The couple played, sliding one after the other down the three brief cascades, out of sight below the bank of the final twist. They reappeared, trudging up the trail, legs black to the knees with mud, and slid down again.

Rain drifted overhead, fell on the three of them, the couple and their watcher, drifted on again. The sun emerged, washed the Slide in brilliant yellow, leaving Renfrew in shadow.

At last the girl unwrapped the food she brought from her trunk, and the two of them ate, feet dangling in the stream. Their backs, splattered with dark mud, were turned toward Renfrew. The boy had constellations of acne scars across his back and shoulders.

Renfrew was growing restless. The mosquitoes were boring in now that the sun had come out and the wind had died. The swamp upriver exhaled a penetrating damp heat.

The girl lay back against the bank and stared into the sky while the boy wandered off upstream toward the swamp, pushed his way into an ohia lehua thicket and vanished from sight. Silence fell.

Renfrew watched the girl for a while; he could see only the top of her head and shoulders. She had one arm thrown across her chest, and appeared to be asleep. He swung the glasses back toward the forest where the boy had disappeared, but there was no sign of him.

He put the glasses down and waited. There was nothing else for him to do. A mosquito settled on his forearm and he spent some time watching it. The mosquito was not large, but he knew the bite would itch like hell later on. He was tempted to smash it, but he refrained. Instead he watched. The tiny proboscis poked tentatively at his skin a few times, then slid in effortlessly. He watched as the abdomen turned pink, then red as it filled.

A gecko was perched on a stone nearby, throat swelling and deflating slowly. Very carefully Renfrew moved his arm toward the lizard. He brought the mosquito close, and the lizard responded by opening its mouth slightly. Renfrew waited some more, wondering if this little drama would have any outcome.

It did. The mosquito withdrew its proboscis and lifted sluggishly from his arm. The gecko moved swiftly and the mosquito was gone. Renfrew watched as the lizard snapped its mouth soundlessly a couple of times and swallowed. Not much of a meal, he thought.

It occurred to him that the gecko had now eaten a little bit of Renfrew, who briefly considered eating the gecko to complete the circle. The gecko threw him a quick look and vanished over the far side of the rock.

Nothing was happening. The girl was still asleep. He checked the time, then spoke into the recorder. "One-fifteen P.M. Male subject still gone. Female asleep."

He picked up the binoculars and watched her sleep. He was about to put the glasses down again when she stirred, changing position. Her arm moved, uncovering her breasts. He grew bored again. He envied her being near the stream. The mosquitoes were probably not so bad there.

That thought reminded him of the mosquito that had

probed his forearm. Sure enough, the spot was red and swollen. As soon as he looked at it, it began to itch furiously.

Renfrew decided not to scratch. He stared at the bite, feeling the itch flow up his arm. It was easier to take than the pig wound. Then the pig wound began to itch. He thought, between the two of them, he would go crazy. He was about to scratch when the boyfriend reappeared, carrying some mountain apples. He stood over her until she stirred and opened her eyes.

Now, Renfrew thought.

The boy sat beside her and they ate fruit, tossing the pits into the Slide. They were talking. Finally the boy stood again, and once again Renfrew thought, Now.

But the boy went sliding. After two or three trips, she joined him. They took two more trips together; the second time they failed to reappear.

"Come on, come on," Renfrew breathed, watching through the glasses, but there was no sign of them.

"Damn." He clicked on the recorder. "Two-forty P.M. Subjects have gone to ground at the bottom of the Slide. This may be it. I'll give them ten minutes, then move in for confirmation."

He slipped the recorder into his pack. Ten minutes later he started down the trail toward the Slide. It began to rain slightly as another shower moved in. He thought if he could move into position above the last switchback where the trail descended to the stream, he would be able to see them at the foot of the Slide.

It took five minutes of hard scrambling before he came around the last bend. They probably feared some other hikers might show up, and wanted their privacy.

The thought was small comfort to Renfrew, but he caught sight of the boyfriend's head and shoulders, then saw them both clearly, so clearly he had to drop back and move more cautiously.

They were below the first small set of rapids.

Renfrew pulled back and waited. It was only a matter of time. He watched the cloud formations moving in the sky. They formed transitory curtains of rain which hung over the swamp for a few moments before they dissolved, to re-form in another place. He could hear the water move down the Slide, the white water of the rapids downstream, the faint hiss of moisture moving on the stems and leaves of the grasses beside him. He was listening for something else.

Finally he heard it. The girl was screaming.

Her screams were thin and far away; Renfrew could barely hear her. It was happening so far away, in a dreamland. Even when Renfrew was lying in the rain shot full of holes, or gored by the boar, death was far away. When he emptied the clip of his M16 and saw the VC heads fall apart in the distance, it had nothing to do with him.

Very leisurely Renfrew moved down the trail until he could see the couple.

The male subject was sprawled in the rapids. His feet and arms were twitching randomly on the rocks; blood began to stain the water as the rock cut his ankles and feet. The girl was still screaming, her hands over her mouth. Renfrew could barely make out her words above the white water whipping over the boy's body.

"What is it?" she was screaming. "What is it? What is it?"

The boy's eyes had rolled back into his head, his mouth had fallen open, and he appeared to be trying to swallow. It was just like the old woman. Renfrew made a note of that in his pocket recorder. The girl had carried the poison or whatever it was. The pair had made love. The boy had died.

Mission accomplished.

Renfrew watched the body go limp. It rocked obscenely, white water pouring over his knees and belly. The head fell back into the water upstream, was pushed up until it faced the sky, mouth and eyes agape as another rain shower began to fall. Water had pooled in the open mouth.

The girl turned and climbed in panic up the rocks beside the Slide. She would be going for help. "What is it?" she kept asking, over and over.

Renfrew waited a few moments to make certain the boy was dead. Then he unsheathed his bayonet and started after the girl.

16

"I don't know why I didn't expect mosquitoes," Chazz said, slapping. "Travel brochures, I guess."

The group trudged single file along a narrow trail. Swamp plants grew low to the ground on either side. Through a mist he could dimly make out the edges of forest. It was not raining, but moisture beaded on Ben Silver's eyebrows and Andrea Silver's short gray hair. There were seven of them on this field trip, including Cutter, the entomologist; Thomas, the sundew man; and Bradlow, whose specialty was arborescence. Dewilliter had declined.

Despite the cooling mist, they were plagued by mosquitoes.

They had stopped at the edge of the bog and looked up. The clouds that moved over and around them were thinning, breaking into lumps, and the pale oval of sun hung nearly overhead.

"This is paradise, anyway," Dr. Silver grunted. "Look around. An isolated ecosystem like this is paradise for botanists and entomologists, of course. Tourists, too. Actually, the mosquitoes are not native."

"Someone imported them, I suppose." Chazz scraped thick mud from his shoes with the edge of his hand and flung the clods into the ohia lehua thicket.

Andrea laughed. "Yes," she said, "someone imported them. A sailor who was annoyed that the missionaries wouldn't let the girls swim out to the sailing ships any longer took a cask of brackish water from the hold and cracked it open onshore.

It was full of mosquito larvae. His revenge on the missionaries."

The sun brightened as the clouds thinned and shredded away. A still heat settled over the swamp. All the plants glistened with the mist.

"This is as good a spot as any, I think," Silver said. "We'll stay here awhile, then go on down to the Slide."

Chazz unpacked a magnifying glass and sample envelopes and strolled around the bog, moving carefully from tussock to tussock, avoiding the boggy ground. Andrea exclaimed from time to time over some particularly symmetrical mound of sedge, calling for Ben.

"Koenig!" Dr. Thomas was gesturing him over to a tiny clearing which cradled the delicate paddle shape of a sundew flower, its sticky spines seeming to grope in the air. Chazz dropped to one knee beside Thomas to observe the plant, and watched as a small crab spider shaped like the crown on the Statue of Liberty began weaving. It was about to attach one end to the tallest sundew. Cutter appeared behind them to watch. Chazz peered through his glass as the spider made its fatal mistake.

There was a leisurely violence in the way the flower closed itself around the spider, which had been struggling for some seconds with a kind of puzzled resolution to free itself from the sticky gum on the inside of the flower. Once the flower was closed, though, the spider was gone, invisible.

"They don't usually like spiders," Cutter murmured. "Usually they work together. The spider made a mistake."

"Sundew eating?" Silver said behind him. Chazz twisted around and shaded his eyes as he looked up. Silver was holding some blades of grass in his hands. "I think I may have found a new species," he said, proffering the blades. "It's a variant of *Panicum*."

"That's nice," Chazz said.

"Yes," Silver said vaguely. "Nice. They used to build with these grasses. Houses, you know. The kahunas were very good with plants on these islands. Knew all kinds of poisons and medicines. Shall we go on to the Slide? It's a different ecosystem there."

"Yes, all right," Chazz said. Cutter and Bradlow joined them; the other two said they might just as well stay here in the bog. The Slide was only a half-hour walk to the east.

"All right," Silver said. "We'll be back in a couple of hours, everybody."

The five of them set off along the trail. Forest sprang up around them, the trees twisted and stunted with the excess moisture. The path seemed to meander aimlessly, as if it were more interested in staying to the driest ground than in actually getting anywhere. Chazz saw unlikely stands of Sugo pine through openings in the forest. When he asked about them, Silver told him they had been planted in a reforestation project. There were so many introduced species in these islands it was difficult to discern which plants and animals were native.

Chazz could hear running water in the distance, which grew louder as they slogged on. Finally they came around a bend in the trail and emerged from the trees. The top of the Slide was at their feet.

"Pretty," Chazz said.

"Used to be something of an attraction for tourists, I understand," Silver announced. "It's been closed to the public for a few years, though."

"Why?"

Silver shrugged. "Who knows? Too many hikers, or the Park Service can't patrol this area, or there's been some violence around here or something. There's a car park about a mile down that way, but the trail is fenced off."

He started to climb across the stream, and the others followed. Chazz let his eye travel along the Slide to the final bend. The top cascade was quite high, and he imagined one would hit the first pool at the bottom with considerable velocity. It looked like fun, and there were fewer mosquitoes here by the stream. It smelled quite fresh.

The group scattered, moving along the trail down the stream, pausing from time to time to examine some interesting plant. Bradlow pointed out to Chazz some of the trees that once were mere shrubs. The climate and soil were so favorable that shrubs became trees.

It was Cutter who found the bodies. He appeared, clambering up the slippery rock and mud of the trail, his face ashen. At first Chazz thought he was having an attack of some kind, because he was gasping and pointing downstream. Then he began to retch weakly, as the others climbed down the trail.

The bodies were arranged side by side on the bank.

The faces had been neatly sliced from chin to crown. The skulls were cracked open and the contents removed.

17

"The man from the Centers for Disease Control gets in tonight." Takamura chewed nervously on a toothpick. The rotors of the big Sikorsky flexed gently overhead. There was no large clearing close to the Slide, and the emergency crew had to put down at the edge of the swamp. Takamura, Chazz and the other biologists were waiting for the pickup team to return with the bodies. The scientists were huddled under the trees a few yards away. Ben and Andrea Silver were both very pale.

Chazz nodded. "It looked like a ritual, Cobb. They were laid out like offerings."

"Yeah. At least this one wasn't a disease. This island is going crazy."

Chazz wasn't listening. "Sure?" he asked.

"Mmm? Am I sure it's going crazy?"

"Are you sure this wasn't the disease?"

"Disease? Doesn't look like it, does it? Throats cut, faces

sliced open, skulls emptied. Looks like some kind of cult to me. Or a madman."

"Maybe," Chazz said.

The sun was low. It had taken Chazz, running all the way, forty-five minutes to get from the Slide to the lab vehicle. He had used the CB to call the police. Everyone else had remained in the swamp; no one had volunteered to remain at the Slide.

Four men with stretchers were toiling back up the muddy trail with the bodies. Chazz did not envy them the job. It was hot and humid here in paradise, and now that it was evening the mosquitoes were swarming.

He glanced over at the Silvers. Andrea was standing beside Ben, one arm around his slumped shoulders. Neither of them looked good. He seemed to be in shock. But then, he had seen the bodies; she had not.

Takamura went over and suggested that since it would soon be dark, the biology team might as well hike on out and get something to eat. The helicopter could take the rest. Silver climbed slowly to his feet and walked off after his wife. The others followed. It would be dark by the time they got back to the lab.

Chazz doubted they would want to eat. Takamura came back as the last of them vanished up the trail.

"Who is he, anyway?" he asked. "The skinny one. He seemed very upset."

"Benjamin Silver. He directed my dissertation research. That was twelve years ago. I haven't seen him since Asilomar."

"Asilomar?"

"A conference center in Pacific Grove. California. Biochemists from all over the world met to hammer out some guidelines for research into what was called 'experimental manipulation of the genetic material of microorganisms.' It seemed quite dangerous then. We were making chimeras, organisms that combined genetic material from entirely different species; in some cases material from plants and animals were combined. People were imagining human beings crossed with bumblebees, lions with snake tails, that sort of thing. Nonsense, of course. The real concern was with disease organisms—cancer viruses, influenzas, bacterial infections created to be resistant to all antibiotics. New and hideous creations escaping from the laboratory."

"Is that a danger?"

"Of course. But between the treaties against biological warfare and the National Institute of Health Guidelines, the danger is minimal. Without the guidelines, the danger is unknown. And that by itself is the danger."

"Dr. Silver was at this meeting?"

Chazz nodded, a gesture nearly invisible in the growing darkness. "He's old-fashioned; a conservative. He was in favor of freedom."

"And you?"

"Oh, I'm in favor of freedom, too; with responsibility, though. There is enormous good to be gained from recombinant DNA. Research should not be curtailed, but it should be done responsibly. The guidelines help define what is responsible."

"I see."

The emergency crew appeared up the trail carrying the two litters. The bodies were covered. Light was nearly gone by the time they loaded them into the helicopter. The rotors started to whine up the scale before everyone was on board. The pilot was in a hurry to get out of the swamp before dark.

As they lifted off, one of the paramedics said, "I've picked up injured hikers this way, but never anything like this. Jesus." The last word was drowned in the roar of the engine. The helicopter tilted forward, turned on its axis and lifted abruptly over the trees.

Chazz looked down. It seemed as if there were no life at all in the darkness below.

Then they crossed a low ridge and he could see the lights of traffic on the coast road, and to the west the lights of Hanapepe, which disappeared behind them as they swung east toward Lihue.

Above them the stars were shining fiercely.

"You haven't said much," Chazz offered later as Takamura was driving him home.

Takamura nodded, but remained silent for some time. He turned off the highway onto the Koloa Road, through a tunnel of huge eucalyptus trees. The stars flickered behind the branches. Chazz could see Sirius flare to the south, the dog always chasing at Orion's heels.

"Your van must be at the lab. You want to go there?" Takamura said at last.

"No. I'd just as soon go home."

After a silence, Takamura said, "I think of Charlie Chan: 'Impossible to prepare defense until direction of attack is known.' I don't know what we are dealing with here. Outbreak of a new disease or random deaths occurring with uncharacteristic frequency? Neither of these is particularly pleasing to a police officer. If this is a new disease, at least it isn't a crime, but there may be panic. The papers will be out tomorrow, and there will be stories on all these deaths, including these two today. And these two certainly are criminal. Mutilation like that requires a special kind of human. From outside the island, I would hope. If there was a cult like that here, surely we would have heard about it."

"*Akua*."

"Oh, the little boy. Yes, *akua*. Come down and eat brains of dead people. Perhaps we have a brain-eating cult here. The police academy in Honolulu had no suggestions about brain-eating cults. There is some racial violence in these islands, Chazz. Too many tourists, too much unemployment, overdevelopment. We have tried to minimize all that here in Kauai. But racial violence is simple—anger, resentment, envy. This is more complicated. I don't believe in *akua*."

"Ghosts? Zombies? Maybe kahuna magic. Silver says they can pray people to death."

"Yes," Takamura said. "I have heard that."

"Suggestion, perhaps."

"Perhaps."

"By the way," Chazz said. "Does the word 'lolo' mean anything to you?"

Takamura thought. "A Hawaiian word, most likely. Doesn't mean much to me, though, why?"

Chazz shrugged in the darkness. "I don't know. It's probably nothing. Something Dewilliter said the other day. He said something about 'lolo.' At least, that's what it sounded like."

"Hm. He's the impressionable young man? Rimless glasses. Rather wild talker, I think. I'll check with Sammy later. Then there is your traffic accident. I'd like to know who he was. Surely not Ronald Smith from Indianapolis. Did you find anything in Dr. Shih's samples?"

"I'm not sure. There was something that didn't feel right in the electron microscope study this morning. There was plant material there, of course, but I don't believe that it was connected with the man's death. I think the pollen was a mistake. It was something else that I saw. It looked like an empty bacteriophage."

"You lost me again."

"Looks like a lunar lander with a stinger. It sticks a tail through the cell wall and injects its own DNA through it. Then it's empty. Sometimes the bacterium is fooled, thinks the foreign DNA is its own. Like I say, that's what it looked like, but such things are not really uncommon. I'll have to do a lot more research on this, study the samples a lot more. That's why I think you need people from Atlanta. It might be a disease. It might be nothing."

They drove in silence for a while. Then Chazz said, "Tell me something. Why do you quote Charlie Chan all the time? Shinawa says you see too many racist movies. He says Charlie Chan is a stereotype."

Takamura considered this question. "It began, I believe, as a kind of irony. The fact is, I loved all detective movies when I was a kid, even Charlie Chan. I saw so many of them, so many times, that I could quote him all the time. Then it amused me to be a Japanese detective who quoted a Chinese detective who was played in the movies by a series of actors, not one of them oriental. Now, you see, I find some quotations very apt. For instance, Charlie Chan says, 'Mind like parachute, only function when open.'"

"I see," Chazz said.

"I hope all these events are not related to one another,"

Takamura said. Then, "Sammy will be picking the doctor up later tonight."

"I hope I'm wrong, but I think you're going to need him."

18

It was early morning; Chazz jogged along the roadside to the Douglass Research Center. He worked his lips and spat. His mouth was gritty.

The murdered kids had been young. The bodies were young. The faces were gone. They were anonymous without faces. The skulls had been broken open with a rock. The rock had been set carefully beside the boy. Hair and blood were still stuck to it. It was a smooth oval rock with a bluntly pointed end, the kind often used to crack open coconuts.

The ancient volcano of Wai'ale'ale was crowned with clouds, but the sky overhead was faultless, as clear as it had been late last night when he watched Sirius flicker through the eucalyptus. Already it was growing warm, with that sense of indrawn breath damp earth often had in the tropics. He trotted on the shoulder, listening to the whisper of sugar cane. Many of the fields had been harvested, the red dirt turned now in furrows. Other fields had new shoots. The green was brilliant in this early sun.

From time to time the dew-soaked webs of wolf spiders sparkled between sugar canes. The wolf spiders were small-bodied, long-legged arachnids which sat in the middle of their webs with legs held together in pairs so they seemed to be four-legged and a good three or four inches across. The webs had caught more sun than prey.

His blood moved sluggishly as he ran. Gradually, though, his head cleared. Fear fell back as he ran. There were more than thirty thousand people on this island. Six deaths out of thirty thousand was not many. New viruses were rare, homicide even rarer, and cults, in the end, did little damage to people outside their own membership. The two bodies yesterday must have belonged to a cult. Some kind of ritual sacrifice to Pele or Lono.

He began to believe it.

The kid in the guard shack was asleep when Chazz stopped, panting, beside it. Once he caught his breath, he rapped on the glass.

"What?" The kid's head jerked up. "Oh, Dr. Koenig. I musta fallen asleep."

"Yeah. Dull night?"

The kid grinned. "Yeah, but the surf's gonna be up today, Dr. K. That'll make up for the dull night. Another shitty day in paradise, eh?"

"Looks to be, all right. So how do you take them, these shitty days?"

"When you live in paradise, you take it one day at a time. That's what we say."

"Okay," Chazz said. "Just don't get eaten by sharks."

"Oh, no." The kid laughed. He gestured at his surfboard leaning against the back of the shack.

"Terrific." Chazz waved, and jogged on down the road toward the sprawling laboratory complex that had been remodeled from old worker barracks. Behind him the kid settled back into his chair. Slowly his chin dropped once more onto his chest. Surfing took a lot out of you.

As Chazz let himself into the building, he thought about the positive relationship between benign climate and general friendliness.

No one was around. He snapped on the hall lights and walked toward his office, pausing every now and then to look at the old photographs hanging on the wall. There were pictures of sugar mills with rail cars and open touring automobiles of 1910 vintage. Men in wing collars and handlebar mustaches leaned on the hoods or against the sides of old steam locomotives. Horse-drawn cane carts were caught by the camera, their drivers staring stiffly into the lens; volcanic rock gardens; an ancient wooden hotel with a broad porch. Rows of Japanese peasants from the 1880s hand-tilling the thick soil. Some of the photos went back 120 years.

Chazz paused, his key out, at his office door, then changed his mind and went to the library to check his E-Mail.

He rocked in the carrel's chair while the modem auto-dialed the Honolulu Telenet number. It rang, chunked as it answered; he heard the high-pitched carrier tone, and the computer logged on. There was a message from Patria. He sagged in his chair.

Patria was arriving that evening. Aloha.

Chazz stared at the screen for several minutes watching the square cursor blink on and off. Patria had left Yucatan. Was it her scientific curiosity alone that drew her to Hawaii?

He pushed back his chair and paced. Suddenly he shouted, a kiai that shook the walls, and sat down to compose his reply. He would meet her, yes. He looked forward to seeing her. He hesitated just a moment, then signed it, "Love, C." He decided in that moment that she was coming not out of curiosity but to see him. This would be another chance for the two of them.

He'd have to get back to the condo sometime today to clean up. Meantime he should take another look at those samples. There might be more empty phages.

He was preoccupied when he opened his office door, and it took some moments before it sank in.

The room was a shambles. Papers were strewn everywhere, his desk was tilted against the wall, drawers hanging out. Books and journals were torn out of the bookcases and scattered.

The window was open. He stepped cautiously through the room, trying to comprehend what had happened. He had nothing of value in here, no secrets.

He leaned out the window and looked at the ground. A bed of lantana bushes grew along the side of the building here. The plants were trampled under the window. Maybe the police could make something of the footprints. Looking along the building, he could see the entire bed was trampled. It appeared the other offices on this side of the building had been burgled as well.

They were not specifically after him, then.

His elation of a few minutes ago was gone, replaced by a feeling of outrage. It was rape, violation; even though this was not his home he felt a smoldering anger in the pit of his stomach.

He took a scrap of paper from the floor, folded it around the receiver and punched in Takamura's number with the tip of a pencil. Later he would find out that this precaution was pointless, but his reaction indicated a change that had just taken place in his life.

19

The newspaper headlines seemed uncertain which death to feature, but the girl by the Slide had been a tourist, and hers was a spectacular murder. That pushed her into a banner headline.

The overall effect of the front page was disastrous. TOURIST DEAD IN FREAK TRAFFIC ACCIDENT; VISITOR DIES fell into three column inches on the lower left; UNKNOWN MAN FOUND DEAD got a full column down the right side; DIVER'S MYSTERIOUS DEATH and WELFARE WOMAN DIES got short bits at the bottom. A file photo of the Slide with a white circle around where the bodies had been found filled front center under the six-column head. The photograph had been taken when the Slide was something of a tourist attraction, and had been cropped in order to remove the unwanted happy picnickers Takamura could remember from the Visitor's Bureau brochure. The words *death*, *dies*, or *dead* appeared on the front page five times in 18-point type or larger.

Takamura dropped the paper onto his desk, turned so Strachey, the man from the Centers for Disease Control, could see it.

"There," he said. "'Events explode suddenly, like firecrackers in the face of innocent passerby.'"

"What?" The young epidemiologist was on his first field investigation. He was busy reading the stories, but the policeman's tone had put his last sentence in quotes, and he thought he should ask.

"Charlie Chan," Takamura said wearily.

"Oh. I meant what events exploded suddenly. Surely this is a weekly newspaper. All this didn't happen at once."

"No," Takamura agreed. "Over three days. Do your newspapers usually look like this? All this carnage?"

"More or less." The doctor shrugged. "I come from a large city. This looks like an ordinary day to me."

"I see."

"Still," the man continued, "so many deaths at once is unusual. The first step would be a talk with the medical examiner."

Takamura nodded. "She's a bit busy this morning, Dr. Strachey," he said drily.

Irony was lost on the doctor, who glanced at his watch. Even after only five hours sleep following his long flight via Honolulu, he seemed fresh and bouncy. "Right. But it's after seven. If we're dealing with an epidemic, we'd better get busy, eh?"

Takamura put both hands palm down on his desk. "Right," he said. The phone rang. He picked it up in a continuation of the same gesture.

Chazz told him about the burglary.

Takamura glanced at the headlines upside down on his desk. He couldn't see any connection to all those deaths. "I'll send someone over. It's most likely a routine break-in. They happen too often, even here. I'll send Sammy, okay?"

"Okay."

"And Chazz, once you're done with Sammy, would you come into town, to the morgue. The CDC man is here, and we'll be talking to Dr. Shih. Bring the slides and anything else you can; I expect he'd like to take a look."

"I'll be there as soon as I can. Jesus, what a mess."

"Yeah." Takamura disconnected, then called Sammy Akeakamai at home. Sammy agreed to get up despite the hour. For the lieutenant bwana sahib.

"Let's go," Takamura said to Dr. Strachey.

It was a glorious day. Dr. Strachey was clearly pleased with his first assignment. They stood on the steps of the county hospital. Dr. Shih had demanded ten minutes to finish up. "It's gorgeous here," Strachey said, making a faintly repugnant sound as he inhaled deeply through his nose. "God, the flowers. I hope this is a long assignment. I'd like to stay here awhile."

"Quite all right," Takamura assured him. "We like it here, too."

"Do the victims have anything in common?"

"The first man, still a John Doe, was a drifter, lived in a homemade tin shack at the end of a dirt road. Heroin addict. The diver lived in Wailanai, a little village near Hanalolo. That's on the south side, about ten miles from John Doe. There was a small stash of cocaine in his boat, traces in his body. Different drug, but both users. We had the freak traffic accident the same day. And a woman near Hanalei, on the north side, on welfare, no known drugs, harmless. She had a small garden. It rains a lot on the north side, a different—what do you call it?—microclimate. An unreliable witness spoke of *akua*, monsters, who ate brains of dead people, and an old car. It doesn't mean much yet.

"All these people, except the traffic accident, died in a similar way. Dr. Shih can fill you in on that. They didn't appear to know one another. We had two apparently ritual murders yesterday. Their brains were stolen. *Akua*? Haha. There have been rumors of a cannibal cult in the hills; we do have some former hippies up there, people from the mainland, haoles. They came to form squatters' communes in paradise, you understand. I suppose there were a lot of drugs in that group once, but they haven't made any trouble in a long time. The park police used to go into Na Pali to run them out. They'd homestead up there on park land. This is a small island, but there are a lot of very inaccessible places here. It's easy to hide. Maybe they've developed a taste for brains. Could they have caught this disease? Could it have driven them mad? Problem is, the rumors all appeared since yesterday, which makes it a pretty thin theory, but I don't have any fat ones. Does that answer the question? I thought not."

The first tentative sense that this was not going to be a routine assignment nudged at Dr. Strachey's awareness. He frowned.

The expression was not lost on Lieutenant Takamura. "Come on," he said. "Maybe we can go in there now."

Dr. Shih was working on the boy, speaking into the microphone hanging nearby. Her gloves were slick with gore as she poked around in the chest. Takamura and Strachey watched for a while until she finished, turned off the mike and turned to them.

"I'm getting tired, Takamura. I want a vacation. You are sending me too many of these." She gestured birdlike at the bodies.

"Dr. Strachey, Centers for Disease Control. He's an epidemiologist, right?" Takamura looked at him for confirmation.

Strachey nodded. "Nice to meet you," he said. It sounded odd since he was standing on the other side of the room. Dr. Shih was gowned and gloved and clearly not pleased to see him.

"Yes," she said shortly. "The girl's throat was cut, carotid artery, larynx, everything, quite swiftly. A very sharp knife. The male, however, died of the same thing as the others before he was mutilated. His was not a ritual death, unless there are some bizarre cannibals living up there in the hills; and if there are, they are very likely eating infected brains. Dr. Koenig's hunch was right. There is considerable neurological damage in the cortices of the first three victims."

20

"Pity," Dr. Strachey murmured. "I was hoping this would be routine. But then it never is, I suppose."

Takamura watched Strachey's eyes, not the object of his attention: John Doe's brain resting on a glass plate. The brain, which looked something like a grayish pink cauliflower neatly divided in half, had several dark blotches on its surface. It looked like a plant disease of some kind, a smutty stain.

Strachey and Shih were conferring, leaving Takamura out as much by their vocabulary as by having their backs to him.

"Evidence of hemorrhaging . . ." she was saying, tapping one of the stains with her forceps. "Inconsistent with cerebral aneurysm . . ."

"Any meningeal involvement?"

"None evident as yet."

Strachey picked up the brain and turned it over. He did not look happy.

"What is it?" Takamura asked.

"It's a brain," Strachey said with forced cheer.

"That's helpful. I meant, should I alert the hospital, call out the National Guard, get the hell out of here? Is this an infectious disease that is going to kill us all, or what?"

"You needn't . . ." Dr. Strachey looked up. "Oh, I see, you're joking. I don't think it's necessary to panic just yet. These cases are too isolated and far apart to suggest anything very infectious. But I don't know what it is, not yet."

"Okay," Takamura said. "I'm going back to my office. I have paperwork."

Strachey had already turned back, and waved his free hand. Dr. Shih seemed to be smiling good-bye over her mask, but Takamura couldn't tell for sure. He left.

His IN box was full, the OUT box empty. He fed a sheet into his typewriter and began his report on the two murders, referring from time to time to his notes. Time passed. He finished the report and put it into the OUT box. Four pages in the OUT box. IN was still full. He took some of the pages and read. There were memos from the sheriff's department regarding an intersection in Kapa'a which had been judged unsafe. There was an announcement of the biannual weapons checkout; a message about an advanced course in Honolulu on antiterrorist techniques.

There was a new directive from the Governor's office regarding Civil Defense evacuation procedures for the outer islands, a concept that always pained Takamura's sense of decorum. There was some kind of military installation on every island. A nuclear device directed at Kauai would most likely eliminate the island altogether. Evacuating everyone to Lihue and providing barges to take them to Honolulu seemed ludicrous. There weren't enough boats for 30,000 people, and it seemed most likely Honolulu would not be there when what boats there were arrived.

The IN box was finally empty. OUT now contained some pressing matters, most of which would find their way into a file cabinet somewhere. Takamura's eyes were closed when Sammy Akeakamai and Charles Koenig appeared.

"He sleeps on the job," Sammy said. "Very uncharacteristic of the Japanese."

"I was not sleeping, Kukui Nut. I was cogitating. There is considerable, if subtle, difference. What of the burglary."

"The slides are gone," Chazz said. "So are the electron 'scope preparations."

Takamura sat up. "Oh?"

"Lots of other stuff, of course. Personal things from peoples' desks. Some computer disks, small electronic devices. Drug cabinets broken into. Weird, because we don't have any recreational drugs around. The pictures are gone, too. Lovely color Polaroids of a phage ghost."

"You think that's what they were after?" Takamura asked the room in general.

Sammy shrugged. "Could be, or they could have just grabbed a bunch of stuff at random. No way to tell. Dr. Koenig locked his office yesterday. The slides were on a shelf by the desk. Pix too. The whole batch is missing. So's a gold pen."

"Why 'they'?"

"There were two of them from the prints and the amount of damage to the shrubbery. Wearing reef walkers. Every shop on the island sells them. No useful prints yet, but Kim is still dusting all over the place."

"*So des'ka*? Well. I guess Dr. Strachey will have to wait until Dr. Shih can prepare him some more slides to get a look."

Sammy nodded.

"One of the problems," Takamura explained, "of being in a small police force is that homicide and robbery fall in the same department. You see, the homicide section seldom has anything to do here, so just to keep them busy we are also given robbery. And, from time to time, vice, narcotics and traffic. We are never bored. So I suppose we'd better solve this one. Isn't there a guard shack at the Research Center?"

Takamura leaned back in his chair, clasped his hands behind his neck and adopted a ready, receptive air.

"Sure." Sammy shrugged. "Guard didn't hear anything. Didn't see anything. It was a quiet night, like most. Said he was really pissed off, because now he isn't going to get to go surfing and today, according to the surf report, the waves at Poipu are going to be perfect. Abso-lutely perfect-o. He said he was going to get a job as a waiter so he wouldn't have so much responsibility. He's got his surfboard at the Hanapepe Police Station, where he is even now struggling to recall anything out of the ordinary that might have happened last night. He won't come up with much. I think he was asleep. Like you, boss."

Takamura twitched his thumb. "The Kukui Nut," he told Chazz. "'Must turn up many stones to find hiding place of snake.' It's time to do the legwork. If I were you, I wouldn't come along. This is the 'When did you see him last and how did he look?' phase of the investigation. Unglamorous and boring."

"I've got to get home, anyway," Chazz said. "My wife is arriving tonight."

Takamura raised an eyebrow. "I didn't know you were married."

"She's a career anthropologist. I wanted a family. So we don't see much of each other these days."

"Soon you will come for Mrs. T.'s tempura. Then you will see a family in action. Perhaps you will come with your wife. We may all learn something then." His eyes twinkled with good humor.

"I'm sure as an anthropologist she'd like that. Observing native customs or whatever."

"So?" Takamura stood up. "We all have our work to do, then. Why don't you come downstairs and meet Dr. Strachey before you go; we can stop off and see if the computer has returned any information to us, which I doubt, but high-tech police work requires occasional obeisance at the shrine."

The computer had spat out a message. According to SAFE (the State Department list of Suspected Agents of Foreign Embassies), the accident victim was not an insurance salesman from Indianapolis, but a probable lower-echelon KGB operative in the Midwest attached to the Chicago consulate.

"I bet he was here on vacation," Chazz said.

21

It remained one of those rare February days made of balm and myrrh. Even the man watching from across the street felt good. When he saw Koenig come out, he stretched and yawned and breathed deeply of this somehow nearly liquid air. He said, very softly, "Hot damn." It was that kind of day.

Chazz paused on the steps, glanced up and down the street. It was, he suddenly realized, Sunday morning. This light traffic would be for the island's bewildering array of churches and temples, with their swirl of overlapping schedules. Some of these cars would carry Portuguese fishermen and hunters and their families to Mass, Chinese families to the Hawaii Chinese Buddhist Society, Japanese shopkeepers to the Honpa Hongwanji or the Soto Mission or the Daijungu Shinto Temple, Filipinos and Koreans and other Japanese to the Methodist church, Hawaiians to any of these, or smatterings of any ethnic community to the Mormon, the Lutheran, the Baptist or Pentecostal.

Whatever God there might be must smile at all the ways He finds Himself worshiped here; perhaps that is the nature of Paradise. Chazz, more agnostic than devout and more Zen than agnostic, felt sublimely tolerant at this moment of everything and everyone. The day was fine, and tonight Patria would arrive. He hadn't realized the void that work and isolation had made. His marriage was a tentative, fragile structure, nearly dead, but perhaps with proper breathing and calm encouragement it might flourish once more.

In this thick yellow sun it was difficult to brood on evil.

The cult must be a small one, a couple of people, three or four at the most. Probably it was from California, where such things were woven into the social fabric, though it had been a long time since this sort had been visible, even in California. This looked like Manson or voodoo. Takamura would find them and that would be the end of it.

And the mysterious disease? A new virus? An old virus mutated? An environmental toxin or toxic waste? Chazz shrugged. It wasn't all that serious, not in this air, this light, these frangipani scents. He could see night-blooming cereus from here, blooms now closed, and banks of poinsettia. The flowers visible from the County Building steps were as various and representative of the floral population of the world as the churches were of its people. Of course there would be an occasional odd disease. But it affected only a few, and those with obviously unhealthy life-styles. Dr. Strachey from the Centers for Disease Control would take care of it, if it hadn't already died out of its own accord.

The burglary too he could dismiss. There was plenty of disaffection, plenty of poverty, plenty of despair, even in Hawaii, to account for a break-in. After all, sugar prices were down again. Tourism was the only other industry left here, and that had been hit hard by economic recession. Someone thought there would be something in the lab to sell.

He believed it, every bit of it. He was smiling as he trotted down the steps and walked over to his rented van. Nothing could disturb the feeling of hope, not the MacDonald's across the way nor the Radio Shack in the shopping plaza. There was a warm and limitless ocean out there teeming with life. There were brightly colored birds in the ornamental shrubs and blossoms heavy with perfume. There was food for the asking.

That reminded him that he hadn't eaten in almost a day; he'd had no dinner last night, no breakfast this morning. He relocked the van door and walked across the nearly empty parking lot of the A & P. He hardly noticed the man across the street, who had been leaning against the glass window of a realtor's office, stretch and then walk aimlessly up the sidewalk. He was a short, stocky, muscular man with a neat dark mustache and dark sunglasses, vital on a day of such brilliant sunshine. He was most likely on his way to church, for he was dressed in sober dark blue slacks and a neat white shirt.

Chazz walked up Rice Street toward a breakfast place called Eggbert's. He passed the museum. Traffic picked up as the day advanced, and the irregular hours of church services brought more cars onto the road.

Chazz looked down Rice before entering the restaurant. There were no pedestrians in sight, but the poinsettias by the Museum were brilliant, the heavy crimson bracts bowing gently in the breeze.

Eggbert's was famous for blueberry waffles. Chazz had two helpings. When he finished, it was nearly noon. Lihue was busier. Most of the churches were emptying, and groups of strollers moved smiling along the walks. He could detect no evidence of panic, no terror of disease and death. God was in His churches and all was well with the world.

The figure idly window-shopping across the street before the display of a Japanese shop specializing in pearls was vaguely familiar; neat blue trousers and white shirt. Chazz shrugged and crossed to the parking lot. The old van took some coaxing but started at last, and he turned up Rice to the Kaumuali'i Highway. He didn't notice the silver four-wheel-drive Subaru three cars behind him.

He turned into the Kukui Nut Shopping Center, a new and thoroughly mainland enterprise filled with the usual tourist boutiques, record store, a Mexican restaurant, Sears and supermarket. He sauntered around for an hour or so, picking up groceries, cleaning materials, a couple of extra pairs of reef walkers. He browsed in the bookstore for a few minutes and finally bought a book on local hiking trails.

At 1:15 he emerged from the end of the plaza and walked around the building to his parking place. He passed a silver Subaru Brat streaked with reddish mud. The driver was reading the newspaper, and Chazz could see the headline and part of the picture of the Slide. The headline was a momentary ripple on the surface of his Sunday tranquility.

He was nearly at the end of the eucalyptus drive when

the Subaru appeared a half-mile back. When he turned off the Koloa Road onto Kapuna, the Subaru was a quarter-mile back, but it had vanished before Chazz got to the complex at number 47.

He parked under the carport. As he carried the first two bags of supplies up the cement walk to his kitchen door, two men in telephone company overalls appeared around the corner. They could only have come from his kitchen.

"Hello," the first man said to Chazz, who had stopped, holding his two bags of groceries.

"Hello," Chazz said. He shifted the two bags of groceries to his left side.

"Hawaiian Bell," the man said unnecessarily, pointing at the insignia on his breast pocket. The other man, holding a toolbox, nodded agreement.

"I see," Chazz said. "Something wrong?" He was ready to drop the bags if necessary. He thought of two men breaking into his office.

"Nope. All square. We had a line out, but everything's working fine again. Sorry if we inconvenienced you."

"Not at all."

They could be from the phone company. He watched them go to the visitors' parking area and climb into a panel truck. It looked like a phone company truck. As they drove off, the second man waved at him.

Chazz shrugged. He saw no reason not to wave back.

22

Takamura was accustomed to the even tranquility of his island; he had an intuitive feel for its psychic life, the rhythm of its cycles of happiness and despair. In his gut he knew the effects of unemployment and weather and good economic news and high levels of tourism. There were times when outsiders discovered his island and money flowed in, along with the people in the funny shirts; and other times when it was forgotten and a somnolence set in. There were times when sugar prices were high and almost everyone had a job; and times when the world markets fell and petty crime and drunkenness increased. Tourists' cars would be broken into more frequently, small thefts would increase. There would be more accidents.

Now, though, there was an anomalous spike on his internal statistical chart. Homicides, cults, epidemics, these things did not fit.

"Who's first?" he asked Sammy.

Sammy, who was driving, shrugged his heavy shoulders, and the little Toyota wobbled on the highway. "Start at the beginning," he suggested. "Up the dirt road to John Doe's house. There are six houses on that road besides his shack. Small farms, most of them. Three Portuguese, a Hawaiian, two Japanese. Everyone should be back from church by now. Maybe somebody saw something."

"Maybe," Takamura said without conviction.

It was too many days ago; too much rain and sun and a minor flash flood had happened since then. One of the

Hawaiian kids who'd been home sick from school thought he saw a car. Was it a big, old dark car? No, it was small, no one he knew. Could have been a tourist, they did that sometimes, drove up the side streets to see what there was to see. There wasn't much up this road; it didn't even have a name.

One of the Portuguese families had been up in the hills looking for a strayed goat that day; no one was home. The other two Portuguese families had been in town. One of the Japanese women thought she might have heard a car. It was very muddy that day; she remembered it rained all night the night before and the car sounded as if it was having trouble with the mud. Not too much trouble, though. A four-wheel drive, she thought. It had stopped to shift into four-wheel drive, then continued more easily, that's how she knew.

The remaining two families drew blanks. No one knew the man who lived in the shack beyond the end of the road, though they had seen him a few times. He didn't have a car; he always hiked up the road with an old backpack. But pig hunters hiked in here from time to time as well. It was possible to live a long time alone up there. Food was plentiful in the hills, mangoes and bananas and breadfruit. No, they didn't know he was a drug addict, though now it was mentioned, he did seem unhealthy, pale, with a strange sheen of sweat on his face. Still, they assumed he was a hunter.

How long was he around? Some said a couple of months, others said a year, maybe. Sure, it was their street, and he was a stranger, but he never bothered anybody and they hadn't seen him very often, just a few times. He kept to himself.

Takamura and Sammy stopped at the shack again. Not much had changed since they were here last. It wasn't raining now, but this far up the mountain it was cloudy. The wild lantana was still blooming. The roof was rusted, the sink was full of mosquito larvae. The smell had faded, though.

Sammy wandered off; Takamura sat on the rickety porch and twirled his porkpie hat in his hands. He could spin it a few times on one finger. He could bend the brim into various configurations.

Sammy returned and sat down heavily on the porch. "There's a dump back there," he said.

"Mmm." Takamura turned up the brim in front and put on the hat. He looked very silly, but neither of them laughed.

"People been dumping junk there for years. Off the side of the road, back a hundred yards. Not a lot of stuff left there. He used the dump for materials." Sammy twitched his head back at the shack.

"Yup," Takamura said.

"You know," Sammy said, "you haven't quoted Charlie Chan in a long time. You worried or something?"

"Yup," Takamura answered shortly.

"We've had junkies before. They bring junk with them from Oahu. It comes in from the Far East. Out back are a bunch of plastic bags."

"I know."

Sammy occupied himself in carefully unwrapping the paper from a minted toothpick. The paper had Japanese characters printed on it. He meticulously rolled the paper up into a small cylinder and put it into his shirt pocket. The pocket was filled with those tiny cylinders. He placed the toothpick between his large teeth and chewed thoughtfully.

They sat that way for several minutes. Takamura twirled his hat and Sammy chewed his toothpick. Finally, as if the thought had occurred to them at the same time, they both stood up and went to the car without speaking.

When they got back to the highway, Takamura asked, "Who's next?"

"Pete Williams. Runs a little dive shop in Hanalolo."

"Okay."

Takamura let Sammy make these decisions. They were the same as his own.

Takamura was hoping that nothing would happen today. He was hoping this run of deaths was over. He was hoping the man from CDC would find a bug with a simple cure; that the cult, or the maniac, had left enough clues so the others working on this case could wrap it up today.

Pete Williams' dive shop was definitely little. Pete Williams sat in one room surrounded by tanks, masks, fins and other equipment. He had a small two-hose compressor that thumped deafeningly by the back wall.

He cupped his hand over his ear and shouted, "Hah?" when Takamura asked him if they could talk a few minutes. Takamura gestured him outside into the street.

It was a little quieter there, and sunny. "Rake Wyman," Takamura said.

Pete nodded. "Sure. What about him?"

"He's dead."

Pete nodded again. "Sure. I know that. It was in the paper. He was using my boat, my Zodiac. I knew it would happen someday."

"Did you?"

"Sure. He went diving alone. Crazy. I think he tooted a bit, too. He was nuts, if you ask me, diving alone like that. I tried to tell him, a hundred times, but he insisted. A good diver, of course, been at it a long time. It was bound to catch up, though. Too bad." Pete didn't sound particularly upset.

"Any idea why?"

"Why he dived alone? Nope, not really. Treasure hunting, I imagine. Might have been looking for a ship. They often do, you know, look for ships, the treasure hunters. You know?"

"Do they?"

"Yeah. They always have some legend, some fabulous sunken ship. He was consistent, too, I'll say that."

"How so?"

"Always went to the same place. Always went to The Slip. Out past the Navy facility. Popular place for diving, but there are other popular places. He always went there. Probably thought there was a ship out there."

"Was there?"

"A ship? I doubt it. Been a lotta divers there. Could be deep, of course, but a lotta divers been deep out there. You never know. Maybe he knew something. You never know."

"No, I suppose not."

"He did find something once."

"Did he?"

"Yeah. An anchor, a propeller, something heavy. 'Bout this

big." Pete held his hands far apart. "I didn't see it. He had it wrapped up. This was a month or so ago."

Takamura nodded, staring off at the ocean. He wondered if all this had any meaning. "Anything else?" he asked at last.

"Not that I can think of, no, nothing else, I guess. He came and went, never talked much. A loner, you know the sort?"

"Yes, I know the sort. Thanks for your help."

"Sure," Pete said. "Anytime." He went back inside. The thumping of his compressor was loud when he opened the door, faded after he closed it.

"I wonder if it means anything," Takamura said as they drove up to Wailanai where Rake had lived. Sammy didn't answer.

The propeller in the garage didn't look much like a clue. It took both of them to load it into the trunk of the Toyota.

23

"You know what I'm going to do?" Renfrew said to the old man, whose eyes flared red when he looked up. "New shoes. I'm going to get new shoes."

The old man said nothing.

"You know what else I'm going to do?" Renfrew mused. "I'm going to buy myself a Jennings bow with silencers and brush deflectors, and a new bow quiver and sights and a couple of dozen graphlex arrows and razorback broadheads. I'm gonna fletch my own goddam arrows. No goddam pig is gonna rip me again."

The old man was silent, rubbing his knees slowly, soothing the ache.

"Hey," Renfrew went on, "you know what else? This wound don't hurt anymore." He slapped his side where the flesh puckered pinkly. "You did a hell of a job. That was quick. Tell me more about this *ana'ana*. Maybe there is something to this stuff."

The old man smiled bleakly. "You're dark, Renfrew, perhaps too dark. *Ana'ana* is a dark art; people do not speak of it much. A nighttime art, very bad. Used only to kill. You should learn healing, Renfrew; that is better. It has to do with the pig sometimes, too, *ana'ana*. You would understand about *O'o-a-moa*, the boar that attacked you."

"Good. And praying to death!" Renfrew smiled. "Does it work?"

"People die, do they not?"

"Sure they do. They're shot, they're poisoned, they fall down, get sick. Do they get prayed to death?"

"That is *ana'ana*. When a man died, ancient Hawaiians said, was it *ana'ana*? They took a pig to the kahuna and said, 'Here is the pig, O Uli in the heavens. This pig is offered to buy the death of him who prayed to death my friend.' 'Is this the pig to procure *ana'ana*?' asks the kahuna. 'Yes,' they say, and the kahuna tells them to let the pig go. What the pig does then, that tells the kahuna who did it. If the pig roots in the ground, then the man who caused *ana'ana* is himself doomed, and it would not be long before he himself was in the earth where the pig was rooting. Pig points to the man, and the man dies. This was believed; men died."

"The pig pointed at me."

"Ah, indeed?"

"I want to learn."

"So." Kalaipahoa laid his finger alongside his nose. "You wish to become kahuna, though you are haole?"

"Yes."

"It's a black art, Renfrew, kahuna *ana'ana*. Deadly."

"I wouldn't use it that way," Renfrew assured him. "Only for good."

"But consider, Renfrew: the boar, *O'o-a-moa*, he turned toward you. He almost killed you. That is a serious thing, a sign. You cannot trifle with such things. There are spirits all around; they have their own purposes, and may mean you harm. They come down from the High Realm sometimes."

"I killed him," Renfrew said. "Who had more power?"

Kalaipahoa smiled again, and his smile was as bleak as before. "Yes, you killed him. That could have another meaning, though. You are bound to *O'o-a-moa* now. His name was Death Rattle. Be sure it is not your death too."

"Don't worry about me. I can take care of myself. Just teach me."

Kalaipahoa brushed his fingers along his bushy white mustache, back and forth, back and forth. "*Ana'ana* is strange," he said, almost to himself. "It can turn back on itself. Very dangerous."

"Teach it to me."

Kalaipahoa brushed his mustache for a while, absently. Then he decided.

"All right," the old man said. "First, a song. I sing the prayer for you. Listen carefully." He closed his eyes and began.

A-a ke ahi, ke ahi a ka po o Lani-pili.
A i hea ke ahi, ke ahi a ka po o Lani-pili?
A i ka lani; make i ka lani;
Popo i ka lani; ilo i ka lani;
Punahelu i ka lani.

"The power," he said, "is in the sound. The language reverberates on the palate, produces vibrations against the base of the brain. You must remember precisely." He chanted again, his voice powerful, resonant, hypnotic.

Then he translated for Renfrew.

The fire burns, fire of the night of Lani-pili;
Where burns the fire, fire of the night of Lani-pili?
It burns in the heavens;
Death in the heavens; corruption in the heavens;
Maggots in the heavens; mildew in the heavens.
Heaven speed the death of the kahuna ana'ana . . .

* * *

"It is not the meaning, Renfrew, the meaning is not so important. It is the sound itself, and the intent you have to use it."

Renfrew learned fast. As the day passed, he mastered one after another of the songs to pray someone to death.

He thought these songs probably wouldn't work, not so well as whatever it was that he had given the girl in her cigarette that later killed the boy; he had seen with his own eyes how fast and effective those things were. Still, you never knew; some people would believe ancient kahuna were responsible. Rumors would be going around. He could use that.

Besides, the old man knew some other tricks that did not depend so much on magic. Maggots in the heavens was all right, but the crushed and dissolved roots of certain plants provided a certain path to death. Meat broiled on an oleander stick would kill, as would an injection of the extract of the seeds of the wiliwili tree. Even the lovely plumeria produced a poisonous sap. The kahuna could bring about death by innuendo, by suggestive extrasensory projection, by burning articles belonging to the victim, by what could only be voodoo, taking a piece of the victim, his hair, his skin, and making his image for destruction. Maybe he could do that. Kalaipahoa said it must be used to fight evil, not do evil. But of course no one thought what he did was evil. Evil was what others did.

But he used a little science too, in case the target was too strong, his magic too weak. He knew poisons, and secret deaths, intimidation and terror in the dark and bloody violence and the fear of *akua*, the brain robbers, the eaters of the soul. Healing kahuna had to know such things, to counter them.

So the day wore on and darkness fell on the mountain. The old man took his apprentice into the forest and showed him how to gather the plants, where to find them and what they did.

It was just the beginning, but Renfrew liked possessing the secrets. He liked the idea of being the human hand behind supernatural terror. There was, it seemed, a secret society of men who still practiced the ancient kahuna magic, some healing magic, others the black arts of death and fear. Renfrew would be one of these, whatever the old man said.

Kalaipahoa taught him that every medicine, every healing herb and root and prayer, had another face: it could cure, but change the dose just a little and it would kill.

And Renfrew, because he was not stupid, understood his lessons well and added this knowledge to all that the United States Marines had taught him, and all that he had learned before that in the streets of Detroit. Renfrew felt the power flow through him, and because he felt it, he thought he was free. He never saw the old man's smile, never felt the yoke around his neck, never felt its weight on his shoulders. Not until it was too late.

O'o-a-moa, though. He was bound to *O'o-a-moa*. He forgot that. The pig had pointed to him.

This, Renfrew thought instead, was his college. He was going to be one of the best. Absolutely one of the best.

24

The men were right. His phone worked fine.

Chazz called Pan Am four times during the afternoon. The flight was on time. It remained on time.

He imagined her at the Oakland airport. He imagined her over the Pacific at 40,000 feet, watching the movie. She would have dinner on board. How long would it be between the time she ate and her arrival in Lihue? Should he have dinner first himself, or wait and take her out?

The condo was clean. The fridge was stocked with food.

Through the living room window, the sun was hovering above the crowns of a clump of coconut palms that grew on the other side of the pool. That meant mid-afternoon. In the other direction was the scrub where he had walked the other night. He called it the Night of the Toads. But now the sun was stuck above the palms, refusing to move.

A breeze so slight as to deny its own existence rustled the leaves of the enormous ficus in the courtyard; they seemed to stir restlessly on their own.

Chazz looked around. There was nothing more he could think of doing. Should he do something about the stolen slides? Should he do something about disease and death?

There was no aikido training today. Shinawa was away for the weekend. Takamura was busy chasing clues.

A few people were using the pool. Off-duty waitresses who didn't surf, people with normal weekday jobs who lived in this complex. Chazz stood in his living room and watched them blankly for a while. Then he shook himself, took his *jo*, his ashwood staff, out of its case and walked up the dirt road into the scrub. There was a clearing where he could work out.

Because the day was fine, the dirt in the clearing was dry, packed hard and relatively level. Chazz in his bathing suit began to sweat as soon as he started doing the 31 *kata*, the prescribed series of thrusts and blocks with the staff.

Muscles leaped under his skin. The wooden stick sighed through the air. He counted under his breath as he went through the series, slowly at first, limbering up. Thrust, step aside, cover; thrust, step, cover, strike. Strike again, reverse, strike, strike. High thrusts and low ones, upward blows, blows to the side of his imaginary opponent's head.

He went through the series once. He paused, then went through it again. He felt dizzy, tired, a little bored. He wanted to throw the stick away; he felt silly.

He forced himself to do it again, a little faster, and as he did his breath began to ease. Sweat poured off him now, the staff moved in a blur, darting forward, whipped overhead to block, swinging in an arc, whistling as it fell. What he began to feel was anger. His muscles moved smoothly, the staff moved as a part of him, circles, thrusts, sweeps.

He switched to the thirteen *kata*, a different series.

He worked for an hour.

When he finished, he felt better. His violence had melted away. The air was clear and warm and sweetly scented. He breathed easily.

Patria's plane would be descending for a landing at Honolulu. An hour between planes, then a half-hour flight to Kauai. Two hours from now. It was a little after five.

Chazz went for a swim. The few people in the pool that time of day gradually drifted inside. He didn't know any of them, anyway, and didn't feel like talking. It was cocktail hour for most. He had the pool to himself.

He swam to the deep end. The water was cool on his skin after the heat of the day. He floated on his back, and an experiment occurred to him. He closed his eyes and slowly let out his breath. He began to sink, stopped. He let a little more air out. He could hear the sound the bubbles made when they broke on the surface. He sank a little more.

He could regulate exactly where he was in the water by relaxing and establishing neutral buoyancy by letting out his breath. He found that to get to the bottom he had to let almost all of the air out of his lungs. This shortened the time he could stay down. The important thing was to be completely relaxed.

He felt the cement of the bottom against his back. The sound of the filtration system was clear down here, faint gurgles and swishings. The game amused him. It was a matter of fine control, flirting with panic. Finally he allowed his feet to drift underneath him, and with a convulsive thrust pushed himself up through the surface, gasping for air, streaming water from his hair. In the moment he broke the surface of the water and opened his eyes, he thought he saw someone watching him, but the water flowed over his face, and when he could see again, the figure was gone.

At six he called the airport again. Aloha #237 was on time. He called the Koloa Broiler and made a reservation. He showered and dressed. It was six-twenty. He could leave now and be early, or a wait a few more minutes.

The phone rang. "Hi," Takamura said. "Good luck tonight."

"Thanks."

"Investigation is under way. 'Bills sometimes more difficult to collect than murder clues,' says the great detective. Not in this case, however."

"I imagine that's true," Chazz said, laughing.

"One or two things of interest, however. Perhaps tomorrow? I could come by the laboratory."

"Great. You can meet my wife."

"I look forward to same."

Chazz went to the airport. He leaned against the wire fence and watched the sky. Aloha #237 was a dark spot against the deepening blue. It swung gracefully around and came in for a landing in paradise.

Part II

INFERNO

25

She was darker than he remembered, and thinner. Her bare arms were wiry and tan, her thin fingers long and tapering where they touched his forearm. She was pointing with the other hand, and he followed the motion to the wall ahead.

"I expected lush tropical jungles," she said. He heard a sliver of laughter in her voice.

"Lush tropical jungles right this way." He waved at the mountains to their left.

"I didn't expect this." Around them was dust, sad trees and an iron-black stone wall roughly piled up without mortar. The heat built up on the dust and rock, rising to rustle the dry leaves. "In a way it's a relief after Yucatan."

"There's nothing left of it," Chazz told her, "except this wall, all the way around. Fort Elizabeth. The Russians built it in 1817."

"Russians?"

"This was their foothold on the island, this fort, and another one on the north side. They didn't do much here, just some sandalwood trading. Eventually they left."

The wall rose above them, black and hot. They climbed it and walked along the top. The earth was brown and hard. The interior of the fort was filled with weeds and trees that whispered in the faint breeze. As they turned the sharp corner of the first spike of wall on the lopsided star shape of the fort, they could see the waters just offshore were studded with reef. Two men stood on the rocks looking out toward the island of Niihau low in the distance.

They walked on. Patria's fingers rested lightly on Chazz's forearm, an almost abrasive thrill of need. Their touching was tentative, reaching across the time gulf between them. The wall wove in and out. They looked down on the reddish water of the Waimea River where it flowed into the sea.

"You know a lot of local lore," she said.

He smiled. "Not really. I bought a book of local hiking trails. We're on one."

"Hi, mister."

Chazz squinted into the sun. "Yes?"

"Hey." The boy climbled nimbly up the dry-construction wall. "Hey." He stood in front of the couple, head tilted up at them. "You were at Sally's. I saw you." He pointed west, toward the river.

"Oh, yes." Chazz squatted down. "What are you doing way down here?"

"Dad works the sugar cane." He twitched his dirty thumb toward town. "Got cousins."

"Sorry about your doll."

The boy shrugged. "It's okay. He died. Like Sally. I buried him."

"I saw the funeral. How do you mean, like Sally?"

"Sure. *Akua*, hey. Eat brains. I *told* you."

Chazz stood. "I remember. This lady is Patria."

"Sure," the boy said. He shook her hand solemnly. "Wife?" he asked, looking at Chazz.

Chazz glanced at her, then nodded. "Wife," he said. The boy smiled, satisfied.

"What's your name?" Patria asked him.

"Mikey."

"Tell me about *akua*, Mikey."

"Big," the boy assured her. "Like that tree. Long, long arms." He demonstrated, bent over, knuckles in the dust. "They come down from the mountains, eat brains." He pointed out the mountains, clear green, and bright for once.

"Monsters, huh?" She was hunkered down now, her eyes on a level with his. Chazz admired the directness of her contact with him. She'd be good with kids, he thought, then let the thought go.

"Sure, monsters. Lotsa kinds, of course. But I don't know if they're real." He was suddenly very grown-up.

"You don't?" Her question was serious.

He shook his head. "Never seen one. But Sally died too, didn't she?"

Patria looked questioningly at Chazz.

"Sally Cameron. An old lady on the north side."

"The north side? Where the other Russian fort was?"

Chazz nodded. "How did Sally die?" Patria asked the boy.

He shrugged. "Dunno."

"But nobody ate Sally's brain, did they?"

"No. Maybe *ana'ana*, hey?"

"Is *ana'ana* real?"

He stared. "Sure," he said emphatically. He ran past them down the wall. At the corner he stopped and gestured them to follow.

Heat pressed tangibly against their soles. The path on the wall rustled, quick with lizards, a sudden nest scattering before them. It was nearly noon, and the heat made a hollow room around them as they walked. Soon they saw the two men by the shore.

Water broke in small nibbles on the jagged volcanic rock and dead coral before the two men. There was something odd about their pose, and the boy squatted down at the star point of the wall with his finger to his lips. Fragments of sound floated toward them like jellyfish in a sea of heat. The syllables were round and foreign, heavy with vowels, heavy as the heat, tangible as the dry grit under their knees as they watched.

Chazz looked at the men. One was an elderly Hawaiian with broad padded shoulders under a ragged Hawaiian shirt and deep gray hair. The other was younger, an athletic, tan Caucasian. His hair hung shoulder-length over the collar of a tan T-shirt. He looked like a surfer in ragged cutoff chinos. The Hawaiian pointed suddenly, with a gesture so fierce and commanding that Chazz and Patria both followed it instantly.

The water had a calm oiliness that went with the heat; the

surface seemed solid, metallic. Across that blank surface something moved.

"*Mano*," Mikey whispered.

"What?" Patria asked.

Mikey half turned. "*Mano*," he said. "Shark."

The fin swept a broad circle just outside the broken water around the reef, trailing the V of its wake. It moved again out to sea, and the older man called out. The fin-wake swerved again, moved in, slowing. The finger pointed once more, and far out, almost invisible against the odd gray sea another fin approached. Soon the two sharks were hanging ten meters away, facing shore.

The younger man moved into the water, wearing reef-walkers, rubber ankle-length shoes. He squatted down in front of the closer shark, and even from the top of the wall they could see the shark's mouth opening and closing just beneath the surface as it rolled slowly onto its side. The dorsal fin made a distant slapping sound when it hit the surface. The two sharks moved slowly toward the man's hand, passed by, moved out to sea.

A moment later the older man walked stiffly, as if his legs hurt, down the shore toward Poo Point. The younger followed; they passed out of sight beyond the spur of wall.

Chazz stood. "What was that?" He didn't know if he was asking the boy or asking Patria.

Mikey smiled a dirty-toothed grin. "Kahuna," he said. "Kalaipahoa is old Hawaiian kahuna. Magic. He called the *mano* in, hah."

"It certainly looked that way," Patria said thoughtfully. "And that is *ana'ana*?"

Mikey frowned. "Don't know. *Ana'ana* is very bad. No one talks about it, you know. But Sally died."

"You liked Sally, didn't you?" Patria was squatting at Mikey's level again. The boy reached out for a moment, as if he was going to touch the smooth helmet of darkness that was her hair.

His hand faltered and drew back. He turned away. "Sure," he said. Then he ran down the wall and away. He was far up the river at the edge of town when they reached the place where they'd met him. When they turned back to the sea, the sharks were gone. Patria put her fingertip on Chazz's forearm again, the nail drawing a line of electricity down the length of the muscle, which jumped as though galvanized.

"I want you," she said softly, as if to herself, half afraid he would deny what was going on between them, after last night, her fatigue – when she had fallen instantly asleep and left him awake on the shore of her sleep.

He said nothing, but moved his hand up to hold her thin fingers in his palm. "Sharks," he said. "Calling in the sharks."

Patria slid her thumb across the back of his hand and gripped it. "Yes," she said, knowing he was talking about hunger.

26

" 'Lolo' means brain," Takamura said. His lean finger rested on a topographic map of Kauai spread on Chazz's table. "It turns up in the word 'pakalolo,' marijuana; they grow it in Maui; not much here anymore. Brain tobacco. And in place names only on Kauai. Nobody knows exactly why, or where it came from. Speculation is that once, long ago, before Captain Cook, some Hawaiian chiefs offered the brains of their enemies to Pele. Apparently a local custom; the legends don't appear on the other islands."

He paused to look at Patria quizzically. She nodded. "It's possible," she said. "Not an uncommon practice. It depends on where a culture believes the soul resides. To the Aztec it was the heart, of course. Ancient Greeks too. Others believe it's the brain. As an offering, the home of the soul is pretty high-value, worthy of gods. And then the practice of eating the organs of your enemy, or of your prey, in order to acquire their virtues, their bravery or strength, is also common."

Takamura smiled. "That's an unpleasant prospect in our present case. We have two bodies with the brains removed. I hope they haven't been eaten. By the way, the Hawaiian word for 'eat' is 'ai.' Same as in aikido, Japanese word for harmony. Also a homonym for love. A bilingual and many-layered pun."

"Love what you eat," Chazz suggested.

Patria pinched him. "Eat what you love," she said, intending the double meaning for Chazz alone. "There are the Foré."

"Who?" Takamura asked. His finger tapped the topographic map as if it were dipping into the Alakai Swamp, a blue-stippled stain sunk into the highest part of the island.

"A Stone Age tribe in New Guinea. As part of the mourning ritual they ate the brains of the deceased. They contracted a disease called kuru, which, it turned out, came from handling the brains. It took years for kuru's symptoms to show up, but once they did, it was always fatal. The practice is long gone now. But it was a case of eat what you love. Or, whom you love."

"Slow virus," Chazz said thoughtfully.

Takamura was talking. "We have our *akua* here, legends of monsters who eat brains. Not their relatives, though. I've never heard of any evidence for it. Stories to scare children. I thought with those two murders we might have cannibals here, but it's not likely. We haven't had a death in ten days."

He put his finger on a series of red circles. "Nonetheless, police work goes on. Here," he said, "was John Doe. His name, by the way, was Robert Lawson Hall, an assumed name. Thirty-seven years old. Born in Hilo as Robert Luria, moved to the mainland when he was six, grew up in Pittsburgh, Pennsylvania, to become a convicted felon of a depressingly ordinary sort. FBI prints and computer search indicated he had a substantial record: burglary, armed robbery, assault, receiving stolen goods and narcotics offenses."

He indicated Hall's shack at the end of the dotted black line of a dirt road.

"And here," he went on, "we have Wyman, the diver." The Slip was off the northwest coast of the island where steep, rugged cliffs fell to the sea, forever undermined by incessant waves and scoured by winter storms. Furrowed like a human brain. "Born in Lahaina, Maui. Former merchant seaman, lived all over the world, it seems. Moved here more than ten years ago. I don't know what to make of him at all. There was a propeller, apparently from an old Navy ship, in his garage." Takamura shrugged.

"Here." He tapped the broad valley of the Hanalei River. "Sally Cameron. And here the two bodies." This red circle was east and inland from Hall's shack. "These episodes quarter the island. No apparent connection among them. Strachey is still looking, but so far he can't find a single common medical clue to them and doubts there is an epidemic. He's waiting for word on some tissue samples he sent back to Atlanta. He has also requested some help. So far with no action."

Chazz watched light fall through the leaves of the bo tree.

"What about kahuna *ana'ana*, witchcraft? I'd like to talk to a kahuna." Patria asked.

Takamura said, "There aren't many real kahuna left anymore. Between the destruction of traditional culture and a couple of hundred years of intermarriage, few pure Hawaiians are left. Some of the old hippies might be interested in traditional folk arts, even the darker ones. Praying to death, poisoning and so on; most of us tend to think nudism and free love are about the wickedest they get."

"And the burglary?" Chazz asked.

Takamura ducked his head. "Nothing yet. We have informants, of course. And as Detective Chan says, 'When money talks, few are deaf.' Someone will try to sell something, and then we'll have them. Don't worry."

"Anything on the traffic accident? Smith, or Jones, or whatever his name was. KGB?"

Takamura shook his head. "Nobody saw him. Nobody knew where he was coming from, though of course it was from the West. He could have been up looking at the Polihale sacred springs. He could have been sitting on a rock somewhere. As you suggested, he may have been here on vacation. There is no connection. He died of a crushed skull."

"And yet," Chazz said.

"Yet what?"

"I'm not sure . . . You know, this island looks a little like a brain. Here are two hemispheres divided by Waimea Canyon, deep irregular furrows, a generally roundish shape."

"To me," Takamura said, "it looks more like a badly made arrowhead." He rolled up his map. "I'll see if I can find a kahuna. Sammy probably knows someone."

Patria smiled for the first time that afternoon. "I'd appreciate that. Perhaps the one we saw at Fort Elizabeth, the one Mikey told us about. And of course there was a ritual aspect to the double murder, wasn't there?"

"Yes, except the boy apparently died of the same thing as the others." Takamura said good-bye and vanished down the corridor. Chazz locked his office.

As they walked to the van, they passed the bo tree. Chazz told Patria it was a fourth-generation clipping from the original. "Buddha's bo tree, the one under which he was enlightened, was the great-grandfather of this tree. A cutting went to Ceylon, and a cutting of that one was brought to Honolulu. This tree was grown from a cutting of that tree, so it is a part of the original."

"What happened to the Buddha tree?" she asked. She had said nothing further of her need or his, but it was the unacknowledged background to their conversation, carrying them toward a kind of home.

"It died."

"What is enlightenment, anyway?" she asked at the car.

"Good question," Chazz answered. He drove a little recklessly, a little too fast.

27

Light barred her back. He traced the path of the river Lacanjá down her spine, the shade and light past Bonampak where the ancient murals were, the jungle ruin she had told him of, clothed in vines, dense dark in the hollows. The river ran smooth here, soft against her banks. He felt his breath catch, the lightest touch of his fingertip against the small vertebral mount, felt the animal life move in the deep waters.

She said nothing, head forward, her dark helmet of hair swept down against the cheek, lost in shadow. Leaves rustled against the whitewashed walls downriver from Palenque, harsh sun filtered through the thatch roof. Where was she, deep in jungle up that river? He thought she had been lost, had found another there. He touched the clasp of the top of her bathing suit, touched it. Felt his fingertip tremble.

Still she said nothing. Her suit was damp; she felt it against her inner thigh, along her ribs. She felt salt and said nothing. And then she tasted salt and knew that she was crying, but he could not see. His fingertip trembled against her spine, the leaftip touch of palm against the window there, where moonlight filtered. Somewhere a gecko chirped, chirped, crouched in the rafters, a presence in this place. Where was she?

He reached with his other hand, touched the clasp again. Suddenly the two halves fell away, two straps hung down along the soft curve of her rib, swayed with her sharp inhalation, the soft hiss. Chazz put both his palms against her shoulder blades, glided over smooth skin, skin not so tan as her forearms, skin barred with light and dark. Skin.

Her hands rested on her knees; she—turned away from him seated on the bed—breathed out slowly, in spasms. "*Bay,*" she said. "Yes."

Chazz bent his forehead down, touched her nape with his brow, his own breath then on her back. His hands moved, one each way, rounding the curve of her along the rib furrows, through soft muscle rocking under his touch. Her breasts. Chazz ached.

He lifted the suit top over her lowered head and she leaned back, into him. She was warm in the dim light, barred with light, a prisoner of shadow. Her back arched her breasts into his hands, and he felt the hard kernels of her grind slowly against his palms. He could barely move, barely breathe. Where was she?

Her head turned, her breath against his own neck, his chin. Her lips moved against his skin.

"*Akna',*" she said. "Our Lady, I have missed you. Where have you been, oh my *bäho'*, my companion?" She spoke raggedly the ancient Mayan tongue, the glottals, the thick syllables, and he heard in them the deep meaning of blood and fire. And so he too stirred. They were standing then, face-to-face, hands lifted first to each other's faces, then more swiftly down, sliding the damp cloth of their suits away.

"*Chich,*" she said, smiling. "Hard. Intense."

"And you," he said as her thighs closed tightly on his hand. "You are soft."

"Yes. Soft." She held his hand, held it hard, the dark hair curled damp and rough against his hand. She pulled herself to him, still holding his hand, and his other hand found the base of her spine, the Lacanjá between deep banks, shifting in the shadows, running swifter here. The muscle jumped and she released his hand to grope backward for the bed.

His face was buried in her hair, against her ear, his breath slow and deep and very warm. "I've missed you," he said, and she could barely hear despite his nearness, crying out as he entered and rocking slowly as they found each other's rhythms where the river flowed, carrying them along beneath rain forest where moonlight slid swiftly through the canopy of leaves. Mahogany spread branches through which the animals called to one another, speaking in tongues.

Chazz could see the coiled shapes of microscopic entities yearning toward one another too, as though the universe itself were one vast pattern of union, one infinitely replicated knot in the process of tying itself from infinitely small to infinitely large. The intensity of his pleasure met Patria's, and they found their center together. He no longer wondered where she was, where she had been, whom she had been with, why she had left him for such a far strange place or why she had come back to him at this time, now, because the river moved swifter and swifter, the sound of it growing too into a roar where the falls would be, and their joined bodies turned in the current, carried, floating toward that plunge.

Her breath grew rough, her arm twined around his neck, hugging his head to her own cheek with such intensity that he felt what was almost fear yet had no desire to move away, to break that terrible hold. Limbs thrashed, her back and pelvis arched bow-taut into him and she shuddered, frozen against him, suspended above the riot of white water in the river as though now they were soaring birds caught in an endless updraft, where she cried aloud a fierce hawk-cry that echoed through the canyon where the river flowed.

Gradually she subsided; her back relaxed, slowly, slowly; and then she breathed again against him, saying, "That was *yawat pixan*, a cry of the soul, oh, Chazz, my God, it's been so long," and she was moving again, slowly wringing from him such intensity of pleasure it bordered on the pain of need; they were the bird again, circling down to blend with the rapids as a leaf floats to the surface of swift water, and there were huge rocks, boulders, tortured land around them with cataracts and channels where the water moved in spouts and fountains, in cascades, eddies, whirlpools and torrents, clear, cold water from the distant mountains where snow fell all the year in a silence beyond belief, while now the sound grew until it filled all the space left around them, and they swept spiraling around the final bend and flew over the falls in a desperate roar of white noise and interstellar static and fell forever into the dark at the bottom of the world. The knot pulled tight.

Then someone cut the knot, and they were two people lying in a bed. The earth turned slowly under a moon that graced the sky and touched their room.

Later she spoke into the silence. "The ancient gods came from the tuberose, so fragrant a flower, called *bäk-nikte'*. It is lovely they come from such a flower. I love you."

He said nothing for a time, staring into the ceiling without thought. His fingers traced a spiral on her opposite shoulder; she shrugged it into his palm and rolled toward him once more. She put her arm across his chest, traced fingernail lines down his rib cage, across his belly so the flesh puckered under her touch, the graying hair damp with their sweat, up the near side. She took his cheek in her own palm, and turned his face toward hers, and kissed him. He kissed her back, and she reached down for him. "*Bäk-nikte'*," she said. "So fragrant a flower." And later she said, softly, "*Chich*," and they made love once more, and their bed was made of leaves that rustled beneath their movements together, and the air was warm and humid as if it were noontime when all other motion was suspended in the heat and wet.

Later Chazz thought about her fear of having children and said something. She shook her head. "It's all right," she said. "Don't worry. Not about that." She watched the moonlight, steeply slanted now, almost down behind the scrub outside. It tracked across the walls, catching a glitter from time to time as if this were a fairyland of mica dust; and then the moonlight faded and the room turned dark.

"Clouds," she said.

Chazz made a sound. "Nothing to worry about," he said. "A rain shower, perhaps. The weather is benign. This is paradise, you know."

He could hear her smile as she said, "I believe I read that somewhere. So what is happening to spoil it?"

For a moment he thought it was something he'd done to the mood, then he knew she meant the reason he'd called her here, their meeting with Takamura, the deaths, and he said he didn't know, not yet, but that something was loose here in the darkness under the sunburst surface of things. Probably, he thought, it was a virus with a new kind of vector, but perhaps she could suggest some other way of seeing it, something that would break the deadlock.

She moved closer to him in the dark. "*Akna'*," she said. "The moon is gone. That would be a bad sign in Yucatan, under the circumstances. Are people spreading this? Witchcraft is often held accountable for inexplicable deaths, but inexplicable means without explanation, and we scientific Westerners have explanations for everything, don't we?"

"Not at the moment," he said. "No explanation. *Akua*, perhaps, those shambling monsters in the dark, out of our nightmares, eh?"

Cool and rational she might be, but she slid her own hand between his legs and held him gently there, for comfort, for reassurance.

Dreamily then, as the darkness deepened, she told him about the formal parting before sleep of the Lacandon Maya. "*Ki 'iba' a wilik*," she murmured. "It means good night. It means be careful what you see."

28

Once Koenig's van had vanished up Kapuna Road, Sammy Akeakamai heaved himself out of the yellow Toyota. He looked up at the sky, which seemed to glower back at him.

He wore a loose short-sleeved shirt patterned with crisscrossing palm leaves of a virulent green on a light blue background hanging outside his baggy white trousers. Takamura had told him it was perfect camouflage if only he were standing still against the wallpaper of the lobby at the Kauai Luau Hyatt. Sammy shrugged when Takamura said that. "Surveillance," he said. "It's my surveillance shirt."

This was surveillance.

Despite what Lieutenant Takamura called his reprehensible clothing and high-poi diet, Sammy was very good at surveillance. Without question, the subject, Charles Koenig, did not know he was under observation.

Sammy looked up and down the road. It was clear. He trotted across to the condominium side and walked slowly along the shoulder. In seconds his shirt was stuck to his back. The air was close and dense. He vaguely envied the Koenigs their trip to Koke'e, where at least the altitude, if not the clouds themselves, would give relief from this unseasonable heat and humidity.

He paused in front of the complex. There was no one in sight. The surface of the pool was flat and dull, without a ripple. The palms leaned away from the prevailing, though at the moment nonexistent, wind. The leaves of the enormous ficus drooped in silence.

A silver Subaru Brat appeared around the corner, moving slowly. The driver seemed to be looking at address numbers. He cruised past the complex, then abruptly speeded up.

Just then a kid came around the corner carrying a long aluminum pole with a net on the end and a coil of thick white plastic hose. While Sammy watched, the kid began to skim the few leaves adrift on the surface of the pool. He didn't notice the overweight Hawaiian by the road. Sammy stood there peeling his damp shirt away from his chest and back while the kid hooked up his hose and began to vacuum the bottom of the pool.

Then he sauntered up to the pool. "Hi," he said.

The kid jumped.

"Sorry," Sammy said. "Didn't mean to scare you."

"Oh." There was an awkward pause during which Sammy grinned at the kid. "Tuesday," the kid said finally. "Pool-cleaning day."

Sammy nodded, still grinning.

"Hot, huh?" the kid said.

Sammy nodded.

The kid vacuumed for a while. Sammy stood and watched idly. There was a faint film of algae growing on the bottom and sides of the pool. The vacuum swept over the thin green and left behind the clear blue. The blue was very close to the background color of Sammy's shirt.

"Gonna be a storm, I heard," the kid said, not looking up.

"Heard that too," Sammy said. "Place full?"

"Huh? Oh, the condos. Naw. Tourism's off this year."

Sammy nodded again. "Live here?"

"Me? Yeah. My father's the manager."

"Had any problem with the phones lately?"

The kid frowned. "Nope. You with the phone company?"

Sammy made a vague gesture that could have been assent. "Got to button down for the storm," he said.

"Oh." The kid moved his vacuum over the final patch of algae and pulled the vacuum to the surface. He unhooked the hose and coiled it on the surface. The water fell still very quickly, reflecting the palm leaves and dull sky.

"You want to check the wires or something?" he said.

Sammy nodded.

"Okay, sure, help yourself. You need a passkey or anything? The housekeeper should be over by the three hundreds now. She's got a key. Tell her I said it's okay. I'm Billy."

"Okay, Billy," Sammy said. "Thanks. You're a big help." He ambled off in search of the housekeeper. It was always better to have inside help.

The housekeeper was a pretty haole girl hardly out of high school. She gave Sammy the key without a question.

Koenig's condo was on the west wing corner. The kitchen entrance was on the back, facing the scrub land next door, undeveloped as yet. Sammy was not likely to be observed.

He moved swiftly through the condo, checking drawers, closets, cabinets. Finally he unplugged the telephone and unscrewed the mouth- and ear-pieces, probing with his blunt forefinger, moving wires aside. He grunted when he unscrewed the bottom plate on the phone and looked at the printed circuits inside. He shook the handset and a small wafer dropped into his palm. He looked at it thoughtfully for a few moments. Then he replaced everything and plugged in the phone again.

Outside the kitchen door he examined the phone wires, tracing them out to the pole on the street with his eye. Satisfied, he strolled back toward the road.

He walked west for a while. An old dirt road went inland here, the low stone walls on either side indicating that this was an ancient cane road, long since abandoned. He walked along the dirt road for a while; the scrub was taller than his head, and he could see nothing to either side. Once the dirt road had bent a little, he could no longer see anything but sky and the twiggy trunks of this old forage.

After walking a few hundred meters, he paused in a small clearing, then climbed onto the stone wall. He was tall enough now to see over the tops of the scrub. The condos were very close here, though walking through that stuff would be a real chore, especially in wet weather. He checked the dirt for tracks. Certainly there had been locals driving up this road. It was covered with an ancient mat of dead toads, but there were no fresh ones. The road had not been used for some time. It was ideal.

He waddled back to the Toyota.

The heat and clouds were increasingly oppressive. This was going to be a hell of a storm when it hit.

29

Patria was explaining her theory of cross-cultural substrates.

"But substrate is a term in microbiology," Chazz insisted. "A substrate is what enzymes and some RNA molecules work on."

"No it isn't." She laughed. "It's an underlying cultural or political structure."

They both were laughing. "Well, I say it's a chemical."

"So are underlying cultural structures."

A wind was picking up the dust by the roadside. Dust devils swirled along the shoulder. There was the promise of rain, but no rain, only heat. Yet they were laughing at the metaphors one science borrowed from another, how quarks get charm and how God does not play dice with the universe.

"Any sufficiently advanced technology is indistinguishable from magic," Patria suggested, and Chazz intoned in answer, "Applied science is a conjurer, whose bottomless hat yields impartially the softest of Angora rabbits and the most petrifying of Medusas—Aldous Huxley." And Patria said, "The scientific method is a cultural substrate."

"What about children?" Chazz asked, apparently irrelevantly.

"Don't bring that up again," she said softly. "We were doing fine."

He lifted a hand from the wheel. "All right."

He turned off the Kapuna Road onto the highway and headed west. "Where're we goin?" Patria wanted to know.

"The Grand Canyon," he said.

"Come on. That's in Arizona."

"Wait and see."

"Ha!"

The road rose and dipped through cane fields and along the bluffs beside the sea. Sunlight fell far away through holes in the cloud cover, slanting in broad shafts onto the ocean surface where it danced in brilliance amid the dark blue of shadow. No sun fell here, on land, locked down by a low ceiling of thick cloud. Dust devils danced alongside the van.

"It was here," Chazz said suddenly.

Patria looked up. "What was?"

"A weird traffic accident. I found him. A real freak."

"The Russian spy?"

"Yeah. Even spies take vacations."

"Sure? Maybe it wasn't a vacation. Maybe it was business."

"Come on," Chazz chided. "What business? There's nothing secret here. They grow sugar." He gestured at the cane fields all around them. "They grow pineapples. Used to, anyway. They grow condominiums." They swung down into Hanapepe. The town was asleep, the stores shuttered. There was bad weather coming. He had to stop twice for signs. At the second sign he looked in the mirror.

"That's funny," he said.

"What's funny?"

"Nothing," Chazz said. The van's engine whined on the upgrade. The passed a Japanese restaurant with Hawaiian architecture and Chinese food. "It's just that I keep seeing that car."

The silver Brat was hidden beyond the turn behind them when Patria turned to look, and did not reappear.

Kekaha was a modern town, with new shops and a prosperous-looking school. He had to wind through the back streets to find the canyon road. The streets seemed oddly deserted. This was not a tourist area, and Chazz couldn't account for the apparent prosperity of the village. Perhaps it was the traffic up to the canyon and the Alakai Swamp. Or perhaps it was the Pacific Missile Approach Network Facility a few miles farther up the road. This could be where the Naval personnel lived off-base. The last building at the edge of town was a bar called The Honeycreeper with a pay phone by the entrance.

The Koke'e Road wound up the mountain in a series of sharp switchbacks. About halfway up he spotted the silver truck again, two switchbacks behind them, following. He pointed it out to Patria. If they were being followed, there was nowhere for them to escape, and the van would be no match for the Subaru. By now they were close enough to the cloud base to touch it.

Soon they entered a gray womb of fog. Narrow streaks of water condensed and ran down the windshield. When he turned on the wipers they smeared the water in an arc across his vision. There was enough dust on the glass to turn the water to paste. He found himself hunched at the wheel, squinting through the smears of mud until finally the windshield wiped clean.

"Maybe we should turn and go back," Patria suggested.

"We're almost there," Chazz said. "We'll just go to the first lookout. You should see the canyon."

"See? See? What're we gonna see in this?"

He shrugged his heavy shoulders. "Could be clear there. Here's the Waimea Canyon Road. It's just a little farther."

He was right. Around a sharp turn he made out the sign for a canyon lookout through the fog. There was a car park at the end. It was empty.

"So," he said. "Here."

Patria hugged his arm. The cloud thinned as they climbed the cement walkway over the ridge to the lookout. Chazz found himself listening for the sound of a Subaru engine behind him, but the silence was complete.

Strangely, he had been right. The bottom of the canyon was clear. The lookout was perched on the face of the cliff plunging 1400 feet to the winding canyon floor, where the river was a dull lead color amid the dark greens. Just overhead the shreds of cloud blew east like tattered ribbon.

The layered rock walls seemed to write in an unknown language the story of millions of years, red and tan, ochre and brown and orange rock absolutely horizontal, thin, layer after layer, winding around the eroded points and ridges, the shallower slopes covered with green broken by outcroppings of cliffside, points and curtains and ripples of endless rock that vanished into the overhead gray.

"It does look like the Grand Canyon," Patria said, leaning over the railing to look down.

The cloud closed in again when they returned to the parking lot, so at first they didn't see the silver Subaru waiting for them.

30

Cobb Takamura looked out his office window at the low clouds and frowned.

The storm warnings had been coming in for days. Tropical Storm Walter was in the central Pacific, moving toward the islands. Satellites charted arctic air flowing southeast out of Siberia. The storm could just as easily move south of the islands as north. Takamura had felt in the warmth and humidity a tropical pressure pushing northward.

In fact, he wasn't thinking about the weather at all. Weather was a big, tangible and familiar force, destructive at times, but known.

Takamura was thinking about the interim report on his desk. It had come up this morning from Drs. Shih and Strachey. It included an enormous amount of technical verbiage, behind which Takamura detected an ominous uncertainty. The deaths were due to disease; that much was clear. That the disease had been induced was far less certain. Hall was a junkie. While his arms were riddled with puncture wounds, so were several other parts of his body. The wound on his leg could have been one of those. None of the others had visible puncture wounds.

He had another report. The propeller in Rake Wyman's garage was from an old Navy wreck, the *Valiant*, sunk off Kauai in 1943. The wreck had never been found. Perhaps he had found it.

Rake Wyman had no puncture wound.

The boy, Freddie Delarota, half Portuguese and part everything else, also had no apparent puncture wound, though the face had been mutilated, perhaps to conceal it.

Whatever it was, it ran a similar course in all of them. Photomicrographs from Atlanta were in the report, side by side with pictures of the victim's brain tissue. The pictures from Atlanta looked almost the same, not only to Takamura's uncritical eye, but to the doctors downstairs as well.

The photos from Atlanta were of sheep brains.

"There aren't any sheep here," Takamura told the clouds.

"Pardon," a voice asked from the doorway.

"Oh, hello, Doctor. I'm glad you're here. Your report is . . ." Takamura paused, groping. "Puzzling," he finished lamely.

Dr. Strachey nodded, expressionless.

"It's quite technical. Much jargon."

Strachey nodded again. He tried a weak smile, let it go. "We often cover ignorance with jargon, Lieutenant. It's a course in medical school. I came up about something else, though."

Takamura sighed. "Yes?"

"There's been a snag of some kind in Atlanta. The help I requested's been delayed. I don't know why." He held up his hands helplessly. "The two of us are overworked down there. We need more help. It's crazy."

Takamura turned back to the window. He clasped his hands behind his back and rocked on his heels. The clouds had not changed. They seemed carved from some durable substance, like monuments. "I'm a policeman," he told the outdoors. "I'm not a doctor. I'm not even sure this is police work. We've had four strange deaths from disease, a traffic accident and a murder. The murder at least is police work. I don't know. Perhaps I should call Honolulu, get some state help for you."

"That would be nice," Strachey said quietly. "You said something about sheep when I came in."

"Sheep. We have no sheep here. To speak of. We don't need wool, you see. Pigs, yes. Chickens and dogs and a lot of goats. Wild animals. No sheep."

"You're thinking of the photos. Sheep get a disease. Viral, called scrapie. Similar to number of other diseases—Creutzfeldt-Jakob, Alzheimer's disease . . ."

"Yes," Takamura interrupted. "I read the report."

"The point is," Strachey said slowly, "the causes of these diseases are not clearly understood. What is known is that they are very slow. They take years to appear . . . once symptoms show up, though, progress is rapid." He picked the report off Takamura's desk. "Look." He put his finger on the reproductions of the photomicrographs.

"Normal brain cells." He tapped a picture. "Round cells, called astrocytes, here. In the infected tissue these cells have swollen, become star-shaped. Sheep brain tissue here, infected with scrapie."

Strachey looked at Takamura. "Our problem is that these people all could have what is called a slow virus, which means they contracted the disease years ago, perhaps decades. The virus hides in the nerve cells, then one day, for reasons unknown, out it comes, killing on the way. Quite quickly, too. We need to find what all these people have in common, in the past." He gave an unhappy emphasis to the last phrase.

"Or?" Takamura said after a moment.

"Or else we have something else, and it's not something I want to think about."

"Think about it," Takamura told him.

"Or else we have a mutant. That's a real problem."

"Why?"

Strachey started to pace the narrow office, back and forth. "Look, we have never even seen the organism responsible for the slow virus diseases. In fact, it probably is not a virus at all, but what we call a viroid, for lack of a better term. Evidence is . . . indirect."

Takamura was relentless. "What's a viroid?"

"A naked virus. It has no protein coat. Consequently it attracts no antibodies. It can't be recognized by the host. It acts like part of the host's genetic material. It co-opts the host's protein synthesis machinery, maybe. And it's small, just a few hundred base-pairs long."

"I don't know what you're talking about."

Strachey sighed. He held his hands in front of him, cupped. "Think of a virus, say a smallpox virus, as being about the size of a large truck. Then a viroid would be the size of your kid's rubber duck. They're small."

"So we're dealing with an organism you can't see?"

"Worse. We can't detect it at all. Not yet, not to my knowledge. It's just that they're the only logical explanation. There is an awful lot we don't know."

Takamura sat on the edge of his desk. He picked up his hat and ran his forefinger around the brim. He put the hat back on the desk and looked at Strachey.

"Who does know?" he asked softly.

"A man named Silver did some work on these things some years ago. I don't know if he's still working with viroids, but he published a couple of papers on possible genetic effects of viroids."

"Really?" Takamura said.

31

Chazz saw the Brat as soon as he started down the far side of the parking lot toward the van. It sat on the main road, blocking half the entry. He could make out two figures inside.

He looked around. There might be just enough room to make it to the highway in front of the Subaru, but it would be close; there was a runoff ditch on either side of the access road, and the van would probably topple if he dropped a wheel into it. If he turned left downhill after passing the truck, the Subaru would have to make a U-turn, but it appeared that all they had to do if he attempted to leave was pull ahead, and he'd be blocked.

A service road blocked off by a chain wound uphill to the left. Two cement paths twisted away from the parking lot, one to the lookout and the other in the opposite direction down the canyon to a picnic area. Otherwise, trees or hillside crowded all four sides.

Another sign indicated there were restrooms up the service road.

"Patria," Chazz said quietly, taking her arm.

"Mmm," she said.

"We have a problem. See the silver Subaru down there."

"I see it. Tourists, hm?"

"It's been following me off and on for a couple of weeks now. Since the day you came. They're blocking the road."

"Charlie, come on. They're not doing anything. Why would they be after you?"

Chazz was unlocking the driver's door of the van. He

frowned. "I'm not sure. Perhaps it's just Dewilliter's vague rumors and sense of foreboding. You never call me Charlie unless you're worried."

"Dewilliter? He's the—?"

"Lobelioids." He swung open the door. Looking through the passenger window he could see the Brat was still there. "I had a hunch we should look at brain tissue, and I certainly don't like the implications of that if something turns up there. Then there was the robbery; things are beginning to stink. Whoever it is may have something to do with the murders. I want you to go up the service road toward the bathroom. Slip the chain off and drop it. The service road may have another outlet somewhere. On Cobb's map these hills are crisscrossed with dirt roads. Once I'm through, slip the chain back on and jump in. If they're after us, we can delay them for a while and hope. If they're not after us, there's no harm done."

Patria started without another word up the tarmac toward the restrooms. Chazz climbed in and started the engine. He was watching the access road. The Subaru was still there.

He put the van in gear and backed out of his parking place. Patria was almost to the service road. Slowly he shifted into first and started down the hill. Was the Subaru edging forward? He was sure they had seen Patria head up to the restroom.

He wanted it to look as if he were coming around the parking lot to wait for her. He stopped beside the service road, blocking the view. The sliding door to the van was not visible from the truck. Chazz climbed back and opened it.

Patria reached the chain. It dropped to the ground. Chazz turned swiftly onto the service road, over the chain. In the rearview mirror he saw the Subaru start up the access road toward the lot. He stopped just past the chain. Seconds later Patria jumped in and slammed the door. The van spun its wheels for a moment, caught, and lunged up the service road. The Subaru swung around behind them and hit the chain. As Chazz watched the rearview mirror, the chain slid up the hood of the Brat and slammed into the windshield, which starred with cracks. He could hear over the whine of his own engine the clashing of gears.

The van clattered up the road, spraying dirt. By now they were back in the cloud and couldn't see.

"That'll stop them, won't it?" Patria shouted.

"I wouldn't count on it." Chazz wheeled around a turn. A side road went off to the right; he debated with himself for a moment, then turned. At least it headed in the general direction of the highway, he thought. He had to slow down; the road was deteriorating rapidly, deep ruts full of rainwater.

The old white van jounced and clattered. The ruts were slick. Streaks and spatters shot across the sides, dappling the windows. Chazz had to stop at one point, so he cranked down the window to listen. Above and behind them he could hear the sound of the four-wheel drive. He smashed into gear and went on. The van began to slide on the worst of the slick spots, fishtailing against the banks.

Ahead the road dipped, covered with swiftly flowing water. The tracks plunged in and out the other side. Chazz gave the van a little extra gas and hit the water, which sprayed across the windshield as the high vehicle began to slip. He fought delicately for control as the wheels lost contact with the bottom, it seemed, and he was hydroplaning. Water seeped under the doors.

Suddenly they were out the other side, the wheels caught in the ruts and the van bounced hard. Chazz cracked his head against the ceiling, hanging onto the steering wheel. Behind them he could see the Subaru start down the hillside toward the flood.

His wheels caught again and they lunged forward, uphill. Water was flowing in a ditch alongside the road. They swung around a bend, and in front of them was empty sky, and far away the opposite wall of the canyon. Across the sky hung a rope with a sign. The sign said STOP in large red letters. Chazz slammed on the brakes and fishtailed to a halt at an angle to the rope.

"Son of a bitch," he said.

His back bumper was against the rope, inches from the dropoff. He inched the van forward, away from the road into the heavy brush, ferns and bushes to the right. The hill had collapsed and fallen away, taking the service road with it. Below was bare slope, talus, dirt and rock. Far down the slide he could see trees and shrubs. Beyond that was cliff and the river far below. The dark clouds were close overhead. The only way out was the way they had come, and even now he could hear the Brat whining in four-wheel drive up the hill.

He threw open his door and ran back to the rope, which was stretched between trees on either side.

The Subaru was getting close. He took out his pocketknife and started sawing at the rope. The Subaru engine was whining up and down the scale as it hit soft spots in the road, ruts and firmer dirt, shifting up and down. They were in a hurry. He hoped.

"I don't see any other way to be in harmony with this," he muttered. "So we'll just get off the line of attack." The rope parted. Chazz threw himself back as the Subaru swung around the final bend.

The driver slammed on his brakes when he saw the empty sky, but it was too late. The little truck wobbled violently, front tires plowing through the dirt and debris; but with the rope gone he'd had no warning, and there was nothing to slow the truck. The front tires slipped over the edge. The truck seemed to pause there for a long moment; then, with slow-motion grace, to tilt down. The passenger seemed to be trying to open his door as the Subaru picked up momentum. In a moment it was gone from sight.

Chazz went to the edge and watched as it slithered down the slope. It made surprisingly little sound. The slope was too steep for them to stop, and they slid out of control through the dirt and rock of the slide. The Brat slithered several hundred meters downhill, checked momentarily in the clump of trees, plunged on.

Patria stood beside him. They watched the Subaru twist down the slope, on and on, until it reached the forest where the tiny silver truck caught sideways in a gentle embrace. It looked like a toy as the doors opened and the two men climbed out. They were going to have a long climb back up to the highway.

Chazz waved, then he and Patria turned back to the van. He drove slowly back to the parking lot. The flooded section did not seem all that deep this time.

He stopped at The Honeycreeper to call Takamura.

32

"Now tell me," Patria said quietly. She looked steadfastly out the window.

Chazz pretended ignorance. "Tell you what?"

She sighed. "Don't be obtuse. What's going on? Why did you call me here?"

He drove in silence for a while. Finally he said, "Maybe it was a mistake . . . You're doing good work, and I've gotten a little stale. I thought I wanted . . ."

"Don't start it," she warned. "I love you, Chazz. I like your mind, which I think you have been wasting lately; I like your body, when you can let go. I like being with you, too, but a family wouldn't get you more interested in your work, and it sure as hell would interrupt mine."

"I know, I know." He tried changing the subject. "I saw your piece in *Anthropological Review*. It was very good."

"Thank you." She stared out the window for a time, watching the landscape reel past, the cane fields, red mud roads, the deep green mountains shrouded in cloud. "It was good, wasn't it? And you know what?" She turned toward him. "I think you're jealous. Yes, you are, aren't you? I hadn't thought . . ."

Chazz frowned. "I guess I am at that. You're excited by what you do."

She brushed the back of his forearm with her long fingers. "Well. So don't think you brought me here. I brought me here. And don't change the subject. What's going on? Tell me. Those people were after us."

He made a gesture of assent. "Okay. I guess somebody is playing rough, and I don't know who. I don't even know why, not yet. I've ideas, bad ones. The fact is, I wanted a family, you, with or without children. That's what I was thinking about. I'm sorry. I didn't know about all this, these people."

"You." She stared at him. Her expression was unreadable. "Well," she said again. The cane fields flashed past. The day was dark and hot.

He passed the Koloa turnoff. Patria said nothing. As they passed the Community College, she touched his arm. "That was something, with the van," she said softly, a ghost laugh in her voice. "The Maya dream together," she said. "Maybe we could learn it, to dream together."

He smiled swiftly. Forest and cane fields gave way to city. The County Building was raked by restless sunlight.

Takamura was in his office. "I'm glad you're here," he said.

"Before you say anything, I need to know if you found them."

Takamura shook his head. "No sign. You don't know who they were?"

"No idea. We didn't get a good look at them. They were a good ways down the hill before they stopped. It should've taken them quite a while to get out."

"Oh, the truck was there. Hanapepe Police waited at the top, but they probably headed downhill to the bottom of the canyon instead. There are lots of trails out down there."

"I didn't think of that."

"Don't worry about it; there's nothing we could do. We don't have enough people. By the way, we did check the registration. It was false—a dead end. Our problems are just beginning, though. I've been making lots of calls today."

"Oh?"

"Strachey thinks we have something called a slow virus."

"Like the Foré?" Patria said.

"Yes," Chazz answered. "You were right. I was afraid of that."

"Why were you afraid of it?" Takamura wanted to know.

"Because they're very difficult to detect, they take a long time to incubate, and often disappear after the damage is done."

"Yes. So Strachey said. He also suggested something he called prions, whatever they are. I've tried getting him some assistance. No one can help us. State Health has a problem on the big island with hoof-and-mouth disease, it seems." He stood up and went to the window. The ancient volcano was hidden by cloud, a wet dirty gray that still refused to give up its moisture. Palm fronds tossed restlessly over the lawn. "Let me tell you a story," he said to the window.

"A story?"

"You might like this one." He flipped one of the slats of his Levolor blind up and down, up and down.

"It seems there was a Navy ship, not large, but with a heavy cargo. In the hold of this ship was a treasure. Five hundred pounds of platinum, though that is not really important.

"When I was a small child in an internment camp, a kamikaze pilot who must have been off course in bad weather over heavy seas saw this boat. He probably was low on fuel and was not going to make it back to his carrier, for he chose to fly his airplane into this ship. Ordinarily he would not have chosen such an insignificant target, but this day he did.

"The ship sank; it took down the treasure too. People have been looking for it ever since. One of those people was Rake Wyman. Apparently he found the ship. Now he's dead."

"Was he killed?" Patria asked.

Takamura dropped the slat of his Levolor blind and smiled at her. "That," he said, "is what we are trying to discover."

"Who?" Patria asked quietly. "And how?"

Takamura turned back. "The platinum would be worth about three and a half million dollars today. That explains why but not who. You know, I think it might clear up," he said. "It often happens that way before a big storm."

"I doesn't make any sense," Chazz said. "A slow virus is an inefficient way to kill someone. It's unpredictable, it takes a long time—decades, as often as not—and even then you can't count on it. Unless."

Takamura said nothing, but he raised an eyebrow.

"Unless this is a deliberately selected mutation."

Takamura sat down.

"That's unthinkable, though. Unless someone has gone 'twist' as a friend of mine would call it. There have been cases. The Tylenol killings, and a few years ago a lab technician killed eight people with typhus bugs. Researchers go around the bend, too. Revenge, delusions. Do we have a madman in this island?"

Takamura stood up again. "Tell me," he asked, leaning over his desk and looking straight at Chazz, "is it possible to make this bug?"

Chazz shook his head. "No. Not easily, at least."

Takamura straightened slightly, but he continued to look at Chazz. "Why not?"

"Two reasons. First, what we're talking about is small, very small, and poorly understood. Second, the rules governing recombinant research were worked out at Asilomar. No one is going to fool around with them."

"I would like to be comforted by such thoughts," Takamura said quietly. "Truly I would. But we have too many coincidences here. Ritual mutilations by a cult, death by disease, a diver after sunken treasure dead in the water. Now someone's after you. Why? Let us, for the moment, assume terrorists, shall we?"

Chazz moved restlessly in his chair. "That would be difficult to assume."

"Nonetheless, Dr. Strachey thinks we have a viroid. These people have died of a neurological disorder, a nasty one. The signs make it look like witchcraft. It is deliberate. I think terrorists are testing a new weapon. They could ransom the world. And with the platinum, they can afford the necessary research."

"Impossible." Chazz was not so certain, though.

"Right. Impossible. I asked Dr. Strachey how much money it would take to set up a laboratory to do recombinant DNA research, to design deadly bugs."

Chazz knew what was coming. "I know," he said holding up his hand.

But Takamura interrupted him. "He told me it could be done for a few thousand dollars. That's all. A few thousand dollars. Anyone could do it."

Chazz was shaking his head. "It takes more than money. It takes a very sophisticated kind of knowledge."

"The kind of knowledge your friend Dr. Silver might possess?"

"Sure, but it also would take a very crazy person to do it. Silver is not crazy. He was at Asilomar. Everyone at Asilomar agreed. There are rules. No one would deliberately break them, not even a crazy."

"They have more than a few thousand dollars, though. They have a few million. That can buy a lot of sophisticated knowledge. Suppose it's not terrorists. Suppose it's greed. Threaten a government with an epidemic of some kind of human scrapie. Greed is not crazy."

"No. I won't believe it."

"Well," Takamura said with a weak smile, "as Charles Chan has said, 'Theories like fingerprints—everybody have them.' What's yours?"

Patria cleared her throat. "I might suggest one. I have done some field work in the Yucatan. Medicine and magic. Magic is often medicine misunderstood or disguised. There are poisons, very sophisticated poisons, from plants. Kahuna magic could use these poisons. Someone could have learned about them, used them. It's a simple explanation. No complicated new diseases, no advanced technology. Simple herbal medicine, bad medicine. Religious reasons, personal grudges, who knows?"

"I thought of that, too," Chazz said. "How many of the victims were Hawaiian or part Hawaiian?"

"The medics can't find any poison," Takamura said.

"Doesn't mean it isn't there," Chazz put in. "Some witch

doctor poisoning people. Or a group, a cult. Some poisons are very hard to detect."

"Or," Patria suggested, "perhaps actual praying to death, real *ana'ana*."

"Oh, come on," Chazz snorted. "The power of suggestion. All the victims would have to know they were being prayed to death, wouldn't they? They'd have to be believers."

"No," she said, "they wouldn't. In fact, if you look closely, it was very important that the victim not know. If he knew he was under a curse, he would hire another kahuna to cancel it, throw it back at the source."

"Are you trying to tell me that this kind of magic works? It's real?"

"Chazz, you are still a materialist. Of course it works."

"Where's your scientific objectivity? Your detachment?"

"You can't study it, Chazz, if you don't believe it exists."

"Now wait a minute . . ." Chazz began.

Takamura's calm voice interrupted. "Please. You two. Thanks so much. 'Ancient Chinese proverb: Do not challenge supernatural unless armed with sword of truth.'"

"Right," Patria huffed. Chazz said nothing.

"Now, Chazz. What is *your* theory? Back to terrorists."

"I don't have a theory. Not yet. But two men were after us today; someone is doing something. Someone with a silver Subaru."

"Yes," Takamura said. "Someone is."

"So, is killing by prayer or suggestion or whatever against the law?"

Takamura shrugged. "Homicide is. By the way, Patria, I've arranged for you to meet Sammy's uncle; though Western-educated, he's said to be one of the best kahuna around. Ask him for me if he is praying people to death."

33

Sammy Akeakamai glanced at the sky over the ocean as he crossed the street. Violet shadows shifted and turned over the sea surface, breaking up the sharply slanted light under the clouds. Dust eddies danced listlessly in the gutters, died down, flared and died again. Sammy thought there would be no storm this night, no wind. It was late in the season for big storms, but the Pacific had been capricious this year, and it seemed certain that Tropical Storm Walter would be coming down in the next few days.

The Honeycreeper was a cavernous bar painted a hideous pale blue inside that induced instant depression in the most psychologically insensitive mortals. Sammy pushed his way through the screen door as if through some palpable resistance.

The light within had the same twilight quality as outside. Deep shadows shifted in a confusing pattern across the plastic tables, the bare cinderblock walls, the sagging bar. Violet-green fluorescent tubes hung listlessly from the ceiling. One of them sputtered from time to time.

The television was throwing off the pastels of an ancient and soundless *Dallas* rerun. Three people sat in mute isolation at the bar, staring over their drinks at the screen.

A solitary man waved from a table near the back, and Sammy maneuvered his way through the obstacle course of empty tables and metal tube chairs and sat heavily across from him. A Primo sat on the table fizzing out its final effervescence. Sammy downed it in one vast swallow and sighed as he put down the glass.

"Thanks," he said. "Just what I needed."

"Sure," the other man said. Several teeth were missing from his smile.

They sat still for a time, resting in an almost tangible fluid of inertia. Finally the waiter materialized at the table and they ordered another round.

"Why do you like this place, Alfie?" Sammy asked.

"You always ask me that. I like the light in here."

Sammy nodded solemnly, and conversation died again. The waiter returned with the next round. They sipped in silence while the small man appeared to be watching the soundless television screen thirty feet away over Sammy's shoulder. Finally he spoke quietly, his head down.

"The community's nervous," he said. "Funny weather, maybe. Some say its kahuna. You know how the old folks are, they want tradition. Others, though, kids mostly, they think it's the base."

"What do you think, Alfie?"

"I think you should talk to your Uncle Paul, Sammy. He's kahuna. He could tell you. There are whispers of *ana'ana*. That guy, the junkie, he sold drugs. The old folks don't like that. Then he's dead. A lot of people weren't sorry; they say he was spooked."

"What about the others? What about Sally Cameron, or Wyman, or the man in the car? What about Freddie Delarota, Alfie? Anything on them?"

"Ah, Delarota, now there was a bad one. *'Aihu'e*, a thief, Sammy. The others, I don't—"

"God damn!" One of the men at the bar shouted suddenly. Sammy turned around. The man in the middle was staring into his beer, muttering to himself. He lifted his head and glared around the room as if challenging anyone to contradict him. The other two at the bar glanced at him, then went back to *Dallas*.

"God damn," he repeated.

This time no one looked at him and he sank back into

whatever lethargy had possessed him before. Sammy turned back to his cousin. "Know him?"

Alfie squinted at the ceiling fixtures. He was a leathery fisherman who had been Kekaha High School surfing champion three years running. That was a while ago now. "Seen him a few times. Navy."

Sammy nodded. He picked up his beer and stood.

"Wait," he said softly, draining his second Primo.

He waddled over to the bar and slipped between the ancient leatherette stools where the belligerent drunk was now peering glumly into his glass. "Gimme another," Sammy told the bartender, who took the glass and walked slowly to the television end where the spigots were. Sammy looked casually at the drunk.

"Hi," he said. The man was definitely a Naval officer.

"Sure," the man said. "Hi. Sure." He didn't look up. Sammy looked away, waiting for his beer. "God damn," the man said. His voice was low and tense.

"Something wrong?" Sammy asked him quietly.

He looked up. "Wrong? Sure something's wrong. I got transferred, that's what's wrong. To goddam fucking absolute nowhere. What's it to you?"

Sammy shrugged. In the fluorescent light, the pineapples on his shirt were purple. "Just wondered," he said sympathetically.

"Oh." Suddenly the man ducked his head. "They're doing something out there," he said. He waved his hand loosely at the television.

"Is that right?" Sammy said casually, looking at the Primo Beer sign behind the bar.

"No," the man mumbled. "I was just about to win. I had it figured out. I had it figured. Twenty points. God damn. God the fucking damn. You know something? Class Three. That's right. Class fucking three." He swallowed his beer and waved for another. The lights drew deep purple shadows under his eyes.

"Why not join us?" Sammy suggested, picking up a new draft.

"Sure." The man stood up. "Collins," he said, putting out

his hand. His eyes were slightly unfocused, but his hand was steady. Hours of practice on the PACMAN simulator, he told Sammy. Missiles over the Aleutians, Ferrets on the beach. The Navy was always testing the Ferrets, which seldom worked. Everyone knew that.

Sammy smiled benignly as he shook the hand. Sammy had a large face and his smile filled it.

Collins talked. TDY wasn't up, he got transferred suddenly, didn't understand why. Why? Had something to do with that building. Whaddaya mean, what building? NBL-212, thass wha building. Scientists working on speedboats, he saw the trials, some kinda paint. They painted the boats, put 'em in the water, watched 'em go. Whizzed along. Slick paint.

Sammy lost interest.

Alfie was bored, too. "You a officer?" he asked, not interested.

"They treat me like a fuckin midshipman," Collins complained. "Do this, do that. Officer of the Day, hell. Goddam Ferret flew, most of the time they don't work. Everybody knows that. Big deal. I lost twenty bucks! No reason to transfer someone. God damn it to hell, I was assigned to fucking paradise, you know? Paradise. Got a little place off base. Got a stereo. Got almost the highest fucking score on the fucking simulator, I had it figured. Then boom. Just like that." He tried to snap his fingers.

"Too bad," Alfie said. He scratched his scraggly goatee with a callused forefinger. The rasp was loud.

Collins leaned forward, crooking his finger at Sammy.

"You know what I think," he said in a conspiratorial whisper.

Sammy shook his head.

"I think," Collins said, rolling his eyes, "that they think that I know something about something they're doing that they think I shouldn't know, that's what I think. And that makes me think they're doing something that they think I shouldn't know, and that they think that I know what it is, but I don't. It makes me mad." His eyes filled. Then his head tilted slowly forward; he cradled it in his arms and went to sleep.

The two Hawaiians sat for a long time without speaking, sipping at their beers. At last Sammy got up to make a call from the pay phone.

34

He was an ordinary man with something familiar about him, the set of his shoulders, the texture of his hair.

His house was ordinary, a bungalow in Wailua down a dirt road, surrounded by banana trees. The leaves hung listlessly in the evening heat, burdened by the heavy air, the moisture. The room was small, ordinary. An ancient black-and-white television on a low wooden table, a green couch with a colorful cloth thrown over it, a cabinet with ordinary dishes. He sat calmly in a vinyl easy chair watching her. His eyes were liquid brown, crinkled with good humor.

"My name is Paul Ulana," the old man told her. "An ordinary person. I'm in the telephone book, I like a beer from time to time. This is an ordinary house. Nothing much happens here, you know: some dust, some stones, a few trees, the sea. The wind blows, the waves break."

"Yes," she said, waiting him out.

"It is not Paul Ulana who interests you," he said. "My nephew Sammy has told me you are an anthropologist. You study healing, medicine, magic. How can science study magic? Either they are the same thing, or they are too different to share words."

She smiled. "Science can study magic if it can get inside."

"Then it must know the language of magic."

"Of course. It's language that has the power. Chants, prayers, spells." She paused. "Curses."

She could detect no reaction. "The mind is powerful," he answered. "The mind can do things your science can't. This is because science is a product of the mind. It is not the other way around."

"I know that."

He smiled. "That's why you are here, of course."

"Of course. For instance, something is happening on this island. Cults, maybe?"

He nodded soberly. "My people," he said. "Some of them are dying. But it is not *ana'ana*. No. If you want to understand, you must open your mind. You must receive."

She nodded.

"You do not want Paul Ulana. You want Kalaipahoa."

"Of course," she said. "Mikey said that name. You were the one at the fort, calling in the *mano*, he said."

He nodded again, not surprised. "Our little cousin Mikey, he has the calling too. He will be a great kahuna one day, if he answers that call. Now, you want Kalaipahoa." His hand lifted slowly from his lap. She watched the hand, the thick strong fingers. "You want to know what Kalaipahoa can do. To know those things, though, you must come with him."

"Come with him," she repeated.

"Come," he said, or she thought he said it; his eyes were elsewhere. When his eyes turned back to her, they were red, as if they had caught the light from a fire that did not exist. "Come," he said again, and she went.

The sea itself had begun to change; she could feel the change in her *unihipili*, in the scent and taste of wind. She tried to look at Kalaipahoa, but he sat absolutely motionless, feeling the change, letting his awareness expand beyond his body, through hers, beyond what they could see and taste and hear. Her eyes closed, or were they hers?

The body was seated by the shore, her body, or his body, or, it seemed, their body. The sea stretched away, the teeming sea. Were fins cutting the surface? Did she see the faces of drowned men, pale and distorted, beneath it?

There was sun, no sun; moon, no moon. Her hair swirled

over her eyes, though her hair was short. She walked through fern forests many times larger than she, and was afraid. She heard the clicking of bamboo stalks overhead, too loud to be so far away. She was drawn thin, stretched along a wire thousands of miles long; she was pressed hard into a small place that was darker than blindness. She sat on the shore, and small waves touched her feet with toothless mouths. There were rocks made before the beginning of things.

Where was Kalaipahoa? She was alone.

Beyond her, behind her, to all sides the shoreline stretched away, rock, dry, dead rock, and desolation. She shuddered and reached for her body.

It began to move, not limbs, not hands or the lift of breath. Instead, she lifted out of it, slowly at first, but with growing speed. The earth uncurled like a fern fiddle beneath her. Yes. Currents had shifted, the tones of blue on blue on blue sang a different pitch, a different pattern. Lime fell in fine silt to the bottom of the sea, like white powder spreading through milk, deep, deep and dark, piled and pressed to limestone. Beneath that deep skin the magma moved, blood-red and hot, a pulse within; and the hot blood of earth pulled down the limestone, dissolved it, moved it. Far above, the sky rang like stone. The air was thin here, and cold. Darkness swept in broad filaments, in curtains of cold fire. She could feel a swelling of magma nearby, *there* in the big island, sluggish wound, the volcano that would erupt with Pele's rage.

Other rhythms emerged, matching the change in blue currents, more strident rhythms, a filling, syncopated beat within the broad, stately movement of mountains and glaciers. Strife coming.

See, the old man's voice said out of the emptiness. The blue, see the patterns there, the shapes where they come together, where they unravel. Trace them, follow with your eye, your finger. Those patterns are the change, the rising wind. Crisis.

I have none, Patria said. No eye, no finger. She screamed then in her mind.

Paul chopped with his hand, palm down. The long white whiskers of his mustache fluttered. "It is nothing. Come."

His voice was loud, and echoed off the walls of his living room. Yet she could not move. He leaned forward.

His grip was hard on her elbow. "You must know," he hissed. "Not only form. Not only ritual. These things are only half. You must understand the other half. Pah!"

"Yes," she said dreamily, wondering where the fire was, where the heat was coming from, why his eyes had reddened so.

"Healing and killing. Maintaining the balance, tipping it this way, that way." He seemed troubled. "You've seen it now."

"Yes," she said, wondering what she'd seen.

"Feel that breeze," the kahuna said, rubbing his fingers together. "This is the calm time, before the sickness comes."

She could feel the breeze then. She heard something. A snuffling sound, rasped breath, the sound of hard feet in the earth. This was fever, delirium. She heard herself moan.

It came out of the ferns, the pale terrible shape. What the boy had said, the *akua*? She fell heavily, tasted brackish water, heard dark colors swell and fade, violet and brown. Eat her brains. No, she screamed, I'm not dead. The rough texture of blankets on her tongue, scraping sounds in the dirt, all fell through her at once.

It was a high platform of stones heated by sun, the size of a football field. This was the altar. She heard the word, perhaps it sounded like a memory, something she'd read, perhaps he said it to her: *heiau*.

"You want something else. Something for yourself." His voice was low, singsong, chanting, yet she understood the meaning. "Something for your marriage. Your husband, something for him."

"Yes," she heard herself answer. "I . . . I do love him. It just isn't working. I'm not ready—"

He made a sound that was dismissal of her objections. "For this, for love, you must sacrifice. There will be pain."

She watched in fascination as he cut a square of flesh from the inside of her forearm. The blood ran slowly in a rivulet to her wrist, so bright in the wind from the sea. She could taste its brightness. The wind blew past her again as she stood on the dark rock, facing the sea.

She felt danger, the desecration of a holy place forbidden to women even before the voice spoke behind her.

"You'll be all right," the voice said.

She opened her eyes. The living room blurred, came into focus. She could smell alcohol, feel its sting.

"I'm sorry," he said, coming into view. He held a swab in his hand. "Let me take care of that."

"I. Yes. I cut my arm. On the altar. It was a ritual, wasn't it?"

He smiled kindly. "I will do my best," he said. "Perhaps it will work out. There is still a little of the ancient magic in these things."

He gave her a bandage. The inside of her forearm was weeping blood again after he'd swabbed it. She could feel the coolness as the alcohol evaporated.

"The Maya dream together," she said. "I've never experienced anything like that."

"You were very good," he said. "You moved easily through the three realms. Your *unihipili* is strong."

"Three realms?"

He waved it aside. "Oh, they're all much alike, I imagine, these subtle structures." Seated across from her once again, he began to explain in a calm voice the metaphysics of kahuna magic. Even later, when she was driving through the night toward Chazz and their apartment, she could not understand why she felt so uneasy, as if she had been warned.

35

The ultracentrifuge was whining down. Chazz tipped back in his office chair and rested his chin on his tented fingers, staring down at the pile of MacDonald's lunch debris on his desk.

Strachey was preparing the last batch. They had tissue samples from all the victims prepared, labeled and catalogued.

"This is it," he said, placing a new set of vials in the centrifuge. He set the dial, and a quiet whine started up the scale. He put his hands behind his neck and stretched. Chazz heard a loud vertebrae crack. "Ahh," Strachey sighed.

"What have we got, really?" Chazz asked.

"We have twenty-five little jars of dense, colorless fluid," Strachey suggested. "The question is, What are we going to do with them?"

"Yeah. What?"

"You're asking me?"

"Okay, I've a hunch. We should purify mitochondrial DNA."

"Then weigh it out? Check for homologous sequences?" Strachey suggested.

"Mm-hm."

"Count the base-pairs? Unzip the strands and look for similar recognition sites?"

"Sure."

"Run them through the sequencer?"

"Yup, all of that."

"What are we looking for?" Strachey asked after a time.

He sat heavily. "A stretch of viral DNA or some free-floating RNA? Intruder molecules of some kind? A retrovirus or a toxin? Pathology is not inconsistent with a neurotoxin, but there were no chemical indicators. Still, the neurotransmitter sites were deformed, weren't they? An autoimmune response of some kind."

Chazz nodded. He rubbed his eyes, then climbed to his feet. His chair creaked when he got out of it. He picked up the vial labeled #1, checked the list. "Robert Hall," he said. "Mitochondria. Let's give it a go, shall we? A test run. If it works out all right, we'll load it up and let her go."

They went into the next room. With a micropipette Chazz put two microliters of fluid in a special plastic container. This in turn went into the sequencer, a machine the size of a large freezer. He switched it on. The computer display winked into life, producing a graphic image of the DNA molecule, the graceful double-helix form twining round and round itself. At the moment, the image was static and stylized, a rough template for the sequencer to work on.

With a quiet hum, the machine extruded the dense DNA molecule. Along the bottom of the screen, text printed out 5′ and 3′, codes for the start and stop ends. A blinking underline cursor waited at the corner, then slowly spelled out the first base pair as the sequencer analyzed the nucleotides. Symbols filled in the graphic representation of the DNA above in primary colors, blue for guanine, yellow for cytosine: G-C pair. The molecule notched up a base pair and rotated one-tenth of a turn. A few moments later the second pair filled in: A-T.

"If it kept up this speed, we'd be done in about a million years," Chazz murmured.

Strachey laughed. "Mitochondria makes for a long, skinny molecule."

But as they spoke, the graphics picked up speed, flashing the letters of the genetic code faster and faster until they blurred. The counter indicated the sequencer was analyzing and storing at the rate of five kilobases/sec. The molecule was twisting off the top of the screen in a blur, the colors of the four bases flashing rapidly as the image twirled.

Chazz tapped the keyboard of a separate terminal and got a reading of 2 Hr 49 mi 2.62 sec to completion: nearly three hours for the sequencer to finish each DNA molecule. Once this run finished, though, they could do four at a time. The seconds ticked off, the hundredths and tenths blurred, too fast to read.

"We're looking for . . . ?" Strachey asked.

"I have this hunch," Chazz said. "The computer will look for homologous sequences in all the DNA. If the agent is something that affects the genetic code and is found in all the victims, the computer will find and display all the matches. We can eliminate known sequences. If there is a sufficiently long stretch common to all the victims, we might have something."

He looked at Strachey. "Or it could be a dead end." Chazz sighed. "It's going to take a lot of time and computer power to do the matching. Fortunately, we have a lot of computer power." He smacked the sequencer. "This baby was rebuilt by one of the technicians here. You'd hardly know it's over ten years old. He's got it connected to the mainframe computer in the basement. Massive amounts of optical storage, Christ, billions of bytes, and fast! Not like the old days, eh?"

"Nope," Strachey agreed. "Five years ago we couldn't have done this kind of problem in under a year or two. Now it'll take three days to do all of them, even the controls."

"It's going to be a long night," Chazz agreed. "Despite gigabytes of computer memory."

It was a long night.

They sent out for dinner, ate absently, worked through the evening. They waited until the first sample was finished and the screen said, "Mitochondrial genome 97.63% confirmed, error checking complete, deviation ±3.6%"

"Why mitochondria, though? Matrilineal DNA," Strachey muttered, watching the screen. "I wonder what that means?"

"Means it's inherited complete from the mother, all the way back to Eve," Chazz said over his shoulder.

"Sure. We've been doing ethnic genotyping with mitochondrial DNA for some time now. Any significance to this matching sequence being in the mitochondria, do you think?"

Chazz shrugged. "Probably not, but it's worth checking."

By two in the morning the rest of the samples were prepared and loaded into the long switchbacked conveyer inside the sequencer. They added in their own purified mitochondria as controls.

Twisted helices climbed off the top of the screen; then, base pair after base pair coming together as the machine analyzed what they were, one after the other, for both DNA strands, each one a check on the other since they were mirror images.

Computer memory filled, dumped to mass storage, filled again; each sample, Robert Hall first, then Sally Cameron and Rake Wyman and Freddie Delarota, moving through the sequencer in turn.

Dawn paled the sky. The clouds were lower than yesterday, yet the storm still held off. Chazz and Strachey barely noticed. By ten o'clock they had put in the final samples.

"You know," Chazz said, suppressing a yawn, "even if we're right about this, I don't get it."

"Don't get what?" Strachey was rubbing his eyes.

"Even if we find something, a sequence they all have in common, what will we have, really? Just the beginnings. Whatever this is might be like oncogenes—they break, they move, they express for cancers. We'd need a huge lab, hundreds of people working on it. And now there haven't been any deaths in a while. How are we going to convince people that we need all these resources?"

Strachey shrugged. "I'm too tired to care now. Let's get some sleep and worry about it later."

Chazz dialed his condominium. Patria's sleepy voice answered. "Where are you and what have you been doing?" she murmured.

"Strachey and I just finished. Christ, it's been a long night. I'm coming home."

"Wait'll I tell you about the kahuna," she said. "We saw him before. I dreamed about it."

"We saw him before?"

"Yeah. The sharks, remember? He's good, Chazz. Really good. He has a lot of power."

"A regular Svengali, huh?"

"You," she declared, "are an incorrigible materialist. That's your major failing."

"I love you too," he said. "See you soon."

"Unh hunh."

36

Chazz, slumped with fatigue, spread the slats of the lab blinds and gazed across the courtyard. On the other side he could see a figure walk down the corridor, a dim outline behind the windows along the corridor where his office was.

"I wonder where he went," he said to himself.

Strachey looked up from the screen, where spirals unwound at a furious rate. They were on their way home, but seemed to have trouble moving. "Who?" he asked.

"Huh?" Chazz shook his head, clearing it. "Oh. Silver. He went somewhere. I wondered where he went. I thought maybe we could talk this problem over with him, then I remembered he left. That looked like Andrea over there."

"Mm." Strachey pressed his hands into the small of his back. "Why am I standing here watching this infernal machine? It'll be hours yet."

"Right." Chazz tried briskness. "Let's go." They hung up their lab coats, switched off the lights and left the lab. Chazz was locking the door behind them when the phone inside the lab rang. They looked at each other for a moment.

"We'd better get it," Strachey said.

Chazz nodded and unlocked the door. Strachey brushed past him and answered. Chazz thought it would be for him—Takamura, perhaps—so he hung in the doorway, half-listening.

But Strachey stayed on, saying, "Yes, yes. Yes, sir." Something in his voice made Chazz look up when he said, "No, sir, I can't do that," but the conversation continued, so Chazz went down the hall to the bathroom.

His fatigue buzzed in him at the same frequency as the ceiling fixtures. The sound of the hand dryer reminded him of the whine of the sequencer. He caught himself staring at the chrome nozzle as warm air blew over his hands, then he realized he hadn't washed them. They were dry.

He shook his head and splashed cold water on a face he could barely recognize as his own, disembodied and haggard in the mirror. It helped a little, but not enough. Something gnawed at him, something about heat and dust, a vagrant image. Somewhere he had been recently. What had Patria said? The sharks. Something about the sharks, the kahuna, the Russian Fort. He walked slowly, frowning.

When he got back, Strachey was hanging up slowly.

"That was my boss," he said. "I've been recalled to Atlanta. I'm to drop this project and fly out. Immediately, he said. I'm to catch the eleven-oh-five."

"You're kidding." Chazz came in and sat down. The sequencer hummed with the final samples. "We're so close."

Strachey shook his head. "There's some kind of emergency. He was vague. It sounded strange, but he said the eleven-oh-five. They've made a reservation. I've got to go. As soon as I straighten it out I'll come back. It's insane. He just wouldn't say anything over the phone. Jesus, I've got fifty minutes to pack and get to the airport."

"I'd better drive you."

Traffic was heavy, cane trucks and delivery vans, streams of cars in both directions. Strachey fretted beside Chazz, caught in the amber density of traffic. As they approached the Kapuna Road turnoff, Chazz suggested they take it and go around. "There may be less traffic that way."

Strachey said nothing, his body tense.

"Forty minutes," he said, looking at the van's dash clock.

Chazz spotted a silver Brat that was approaching from Kapuna Road, and though he knew it couldn't be the same one, he avoided the turnoff. He watched the Brat turn west onto the highway and vanish around a bend. He noticed his knuckles were tense on the wheel, and deliberately relaxed.

"Tell me, Strachey, do you believe in magic?"

Strachey stopped chewing his knuckle to look at Chazz. "Magic? Oh. Suggestion?" He shrugged. "There's a lot we don't know about the way the mind interacts with the body. Certainly, attitude has a lot to do with healing. But magic? No, I don't think so. Not if you mean remote control, hexes, spells, that kind of thing. Disease always turns out to have an explanation."

Chazz nodded. "My wife thinks I'm a materialist."

Strachey was chewing his knuckle again. "I wouldn't know about that," he said absently.

While he waited for Strachey to finish throwing his clothes back into his suitcase, Chazz said, "Somebody's doing this, Strachey."

"Doing what?" he answered, slamming the case shut.

"Somebody's getting rid of you. Somebody's afraid, somebody who can call the CDC and have you recalled."

Strachey stared at him. Then he shook his head. "Impossible," he said. "I admit this is odd, but that's impossible. It doesn't work like that. We have a job, a mission, CDC does. It can't be subverted. No, I won't accept that. Something else is going on. You said it yourself: there haven't been any deaths in a while. Maybe this has blown over."

"I hope you're right."

On the road approaching the airport, low gray cloud and leaden sea stretched to an infinity without horizon. There was no detail anywhere in that emptiness, as if time had come to a halt, motion itself had ceased. Only the old white van moved through a static world drained of life. They parked and walked to the terminal through an oppressive silence.

Chazz stared listlessly at the empty sea while Strachey checked in.

They shook hands at the gate. "I never even got to the beach," Strachey said. "A trip to Hawaii, and I don't think I even saw a coconut."

"I'll send you one," Chazz said. While Strachey boarded, Chazz wandered over to the pay phone and called Patria to let her know what had happened. He nearly replaced the receiver before the first ring when the thought *She's not going to answer* drifted through his mind. After seven rings he hung up.

"She's taking a shower," he said to no one in particular.

He wandered back to the fence. Strachey's plane was pulling away, dust billowing around the trees on the other side. Chazz considered calling Takamura to tell him they had just lost their medical expert, but he leaned there a little longer, watching the DC-9 taxi to the end of the runway. In a moment it roared into the air and vanished quickly into the clouds. They were lower than they looked. He supposed the ceiling was no more than a few hundred feet.

In the parking area he caught himself looking around for a silver Subaru. He saw nothing suspicious. Just the usual assortment of taxis and rental cars and hotel buses. He paused at the pay phone again, but there was still no answer. When he tried Takamura's office, the operator said he was out. Sammy Akeakamai was also out. Would he like to leave a message? He told her Strachey was gone. He called Patria again. There was still no answer.

37

He drove slowly toward town, gray sea at his back. The radio told him the storm was coming, something he could feel as the air grew dense and heavy. Strachey was gone, and he would have to process all the information from the samples himself. Who had the power to have Strachey recalled? Or was this really just chance: something else came up, some epidemic in New Jersey or Texas which only Strachey, a young and inexperienced epidemiologist, could handle?

Who, for that matter, were the two men in the silver Subaru?

Where was Cobb? The County Building was on his left, and on impulse he turned into the lot.

He was on his way to the pay phone in the lobby when Dr. Shih called to him. "Dr. Koenig! I'm glad to see you," she said, bustling up to him. Instruments winked in her pocket. She tilted her head, looking up at him. "You look awful."

"I've been up all night. What are you doing over here? Shouldn't you be down in the morgue?"

"Yes," she agreed. "I'm bringing over my final report. I hope. Have you found anything yet?"

He shook his head. "It'll be a few days. We're looking at an enormous amount of information. And Strachey's gone."

"Gone?"

"Recalled. I just took him to the airport. Back to Atlanta."

"I don't understand that. They were cooperating, the CDC. Why would they call him back now?"

"I don't know. Have you seen Cobb?"

"Not today, I haven't. And you'd better get set. Walter's coming."

"Walter?"

"Tropical storm. I still can't get used to these men's names." She smiled. "I guess I'm old-fashioned."

Takamura wasn't in his office. The sergeant on duty said he was on his way in, though, and should be there in a half-hour. "He and Sergeant Akeakamai went down to Koloa for something."

"Koloa?"

"Yeah."

"Can I use the phone?"

"Sure."

There was still no answer. By now she would have been in the shower for almost an hour. Chazz took the stairs two at a time.

She should have answered. Unless she was at the pool. Looking at the sky made that prospect unlikely. Cane trucks clogged the road, slow and lumbering, loaded with stalks brown as winter despair. They must be bringing in as much cane as possible before the storm hit, which meant, Chazz supposed, the growers were expecting storm damage. He honked impatiently and passed when he could, but the seconds crawled as if their backs were broken. At last he left the highway, taking the turn through the eucalyptus tunnel on two wheels. He took the Kapuna Road turnoff the same way.

There was tangled darkness in the roots of the ficus in the court, noticeable as the day grew dim; the leaves no longer stirred restlessly, their sibilance stilled. The tree seemed suspended or trapped in a gradually congealing amber.

The swimming pool was deserted. He ran around it to his apartment.

The back door was open.

He paused, took a deep breath and moved silently alongside the wall, listening intently. Sounds came to him, bird calls, the distant throb of a pump, wind in the leaves gusting from time to time. The light was strange, darker than noon should be, with a blue-gray tinge that smelled of storm. He reached the doorjamb and listened. Nothing out of the ordinary. The television was on, tuned to a soap opera.

He peered around the jamb into the kitchen. A cereal bowl sat on the table. The residue of Cheerios stuck to the insides, streaked with drying milk. The plastic bowl was an intense red.

The kitchen was empty. He pulled the door shut behind him and moved to the folding doors to the living area. One was open, the other closed. He peered around the edge again.

The television was louder here. Bill told Marie that he loved her, despite her condition, no, because of her condition; they had to seize what time they might have left. Swelling music introduced a commercial.

He moved into the living room feeling paranoid. Then he remembered the Subaru twisting down the slide.

Their bedroom was across the living room off a short hallway by the front door, facing the central court. Opposite, the bathroom door was wide open. He could see the mirror over the sink reflect the shower. Empty.

The bedroom was all that was left. The door was almost closed. Could he hear someone breathing behind it, waiting for him? The lights were off in there, the curtains drawn. The narrow space along the edge of the door was dark. The light switch was to the left.

He moved forward. The carpet in the corridor muffled the sound of his feet. The commercial, slightly louder than the program itself, covered any incidental noise he might make. He listened, but heard nothing over the jingle. He kicked as hard as he could, lunged through the door and snapped on the overhead light with his left hand, spinning and stepping back at the same time. If anyone was behind the door, he was ready.

There was no one there. The room was as empty as the rest of the apartment. Abruptly, he felt foolish. No one was here, nothing had happened.

She'd gone out, that was all. He sat on the foot of the bed and watched the soap opera for a quarter-hour before he stirred himself enough to turn it off. When he did, it was awfully quiet, and in the quiet he realized that Patria never left the breakfast dishes out; and that her rented car was parked in front; that she had been waiting for him to arrive so she could tell him about her meeting with the kahuna; that she was gone; that waiting was all he could do now, as he thought about a silver Subaru turning onto the highway from this road earlier that day. He wondered how many of those trucks they had. He knew the phone would ring. He knew what the call would be about.

When it rang, he jumped anyway.

An unfamiliar voice reminded him that his phone was tapped, so he'd better not make any calls on the way. If he wanted to see his wife again.

38

Billy the Kid was beside the pool when Chazz came outside.

"Hi, Dr. Koenig," he said, snapping a chair cushion together and tossing it onto a pile of others. "Gotta button down for the storm. Radio says it'll be here this afternoon. 'Bout time, I say. We been getting ready for days now."

Chazz said nothing and Billy paused to stare at him. "You okay?"

Chazz made a quick gesture. "Yeah. Have you seen my wife?"

"Not since when she left this morning."

Chazz pushed his hands into his pockets and leaned back against a palm tree. "When she left?"

"Sure. Went off with two men. Looked like cops to me. Neat, you know what I mean?"

"Not really. What do you mean?"

"Clean shirts, pressed. One had a mustache. The short one. The other one looked like a weight lifter."

"Either one an oriental or Hawaiian?"

"Nope. Both haoles."

"Do you remember what kind of a car they had?"

"I don't know. No, wait. I think it was one of those surfer trucks, you know what I mean? A silver one. Why?"

"Could I use your phone? Mine seems to be out of order."

"Sure." Billy tossed his hair in the direction of the manager's apartment. "It's open." He went back to snapping the cushions.

Chazz tried Takamura's office again, but he still wasn't in. He left his name with the dispatcher.

He hurried through the courtyard, past the pool where Billy was staggering under a stack of yellow cushions toward the storage shed.

"What's up?" he asked from behind the cushions.

Chazz did not answer. Absently he noted the first raindrop smack the surface of the pool, spreading ripples on its smooth surface.

By the time he climbed into the van, rain was spattering the pavement in quick, wet gusts. He clashed the gears on his way out.

He'd only gone a mile when he began to wish he'd taken Patria's rental instead of the van. It was slow on hills, cumbersome in the gusting winds and treacherous on the rain-slick highway. He was almost out of gas, and would have to stop.

He filled up at the station in Puhi. In Kapa'a he turned as instructed onto the Ma'alo Road toward Wailua Falls. Just before the falls, a private road would bring him in the back way to the Keahua Arboretum, a park which extended up the volcano at Wai'ale'ale. The roads were already slick with runoff, and the van veered back and forth between banks on either side thick with staghorn fern. Forest grew to the edge of the road that twisted along the ridge backs.

Finally the vegetation thinned to open parkland with scattered trees. The road wound downhill and stopped at the north fork of the Wailua River. Swollen water poured over the top of the bridge: a flash flood.

Chazz got out. Rain was falling harder now, thrown in sweeping horizontal sheets across the open space. There were no other cars in sight, no people visible. He was alone in a world of water and dense jungle. Somewhere ahead of him was a message. They were taking no chances.

The trailhead was upstream to his left. His message was in a wooden box containing maps of the trail.

He was to continue across the river past the reservoir. At Kapa'a he was to head north. There was a papaya stand near Moloa'a Bay. He was to say he was Mr. James.

Rich brown water poured across the cement of the bridge.

Where the water caught up against the pilings, the currents were a foot deep or more, spouting up and across, and along the edge a lip of swift water had formed. Even on foot it would be impossible to cross. Apparently they hadn't anticipated the storm. He would have to return the way he had come.

He was half an hour behind their schedule when he reached the papaya stand. The man handed him the envelope for Mr. James. "Just closing up," he said laconically. "Storm comin'."

In the van, Chazz opened it. The paper was wet from the rain, but the neatly typed instructions were clear. In Hanalei he would hire a Zodiac and go past the point of Kalalau Beach.

To his right the ocean was leaden, punctuated with whitecaps streaming spume, sullen with deep troughs between the breakers. He did not relish the idea of going out in a boat, especially an open one. The kid in the office at Sailor's Cove Zodiac Rentals was expecting him.

"Yessir, Mr. James, right? He said you'd be along."

"He?"

"Sure. The developer. He said you'd be along. You're late, actually, but don't worry. We'll get you out there."

"Fine."

The kid held out a hand. "Geoff Smith. My friends call me Smitty." He had blond hair and a red sunburned face. Square jaw, square brow, square shoulders, lean swimmer's body.

They walked down to the beach. The sea was calm inside the sheltered cove, but nothing stopped the rain. Smitty handed him a slicker and they climbed into the small rubber boat and headed out to sea. The waves were larger than they looked from the road, but Smitty was grinning through the drops, his yellow hair plastered to the fine bones of his skull. The boat leaped off the waves and crashed into the troughs.

Try blending with this, Chazz told himself as they smacked onto the cement-hard ocean surface. Somewhere up ahead was Patria. Somewhere. And the "developer." Presumably Smitty thought he was looking over the real estate, although everything from here to the end of the island was public land.

39

Ulana sat watching for a long while. He thought now that perhaps he had made an error, many errors. Around the younger man was a dark aura, an aura of the *ana'ana* that drained away mana, that pulled toward itself something violent and despairing.

He sighed. The end was close, so close; perhaps this mess could still be saved. "Renfrew," he said.

Renfrew lifted his head from his task. "Kalaipahoa?"

"You've studied well." There was no irony in the words.

Renfrew's smile was sharp and fast. He wove grasses and feathers through bits of shell, his fingers still clumsy. The old man was powerful, but a fool. Automatically Renfrew suppressed the thought. He may be a fool, but he was sharp, cunning. He knew what you were thinking.

"You are the fool, Renfrew."

The heiau was a sprawling pile of irregular volcanic stone laid out in a broad rectangular platform exposed to direct sunlight most of the day. The temple looked across a stretch of desert cut only occasionally by fence toward the ocean. Over the ocean now massed cloud as black as Renfrew's solitary nights. Overhead the cloud moved swiftly, tearing around the tops of the radio masts, all that was visible of the PACMAN Naval Facility down below.

Paul Ulana stood, holding his knees. The pain was not too bad, but his time was short, though he couldn't see clearly why. Death was close, though. "You won't succeed," he said.

Renfrew didn't answer. A crude head began to take shape under his fingers, a head of shell, eyes of stone, a cowrie grin.

Renfrew spoke softly. "No, Kalaipahoa. I will succeed. I study, practice. I work."

The sound the old man made was soft and contemptuous. He walked away to the edge of the heiau, looked out west to the massed cloud streaked now with occasional lightning.

"The god comes," Kalaipahoa said. He lifted his hands to the carved wooden post set into the edge of the platform. He spoke in rapid syllables to Ku-waha-ilo, coming swiftly toward them now, his presence tangible, visible, potent with mana. Behind the old man, Renfrew worked on his doll.

"Ku with the maggot-dropping mouth," the old man called, and was answered by a distant roll of thunder. Renfrew did look up then, saw the old man's hair stirred by the breeze, a sudden gust lifting the tail of his shirt. "Ku big eyes! Ku strolling around in the rain!"

The mutter of thunder retreated, the rising breeze died away, and heavy stillness fell on them again. Kalaipahoa sighed again and sat beside Renfrew. He was holding a small leather sack, which he put down between them.

"The old ways are dying, Renfrew. The old ceremonies, the old power—all almost gone. Look at this place, we had to rebuild as best we could. We should have built a new heiau here, but there was no time, not enough people. We should take days for the ceremony; we should chant the prayers; we should build the koa prayer tower, dress it with white tapa, pray there. But there are not many of us left. You, I thought—"

"I have the power, Kalaipahoa." He looked at the pigskin sack forgotten on the warm stones. "Don't worry."

"Yes," the old man said, pressing his knees, not looking at him. "You have the power. You should beware, though. Arrogance kills two ways. You do not really believe. That is a danger."

This time it was Renfrew's sound that was contemptuous, but Kalaipahoa did not react. Renfrew reached out to the sack, put his hand on it. Instantly, and without looking, the other's strong hand was on his. "Not yet, Renfrew," he hissed. "I'm not gone yet."

Renfrew pulled his hand away. "It's hers, isn't it? Koenig's wife?" Renfrew's smile remained this time, and it was the cowrie smile of his doll, empty and humorless.

Paul Ulana stood and walked away, taking the sack with him. Renfrew turned to follow with his eyes.

"Kalaipahoa," he called after him. "Your god, your Ku maggot-mouth, he's coming."

Kalaipahoa turned. "No, Renfrew," he said solemnly. "Ku-waha-ilo is *not* coming. He, the man-eater, he is already here. Soon, as he did when the body of Hakau was laid on the altar, he will come down in a pillar of dark cloud with thunder and lightning, and the tongue of the god will wag above the altar."

"He'll want a sacrifice, eh, Kalaipahoa? He will want a human to die?" Renfrew's lips were smiling still at his private joke.

Now Paul Ulana knew he had made a mistake. Renfrew was agitated, dark violet shot through his aura, his mana swelled and swirled.

"This is not just a storm, Renfrew. The man-eater is here!" He turned and stood at the edge of the heiau again. "I know what you're making, Renfrew. I know whose doll that is." Kalaipahoa looked out to sea where the clouds were.

"Yes, of course," Renfrew said behind him. "It's yours."

He chopped at the back of the old man's neck with the edge of his hand. Ulana went down easily, all the strings cut. His body tumbled down the slope away from the heiau, slack as death. Renfrew opened the sack. The scrap of skin looked like a bit of dried apricot stuck to gauze.

Renfrew watched for a time when the body came to rest. Many minutes passed before it moved, and one hand reached painfully for the ohia tree nearby. Finally the old man pulled himself to his feet, looked up the slope into the cloud and black stone, where Renfrew was a shimmering pool of darkness against the sky that turned and evaporated.

Renfrew had not stopped smiling as he slipped the doll inside his pocket, picked up his bow and, holding the pigskin pouch, ran down the trail toward the west.

40

The Zodiac slapped water with a jar. Spray flew; the inflated rubber sides glistened. Despite the intermittent rain, Chazz tasted salt continuously. His shirt was soaked, his pants were soaked, the boat couldn't move fast enough. They wouldn't harm Patria, he thought. They wanted him.

He tried talking to Smitty. The jarring and lift of the boat made conversation difficult, but he learned the man had shown up that morning to inquire about Zodiacs. He wanted Dr. Koenig to meet him beyond the end of Kalalau Beach to look at the next valley. Smitty said there was one narrow but very deep valley after another around the northwest corner of the island, all desert. Besides that was all state park out there: Milolo'i and Nu'alolo Kai Parks: a series of steep cliffs where the Pacific currents and prevailing weather had cut into the volcanic rock, undermining it until it collapsed into the sea.

The seas were heavy and growing worse. Cliff tops faded into the dense fringed gray of the clouds, and sheets and veils of rain swept into the face of the cliffs, furrowed and twisted by erosion. Runoff made silver trails down the sides to meet the foam where waves crashed into the black volcanic rock. Chazz hung on to the ropes looped around the sides of the flexible boat and shouted at Smitty.

"It's getting worse!"

The surfer nodded but said nothing. His mouth was tight. The wind was picking up, the seas were rougher by the minute, rain blew into their faces. This was the leading edge of the cold front; the temperature was dropping steadily as they plunged on. Because the shore dropped off steeply here, the waves broke close to the cliffs, and Smitty tried to hug the coastline.

They passed a cave thrashed by surf, the spray from broken waves reaching to its top twenty feet above sea level. Through a gap in the rain, Chazz could see that the surface was relatively calm inside, and had he not been pressed, he might have argued for trying to ride out the storm in there.

After an hour of this punishment, they came around a point. A beach extended out of sight into the gray mist and rain. Palms thrashed violently in the wind that curled over the next ridge; rain beat against the sand, pounding it flat. Waves broke a lot farther out from the deserted beach than they had by the cliffs, and Smitty had to steer out to sea to avoid the whitecaps.

"Wind's shifting to the northwest," Smitty shouted over the roar of the surf. "Means the cold front is passing. The weather's gonna get worse."

"Worse than this?" Chazz shouted.

Smitty nodded without saying anything. He pointed at the next point as he headed away from shore to pass around it. Spray was flying horizontally.

The Zodiac tipped violently in a sudden cross-surge, and Chazz had to grab at the rope again. The point sheltered a shallow cove where the waves broke a little less viciously, and Smitty gunned the motor, heading toward the small beach. Just before they reached the sand, he pulled up the motor and the Zodiac rode a breaker in and ground to a halt. In the sudden silence, Chazz could hear nothing but rain hissing on the sand, and the wave they had ridden in hissing back into the sea.

There was no one around. Chazz climbed painfully out of the boat, wondering suddenly where the hell Cobb Takamura was at this moment. It was a question whose answer seemed very remote. He shivered in the sudden chill, startling after the oppressive heat of the past few days.

An enormous lava tube twice the height of a man extended at an angle into the cliffside off to his right. He would be in there. It was the only visible shelter. Cliffs rose precipitously into the cloud. The cove was at the mouth of a shallow and very narrow valley. A small, intermittent stream flowed down the point of the valley and spread out across the beach. The lava tunnel was across the stream.

Smitty, hunched in the rain, said, just loud enough to hear, "This is called the Valley of the Lost Tribe."

The beach had been pounded by rain, and there were no footprints. They had to be inside the tube. Unless this was a wild-goose chase to keep him occupied.

He cursed himself under his breath for twenty solid seconds as the rain plastered his clothing to his skin and his hair to his head. Then he realized Smitty was talking to him.

"The tunnel goes through," he was saying. "There's another cove, no beach. We can't stay here long; the storm's getting worse. I don't believe your friend is here."

"Any way to climb out?" Chazz asked, pointing up the valley.

Smitty shook his head. "I don't know any. People don't try it often. Couple of years ago, two kids tried coming down from Koke'e. They had ropes, climbing gear, everything. They got stuck on a ledge and had to be rescued." He shrugged. "There may be goat trails up there, or maybe old Hawaiian paths no one remembers anymore. These cliffs are bad, though. There aren't many ways up to the top from this side, if any."

Chazz stared into the tube, but the darkness was complete and rain slanted into his eyes. He turned away and sat on the edge of the boat, hunched with his back to the rain.

"There are stories, of course," Smitty said. Chazz noticed that his teeth were chattering.

"Stories?"

"You know, legends. Supposed to be a royal Hawaiian trail over the top. I don't think anyone's ever found it, though. Not that I've heard. The sort of thing people talk about at night, you know?" He shrugged again, but it turned into a shiver. "How long do you want to wait here?"

"I'll check the cave. They can't be anywhere else. If they're not there, we'll go back."

A hooded figure wrapped in rain gear appeared at the mouth of the cave. He cupped his hands and shouted. His words were torn by wind and the sounds of rain, but came through distinctly.

"Koenig!" he called. "This way." He gestured to Chazz. Then he shouted at Smitty, "You'd better get on back. We'll be fine."

Smitty looked dubiously at Chazz, who nodded.

As he crossed the stream he could hear the Zodiac sliding down the sand, and finally the sound of the motor starting up over the breaking waves. The sound faded away. It was gone by the time he reached the tunnel. The figure had vanished back inside.

41

The temperature had dropped a good fifteen degrees in the past hour and a half, but Renfrew didn't care. He loved the lashing rain, the torn palm leaves turning end over end along the trail or wrapped around the wet trunks of ohia lehua, flapping.

At this altitude he was well into the clouds; dense gray-white turbulence still thrashed, moisture condensed out of the cloud onto his clothing in large droplets, but he was above the worst of it.

Soon he would get to the cabin. This meant that he'd have

to unpack his new Jennings bow, expose its exotic woods and alloys to all this bad weather; Renfrew really didn't like that, but there was nothing he could do about it. The plan required it—his plan.

The trail, barely visible under the best of conditions, was nearly indecipherable by now: the fog, the rain and wind and blown leaves and debris, the overgrowth of a wet winter, had nearly obliterated it. Renfrew knew the trail, though. He barely glanced down, moving at a jog through the ferns that touched across the trail so they swished and left glistening streaks of fresh damp along the knees of his fatigues. His bow, cased, slapped his shoulder.

Renfrew touched the small aerosol canister through the cloth of his trousers. The handwritten label had read "Lolo Four: Collins." The vial, sealed into his patch pocket along with his small shell, straw, wood and feather effigy of Paul Ulana, slapped his thigh. So small.

He wondered distantly why he never thought about death.

He assumed it was because he was moving. Because he liked to run. As long as his body was moving, he was not dead, and as long as he wasn't dead, his own death was no concern of his. To have the power of it, that was enough.

It was cold now; his breath plumed out his nose when he breathed, and he liked that sensation, the cold moving in and warming, hot by the time it hit his lungs, heavy and damp and warm when he exhaled and it condensed into lovely clouds that were torn away by the wind of his passage and the scudding of the clouds until they were part of the clouds too, moving on, eastward, blown on out over the Pacific to swirl and dance and rain onto the sea.

The trail, which followed a ridge northeastward, fell away to his left as he ran. Below was a shallow, narrow valley, and ahead, invisible and down four thousand feet, would be the ocean, heaving at the flank of the island as it always had, eating at it endlessly, endlessly patient. Someday the ridge he ran along would collapse into the sea; someday the valley would be swallowed up; someday this would be cliff dropping straight to the surge, and the surge in turn would eat at the bottom of the cliff until it collapsed into a slope again, with a valley chiseled by stream runoff and wind and the limitless working of the water.

This was paradise to Renfrew, this moment, moving, legs moving, chest rising and falling with each breath drawn in and pluming out again, arms working, muscles smooth as oil, even the puckered flesh of his side where the boar had hooked him tugging when he breathed, reminding him he was alive in a dangerous and impermanent world, that he was dangerous and impermanent and now he moved, he ran, and the ridge was there for him to run on, and the moisture-heavy air was his to breathe, and the staghorn ferns were there to slap their own freight of water onto him.

He thought briefly about the old man, about Kalaipahoa, the poison god. He'd know what Renfrew was doing, and had done nothing to prevent it. Why? Renfrew had not wanted to kill him, not yet. He had the effigy, and he wanted to test his own power. The old man had power; the way he had called in those sharks! But Renfrew had power too. He wanted to test it. That would come.

Renfrew ran on.

Soon, though, too soon, the cabin appeared out of the mist, heaved up a timbered bulk, not large, but large enough to square the riot of life, impose its own reminders. So Renfrew slowed, and slowed his breath, and changed his posture in the world, separated himself from the elements, unslung the bow case.

He stood under a huge twisted ohia lehua, a ubiquitous plant with endlessly varying form but with unvarying gloom in the wet upland forests. This one was old, its limbs gnarled, leaves dark, bark wet gray, and tall. The trunk was Laocoon-twined with knotted roots matted into ridges and gullies. Here and there seedlings sprang from the roots themselves, and their leaves, also dark, tossed restlessly, as though tormented by the persistent cloud and rain.

He slipped the Jennings from its case; effortlessly he assembled and strung it. He notched an arrow. With his left hand he pulled his scarf over his lower face.

He paused for a moment at the door, going over his checklist. Today he had Koenig's wife. Soon he would have Koenig. That was the end of his job.

Tomorrow he would do Collins. There would be no problem. It was routine. If all went well with those two jobs, he'd finish his education with Kalaipahoa. He would graduate and take the old man's place. Hell, the old man was fading already. His knees were bad, he could hardly walk, he couldn't even cure himself. Renfrew would take his place, have the kahuna power on this island. He would be feared, respected, obeyed. He would be the kahuna *ana'ana*, the poison god. He would be Kalaipahoa! Then he could go hunt pig if he wanted. He could do anything. Just keep moving.

Renfrew smiled behind his face covering. Then he opened the door and went in. The group in the cabin looked up when he entered. Their expressions gratified him.

42

The sudden absence of rain and wind inside the lava tube, where the man's words echoed and rebounded, disoriented Chazz.

"Dr. Koenig," he said. "I'm so glad you could come."

"I didn't have much choice," Chazz replied. As his eyes adjusted, he could make out a faint impression of the rough rock wall ahead, though he couldn't tell whether the light fell from behind him and he was in a cave, or came from the other end of a twisting passageway. The figure retreated. He was apparently confident that Chazz would not attack.

Of course, they had Patria; that guaranteed his safety. Chazz followed.

The floor was damp and rough. A small stream flowed down the middle back toward the beach; they were ascending. The stranger spoke without turning; Chazz had to strain to make out his words.

"These tubes are quite interesting," he was saying. "They're formed by a kind of lava called pahoehoe which cools more rapidly on the surface than inside. The surface solidifies and the hot central flow continues, leaving tubes like this behind. Just up ahead, now."

Chazz said nothing. The tube opened to daylight again, a daylight filled with rain. The figure stopped just inside the tube and turned back to Chazz. He pushed back his rain hood and held out his hand.

"Dr. Koenig. Ward Freeman. I'm an admirer of yours, you might say. Your work on ribosomes is very impressive."

"I don't recognize your name," Chazz said. He didn't take the proffered hand.

"Oh." The man flipped his hand over, dismissing the comment. "It's not my real name. Security. Ridiculous, but they insist." He uttered an amused sound.

Freeman was pale, with a narrow angular face and short-cropped, almost white hair. He was in his late forties, from the deep lines alongside his mouth and the creases in his forehead. Yet, it was the kind of face it would be difficult to dislike. He smiled; it was an engaging smile that expressed admiration and respect.

Suddenly, in the warmth of that smile, Chazz realized how tired he was, how long it had been since he had eaten or slept. He'd been up all night. "Who are they?" he asked.

This conversation had a curiously disconnected and unreal air, so calm and rational, so offhand. Fatigue.

Freeman frowned briefly. "We have to wait a few minutes; you're late, you know, but they're later. The storm has screwed up the schedule."

He gestured at a pile of rocks and they sat. Chazz slumped as the weariness he'd been keeping at bay swept through him.

"You're tired," Freeman observed. "Of course. You've been up all night, and you're worried about your wife. Of course. I had nothing to do with that. I objected, but of course they don't listen to me. I'm a scientist." His tone was earnest.

Chazz said nothing.

"She's all right, though, your wife. I do know that. She's all right. Well taken care of. We'll be going up soon, don't worry. If you're worried." He seemed genuinely concerned.

"Of course I'm worried," Chazz snapped.

Freeman held up his hands. "Of course. Of course. It's just . . . complicated. I told them this wouldn't work."

"I don't know what you're talking about."

"No." It was a statement. Freeman lapsed into sudden gloom.

Outside the entrance, rain fell. Chazz could hear waves crashing on rock. There was no beach visible, and he couldn't see the water, just jungle and rain.

After a moment Freeman brightened. "Did you notice these stones?"

He patted the pile of rock they were sitting on. "They were built this way by the natives. They've been piled up like this for seven or eight hundred years. The tiny valley out there was terraced. It's all overgrown now. You can hardly tell anymore. There's a little stream, and they used to grow taro here and in the other valley, the Valley of the Lost Tribe. You can still find a taro plant if you look hard. I love this island." He had both hands palm down on the stone on either side of his thighs. It was a curiously naive gesture. It opened his coat. Chazz could see his gun.

"You're quite the tour guide," Chazz said.

"What? Oh, I guess I am, aren't I? Well." He looked at Chazz expectantly. Chazz said nothing.

Freeman shook his head. "This isn't easy, you know. Not at all. But they'll be here soon, so I should begin. We have a project. I suppose you know that by now. A project."

"No."

"No? Oh, I see. You don't know. You've been working in the dark, as it were. It's a recombinant DNA project. They tapped your phone. I tried to tell them you were a responsible scientist; that you were a patriot, too."

"Strachey is, too."

"Who? Oh, the CDC doctor."

"He was recalled. Because of this project."

"You can't mean you think they did that? No, they couldn't have." He leaned forward, frowning. "Unless–" He sat up. "No, it couldn't be. If he was recalled, it was the Centers for Disease Control. This project doesn't have anything to do with diseases."

Chazz barked a laugh.

"No, seriously." Freeman dismissed the notion. "What we're doing, it's simple. Dolphins."

"Dolphins?"

"Cetaceans exude an oil from their skin. All over. It leaves a sort of oily ghost in the water when they swim, reduces friction. They swim faster, see?"

"Okay."

"We've been developing a strain of *E. coli* that sticks to hulls. They express the dolphin genes for the oil. Same principle. The boats go faster. This is classified information. The other side got wind of it somehow. You understand, some kind of a security leak. It's created a real mess. How far do you go to stop the information from getting back to the other side? One thing leads to another. Pretty soon the mess is worse, not better."

"It doesn't sound like a secret worth killing for. Or kidnapping for."

"No one's been *killed*, Dr. Koenig. The kidnapping, well, let's say they are trying to be more persuasive. I don't think it's really kidnapping, you see. It's national security. Submarines could gain a ten- to twelve-percent increase in speed. That's a secret worth keeping, Dr. Koenig. They won't know where our subs are, so we have an advantage. You see? But then, we want them to know we have an advantage; then it's called deterrence. It's complicated, and it goes on all the time."

"Are you trying to tell me the old woman in Hanalei was

a Russian spy? Or that pathetic junkie from Pittsburgh? Or Delarota? He was nineteen years old!"

"Of course I'm not trying to tell you that. No, no. That was all a mistake. An accident. They weren't killed. Not deliberately."

"The bugs got out? What have you people done, Freeman?"

"I can't say any more. We're hoping you'll help us, Dr. Koenig. We have something on the order of an emergency. Here are the others. We still have a two-hour hike ahead of us, I'm afraid."

Two men gestured from the back. Freeman led Chazz, and the other two fell in behind him. His three escorts said nothing.

They hiked through the rain up a hidden switchback trail into the clouds.

43

Despite her fear, Patria took careful mental notes. She tried to consider this as just another field experience; dangerous, perhaps, but no more dangerous really than her three weeks with the Jivaro, or the brief side trip she had made in the Yucatan when her guide had mistakenly led her into a small group of his own mortal enemies.

The two neat men had appeared at the apartment and gestured her outside. They spoke quietly and politely, telling her that Lieutenant Takamura had sent them to bring her in to town. They drove toward Lihue, stopped at the shopping center and changed to an International Harvester Scout. By then she knew it was not Lieutenant Takamura they were going to see. The two neat men had driven west again, turned up the canyon past Koke'e onto a twisting and very rutted dirt road. These other two men had met them, and they had hiked for an hour or so until they got here. The Scout drove away.

The big one had a gun and she had asked no questions.

It wasn't clear what they wanted. The pudgy one seemed ill at ease. He did not appear immediately threatening, and had smiled at her nervously a couple of times.

The other, the big one, never changed expression, never smiled, and seemed in some indefinable way to contain an abnormal indifference to other people. She thought if there was tangible danger it would come from him, because he was not normal. Yet he had done nothing overtly threatening either; he had never drawn the gun. Patria simply knew she had to do what he told her to do.

He was now sitting on the other side of the cabin, arms folded across his overdeveloped chest, his enormous biceps bunched into hard ridges. His wide chin grew down into a thick neck, and although his eyes were quite close together, she thought it would not be a good idea to conclude from that evidence alone that he was stupid. His eyes were wide awake and watching.

Outside the clouds drizzled steadily.

The light in the cabin was bad. There was no electricity, and the daylight was a faded gray filled with dancing spots of darkness; it was right on the edge of a shift from day to night vision. Patria tried to consider what kind of culture she was in just now, that avoided light, kidnapped people, had vague and menacing purposes, waited.

They didn't want her, that was certain. They had her, but she was a means, not the end. They weren't interested in having an anthropologist on their team. So they wanted Chazz. They were waiting; she presumed they were waiting for him. Which meant they must have contacted him, which in turn might mean that he had somehow contacted others—Takamura or the other one, the Hawaiian. Yet they seemed to be, if not clever, at least well prepared; and it was certainly possible they could have prevented that.

She should not, therefore, assume there would be a last-minute rescue. She must appear to acquiesce, be passive, and watch for an opportunity, a moment when their guard was down.

They were in the mountains. She was sure she could not find her way back down alone, not in the dark. Patria was very good on the trail, but she had no compass and the trail was bad, nearly invisible even in daylight. There was no real point in trying to escape. Wait and see.

She heard a sound outside. Someone was coming. No-neck didn't move or give any sign he had heard, but the pudgy one stared at the door somewhat apprehensively.

The door opened, and she recognized in the furtive shape standing there the real danger.

It must have showed on her face, the fear, for the man gave a nod, as if satisfied. His bow was strung, an arrowhead wickedly barbed with razor vanes gleaming in the gloomy half-light of the cabin.

The pudgy man said, "They're not here yet. Where are they?"

The barb moved fractionally, and the pudgy man drew back. After a moment he turned to stare gloomily out the window. It was growing darker.

Patria sat up straight and looked at the hunter; she would conceal her fear.

What was the hierarchy in this room? The hunter was in charge, yet his motives were still obscure. What did he want? What was his connection with the murders? She noted the bayonet at his web belt, and thought of the Canadian girl with her throat slashed. Was he working for someone else? Was he a middleman, an errand boy, a hired hand? Did they want ransom, or did they want the help of a scientist like Charles Koenig?

The pudgy person was not directly under the hunter in the pecking order; perhaps he was irrelevant. She discounted him for the moment. That left No-neck as the employee. He would do what the hunter told him.

Was there a way she could establish some authority?

Certainly not by appearing frightened, nor by asking questions. In fact, she did not trust herself to speak at all.

Ignore No-neck. Disregard Pudgy. Establish a bond with the hunter.

Patria smiled at him. His face was covered, and she could see no reaction. His eyes revealed nothing. They were brown, she thought, or gray. His forehead was clear, plain, blank. No lines, no marks. His eyebrows were straight, nearly connected. The hair visible under his cap was long, tied back.

The door was still open behind the hunter; the mist was close and wet. She could barely see the huge tree in front through the fog. Just a dim outline, really. Something moved there.

The hunter casually pivoted, lifted the bow and loosed the arrow in one motion. There was a brief whirring sound, a squawk, and then silence. He trotted outside and returned a moment later holding the arrow. The barbed tip protruded from a wild rooster. Its tail, once its pride, was already lusterless. The hunter tossed the rooster at the pudgy man, who scurried aside. The dead bird fell to the floor under the window. The pudgy man did not return to his moody staring; he looked in dismay at the dead bird skewered on an arrow; then he sat on a wooden bench against the wall.

No-neck had not moved at all. His biceps bulged in the dim light. They heard footsteps outside, and four men entered.

One of them was Chazz. He looked exhausted.

44

"We've lost them." Sammy heaved his bulk onto the edge of Takamura's desk and settled with a sigh. "Gone, poof, like that."

Takamura said nothing. He noticed that his foot was jiggling, a very bad sign. Takamura was seldom nervous. He'd seen too much to be nervous.

Sammy noticed the foot, too. Takamura stilled the foot with an effort. Finally he whispered, "Damn."

Sammy nodded. "The van is parked outside Sailor's Cove, boat rentals. We've talked to Smitty, a surfer. He dropped Koenig off past Kalalau, barely made it back before the storm hit hard. There was a quote unquote developer asking about boats, signed up Koenig. Smitty didn't know him. Late forties, white hair. They have organization."

"I know." Takamura sighed. "The weather?"

"Awful. This storm's going to be the worst of the season. It's still building."

"Any ideas?"

"One." Sammy stood up again, too restless to stay perched on the edge of the desk.

"Well?"

Sammy shook his head. "It's a legend, really, nothing firm. There might be a trail."

"Go on."

"If they went through the lava tube from the Valley of the Lost Tribe, there might be a way to the top. They might know about it."

"Might? So we should be looking up here." Takamura went to the wall map. He traced the valley up from the coast with his delicate forefinger. "Somewhere up here, in Koke'e. Most of this is park. Not much private land, but there are some old cabins in that area grandfathered in. Long-term leases and such. Some are probably very old, maybe not even recorded recently, eh? They'd have to have a cabin, wouldn't they?"

Sammy nodded. "I'd think so."

"It would have to be unused, possibly unknown. We need the old real estate records. Damn, Samuel, this is a small island!"

"You're calling me Samuel, boss. That's a very bad sign."

Takamura smiled grimly. "I can understand how we lost Koenig. Even with a tag on his car, a few elementary precautions would shake us. They took the opportunities. But why did we lose Patria? She was the bait, after all."

Sammy shrugged again, a heavy gesture. "We were worried about Koenig."

"Not good enough. They waltzed in and impersonated us. Waltzed out again. Changed cars once at the shopping center and we lost them. Damn. What about our call to the FBI? This is a kidnapping."

Sammy snorted. "They said they can't come into the case because the agent assigned to Kauai is not on Kauai, he's on Maui helping the drug enforcement people investigate marijuana traffic; and he couldn't get here even if they considered it an authentic case, which they don't. The agent in charge suggested Koenig and his wife went hiking."

"State Police, National Guard, anything come through there?"

Sammy shook his head again. "No luck. We're blocked."

"I know. Besides, flights are canceled because of the weather; the airport is closed. The island is isolated. Our problem is no longer medical. Perhaps it never was."

They went down to Records, a long, echoing room filled with endless wooden-fronted cases full of ancient gray cloth-bound books. The ceiling fixtures were circular incandescent dishes. For economy, every other one had no bulb.

Sammy took one aisle and Takamura the next. They spent twenty minutes with the old maps and deeds.

Finally Sammy appeared at the end of the aisle and waved. His blunt fat fingertip rested on a map. Takamura nodded. "Let's go."

They made a photocopy and left the building. Takamura drove quickly but carefully. Sammy was on the radio most of the time.

Rain was sweeping in sheets across the roadway. At Sinner's Head there was a four-car accident, and Takamura had to drive along the shoulder, fretting.

"I suppose it's a good thing," Takamura said as they drove through Hanalolo. The town was dead; deserted. "Choppers would be useless even if we had good weather. Did you get everyone?"

Sammy grunted assent.

Takamura shook his head. "I don't like it. I don't like the risk. They'll all be there by now, assuming this is the place, which it may not be. We don't know how many of them there are, how well prepared they are, or how well armed. I don't like it."

Sammy said nothing. Takamura was thinking.

"On the other hand, there can't be too many. Not more than ten. Probably less. This is not a big cabin, and too many people make lousy conspiracy."

He drove on, still thinking.

"On the other hand again, they'll be very well prepared, and very well armed."

"That's the third hand," Sammy said.

Takamura looked at him and grunted. "These are professionals. Whoever killed the kids, planned the kidnapping, he was no amateur. A vet, probably. Trained right here at home; for Vietnam? Likely. Well trained, well armed. Well, 'Kitchen stove most excellent weapon—good for cooking goose.'"

Sammy snorted and Takamura looked over at him. "You're wondering who's got the kitchen stove?"

Sammy looked at his boss. He was expressionless. Then he nodded. "And who is the goose."

They took the Waimea Canyon Road. When they started to climb, Takamura stopped fretting. The others should be there already. He'd called from Lihue, and Sammy had radioed ahead. When they merged onto the Koke'e Road, Takamura said, "We have the kitchen stove, Sammy. And they are the goose. And you are The Kukui Nut."

Sammy smiled. It was action at last. Moving. Up the mountain to a cabin at the edge of the Alakai Swamp. It was getting dark, and the rain still poured in smooth sheets down the windshield whenever the wipers paused at the end of their cycle, only to be thrown off in wild spray when they swung back across the glass. The rain pattered on the metal roof of the police car, hissed under the tires as they cornered.

But they were moving, and Takamura had called him The Kukui Nut.

45

Chazz, slumped on the ratty couch beside Patria, had trouble adjusting to the gloom of the cabin. Patria stroked the back of his hand slowly, and something in the touch revived him. He listened to the room without moving.

There had been, besides Patria, three other people in the cabin: a muscular man with cropped hair seated impassively in a straight-backed wooden chair tilted slightly back against the wall; a familiar pudgy man with his back to them was staring out the window; and a lean figure in combat fatigues with an elaborate hunting bow. He added Ward Freeman and the other two who had brought him here.

He rested his head in one hand and watched through slitted eyes.

No one spoke. His escorts arranged themselves around

the perimeter of the room, as if the center were a stage just before curtain time. The darkness increased rapidly; rain drummed on the roof; and the sound matched the darkness, a noisy, chaotic clatter. Finally the hunter nodded, and the muscular man stood up. He stretched briefly, cracking his elbows. Then he used a long match to light two kerosene lamps. He set them down on a table so they threw their light across the room.

Chazz spoke softly. "Dewilliter! I might have known."

The pudgy man turned and looked sourly at Chazz. He shook his head. "I tried to warn you, Koenig. I tried."

Chazz laughed wearily. "A sense of foreboding on the horizon? Disquieting rumors?"

"Time. We needed time," he said. He sounded bitter.

"Lobelioids?" Chazz said it almost to himself. Lobelioids were harmless plants. The hunter held his bow slightly cocked, ready. Chazz had no doubt he could use it. He wished he knew more about bows. Zen archery.

The thought almost made him smile. This did not look like a Zen archer. This looked like a killer. He could feel Patria's fear of him, her need to tame him and her fear. She sat stiffly, stroking the back of his hand. Chazz could feel tension rise in the cabin. No one spoke.

"So," Chazz said at last, pushing it a little, "you've abandoned lobelioids for gene-splicing?"

Dewilliter smiled grimly. "Not really. Lobelioids suffer from a spindle viroid. I'd been looking into it, you know. Really. Not very practical, you might think. Not much to build a reputation on. But useful."

"Dewilliter," Ward Freeman said pleasantly. "You talk too much."

Dewilliter bit his plump lips and looked uneasily at the dead rooster on the floor. Chazz followed his gaze. Patria saw where he was looking and said, "The hunter. He's a good shot. Very fast."

Chazz nodded. "Impressive."

The rain swept noise rising and falling in waves across the roof, against the windows, into the water-soaked ground outside. The air in the cabin grew close and damp with bodies and tension.

"Why did you need time?" Chazz asked. He directed the question at Freeman.

Freeman appeared to think it over. "It's complicated, Dr. Koenig. Very complicated, more than you know. They're working on it, the other side, the Soviets, you see. We know that. They're working on it, and they may be ahead of us. We can't let that happen."

"You told me. And you want them to know you're working on it, too, and they know you want them to know. I don't believe a word of it."

"But it's all true! The boats go faster! It's just that there was an accident. These things happen. We took precautions. The best. We have funding; the sky's the limit. This is an important project. Very important. Something slipped up. No one understands it, how it happened, or even why. We have a P-4 facility. We took every physical precaution. We used standard K-12 bugs. It shouldn't have happened."

Chazz rubbed his temples. He could barely hear Freeman over the sound of rain and wind. He felt crushed into a bubble of fatigue.

"That's why we needed time, Koenig. The bugs got out. They mutated. People were, ah, affected."

Chazz spoke to the floor. He spoke slowly and dully. Freeman leaned forward to hear. Even Dewilliter was listening closely. "The bugs slashed two throats. The bugs cracked open their skulls and removed the brains. The bugs laid out the two bodies, a young couple, a woman and a man, beside the stream. Their faces were sliced open. I saw them."

Patria stopped stroking his hand, dug her nails into the skin. Chazz turned his own hand over and squeezed hers. He understood. The hunter. He hadn't missed the knife at his belt. Chazz put his other hand to his temple, cupped his head in a cradle of his palms.

Freeman turned away sourly. He spoke to one side, no longer looking at Chazz. "We need your help."

"You didn't ask for it. You can't force someone to help."

"We couldn't ask you. We knew your politics. You were

at Asilomar. You were very vocal there. You voted for containment, restraints. You *argued* for them. Restraints would be fine if everyone played by the rules. In the real world some people don't, though. You underestimate the enemy. You'd be stopped by the rules. We can't afford that. We can't afford to be stopped by rules. *They* aren't!"

"But the bugs escaped," Chazz said quietly. "People died. Some of your bugs. Others were murdered. That makes it less of an accident, doesn't it? That's why we have rules, Freeman. Rules are to protect people from dying."

Freeman shook his head. "You still don't understand. We're protecting people. We must. It is our job, our responsibility. Sometimes sacrifices must be made."

The hunter spoke for the first time. "We're getting nowhere," he said. His voice was a flat, even tenor, slightly muffled by the handkerchief over his mouth.

Chazz could feel Patria tense beside him. The kerosene lamps splashed light against the textured wallboard.

Both lamps were on the table; beside them was a Thermos of coffee, a small wisp of steam twisting from the open top. Chazz found that fact interesting. He was faced with what physics called a three-body problem: two lamps and a Thermos. Two human bodies had to get away from this room. That problem was complicated by the presence of other bodies. How could he use the others to advantage?

In a sense the problem was spiritual. His head was still cradled in his hands, fingers slowly massaging his temples. He needed not to think. He needed simply to be. Awareness expanded around him. He felt the placement of bodies, the currents of aggression, fear, ambition, hostility, intent. Some intent was directed toward him and Patria. It was not good intent. He needed to cut the thread of that intent. Weapons meant nothing without the intent to use them. The bow and arrow, the knife, the guns in the room. They were objects, inert, dead. Only intent could make them kill.

He faced Shinawa, the live blade winking in a similar light. Intent.

You must be ready to die.

46

"Could I have some coffee?" Chazz asked. "I can't think straight."

A Thermos was produced. Chazz settled back on the couch with a sigh, sipping. "You know, Freeman, you're either an idiot or a liar."

Freeman frowned.

"Which is it?" Chazz was smiling pleasantly. Beside him Patria was alert and tense.

"I'm not sure I follow." Freeman spoke slowly. He looked at the hunter, who had pulled back his bowstring a bit, the steel tip of his arrow absolutely steady in the yellow light.

"Well, take Dewilliter," Chazz went on. "He knows what's going on. You see, people are dying in other ways. Not just bugs. That means this is not an accident. Do you know why, Dewilliter? He's shaking his head. Dewilliter isn't in on the real secrets. I'll bet even the hunter here knows the score." Chazz paused as the barbed tip lined up on him; it was answer enough, though, that small motion of the arrow. The hunter knew. The bayonet at his belt gave him away; that movement of the arrow tip confirmed it.

Freeman caught it. He turned to the hunter. "What does he mean, Renfrew? What is he saying?" Patria had heard the thick undercurrent of anger in Freeman's voice.

She glanced at No-neck, who remained impassive. The others were alert, but confusion was increasing. The team lineups were dissolving.

Renfrew said nothing. For the first time he was uncertain.

The lines of authority were not clear. He was supposed to apply pressure on Koenig. That was his current mission. Pressure. Ensure cooperation, those were his orders.

Tomorrow he would kill Collins. This was obscuring his mission. Therefore he would have to stop it.

"Shut up," he said quietly.

Chazz held Patria's hand; he laid his forefinger along hers and gently pointed them together toward the door. She glanced at him.

Freeman was saying, "I have a right to know."

"No," Renfrew said. He nodded at No-neck, who very carefully put the front legs of his chair on the floor and sat straight. "You don't." The arrow backed him up.

Freeman turned away, frowning. "Dewilliter," he said, "what does this mean?"

Dewilliter shook his head. "I can't say, Ward. Honest. You're on the Cetus team. You tell me."

"What does that mean? Does that mean there's another team? Is that what it means? There's another team?" Freeman was shouting.

Dewilliter shrugged helplessly. "I can't tell you, Ward. I really can't."

Chazz was leaning forward wearily, elbows on his knees, the cup of hot coffee cupped in his palms.

Freeman turned to Renfrew. "He's saying there's another team. Inside two-twelve."

Renfrew drew back on the bowstring. Freeman took a step back, holding up his hands; the arrow twanged vibrating into the wall beside Dewilliter. At the same time Chazz threw his coffee into No-neck's face, pushed Patria toward the door, and in two steps was across the small room.

He moved swiftly toward Freeman by the window. The man, still surprised, backed away, and Chazz pulled the arrow from the thin wallboard. He drew its barbed point lightly across Freeman's throat, leaving a thin red line. Freeman spilled back into Dewilliter, mewling in shock and pain.

Renfrew was trying to notch another arrow in his bow as Chazz swept his forearm across the table, sending the two kerosene lamps flying. Dewilliter and Freeman had fallen against the wall; the three escorts were moving toward Chazz.

He saw Patria vanish through the door as the three closed on him, then he went inside himself, moving toward the closest of the three escorts. His right hand came up, the heel of his palm rising from beneath toward the man's chin. Just as the first kerosene lamp snuffed out, the man saw the hand coming toward him and lurched back, losing his balance. He toppled into the second attacker and the two fell to the floor.

The second lamp exploded against the base of the far wall in a rush of flame. Chazz spun delicately around the two toppling bodies, lowered himself as he pivoted and picked up the third man across his hip, tossing him into the struggling heap now visible in the leaping kerosene flames on the far side of the cabin.

No-neck had cleared his eyes by now, but stood uncertain whether to fight the flames splashing up the wall and against the ceiling or come to the aid of the three men. He decided after momentary hesitation to rush at Chazz, who waited until No-neck was almost upon him, then dropped down and sideways, leaving a leg out. No-neck tripped and fell heavily. Chazz scooped up No-neck's wrist and swept his arm in a circle. There was a sharp crack and the arm fell away limply.

Chazz scanned the room, but for the moment all attackers seemed to be otherwise occupied. Dewilliter and Freeman were struggling with the window, urged by the spreading flames. Suddenly the spilled kerosene from the first lamp ignited and another *crump* of flame joined the fire. He heard the sound of breaking glass.

There were incoherent shouts outside. Chazz let out a tremendous shout as he hurled himself out the door into the rain. In the midst of his aerial flip beyond the threshold, he glimpsed Dewilliter and Freeman frozen in outline against the flames. The window was smashed; they were both trying to climb through it at once.

It worried him that he couldn't see Renfrew anywhere.

47

As soon as he saw the flames, Takamura stopped running. He held out his hand, and Sammy, behind him and to his left, ran into it and stopped. There was no way to contact the others in the mist and rain without breaking radio silence.

Takamura pointed toward the dim orange glow in the middle distance. Takamura shook his head. He leaned toward Sammy. "Fire," he whispered. There was little chance he would be heard over the wind now moaning through the trees, but he took no chances. It was bad enough that his entire force consisted of him, two traffic patrolmen and three park rangers who had little taste for this sort of police work. It was not worth risking a warning to the quarry here. Yet there seemed little choice. The cabin was burning.

He cupped his hand around the radio and whispered, "This is Hawk One. All units. Hold back. Do not execute. Repeat, do not execute."

The response almost deafened him. "What? Please repeat, Hawk One. We can't hear you."

The words were audible without the radio.

Something was happening at the cabin. The door was open and figures were pouring out. There were confused shouts.

"All the demons of the seven hells," Takamura said softly, running toward the cabin. He pulled out his gun as he ran. Sammy moved in his swift waddle beside him. Takamura heard the sound of breaking glass, the hiss of moisture on open flame, his own breath. He saw a figure near an ancient ohia lehua tree moving toward them and halted.

"Stop," he called. "Stop or I'll shoot." The figure ducked behind the tree, and Takamura lowered his gun. "Don't shoot," he said to Sammy. "That could be Koenig."

They moved slowly just within the line of trees parallel to the cabin, edging closer without exposing themselves. Yet the confusion at the cabin kept urging Takamura on. Finally he broke from the trees and moved toward the cabin. He could make out two people moving away toward the woods. He shouted, "Stop," but his shout was only one of many; the figures vanished into the trees and mist without pausing.

More people appeared at the door to the cabin. Sammy moved swiftly toward the door. He appeared out of the fog like an apparition, and two of the men stopped when they saw him. They were reaching for their own guns when Sammy very quietly told them to raise their hands. They obeyed, moving away from the increasing heat of the flames.

There was enough of a suspension of the shouting for the whirring sound of the arrow to be plainly audible. It made a hard, brutal sound when it hit Sammy's body. He watched, surprised, as the gun fell from his hand; he sat suddenly on the muddy ground and reached for the arrow sticking from his chest.

Takamura hadn't seen Sammy get hit, and the men in front of the cabin scattered as soon as they realized their captor was down. Takamura fired a shot in the air, but the sound, ordinarily so loud and authoritative, was a muffled *sput* in the swirling mist and rain, the roar of flame and wind. Smoke billowed from the cabin, and his eyes were tearing. He tripped on Sammy's outstretched legs, recognizing him only when he bent down.

"Sammy!" Crouched beside his partner, Takamura held Sammy's shoulders. Sammy looked at him with pain-filled eyes.

Men appeared around the corner of the cabin, sidelit by the flames. "We got these two," someone called. Takamura nodded, a gesture lost in shadows.

Takamura looked at the two prisoners. A tall man with very pale hair, and a shorter rather pudgy one. Neither looked particularly threatening. He nodded. Gradually the patrolmen and three rangers gathered around. Takamura was not prepared to try to remove the arrow. A ranger tended Sammy, checking the wound. He looked at Takamura over Sammy's shoulder. The look said he didn't know.

"I'll hike back," one of the others said. "We need a doctor."

Sammy winced when he spoke. "No," he said. "Wait. There's a hunter. Dangerous."

"I know this area," the ranger said. "Don't worry." He looked at Takamura, who nodded. The ranger melted into the fog.

Sammy didn't notice him go. He sighed. "'Man has learned much who has learned how to die,'" he quoted.

Takamura smiled. "Charlie Chan does not die," he said. "Neither does The Kukui Nut. Too tough."

Sammy waved a hand, then winced. "Maybe," he said.

The roof of the cabin collapsed while they were moving him and a shower of sparks vanished downwind into the mist.

"Any danger of this spreading?" Takamura asked the ranger.

He shook his head. "Not this year, certainly. Probably never. I'm surprised it's burned this long."

Sammy grunted. "At least it keeps me warm," he said.

"Be quiet, Kukui Nut," Takamura said.

"Yes, boss."

"You're going to be all right."

"Yes, boss."

"So shut up and rest."

"Yes, boss."

"Take care of him," Takamura said. He went over to the group huddled under another clump of trees. Water dripped steadily from the leaves, but it was slightly dryer there. "Who are these two?" he asked. He took off his porkpie hat and looked at it sadly. It was sodden and shapeless. He ran his finger around the limp brim, removing water. Then he put it back on.

"This" —the patrolman guarding them gestured at Dewilliter— "claims he has nothing to do with all this. The other won't say anything."

"Are you in charge here?" the other asked Takamura, ignoring the patrolman.

Takamura nodded.

"I must warn you," he said. "You don't understand the implications. This is a national security matter."

"My partner," Takamura said slowly, "is over there with an arrow in his chest. It is possible he will die. That is more than a national security problem. That is a personal problem. For him, and for me. There are other matters – kidnapping, murder, attempted murder, robbery, breaking and entering, probably arson and several dozen other crimes. I'm responsible for the security of this island; I really don't care much about national security at this particular point, sir. You two are under arrest. When we catch them, the others will be under arrest as well. Then, perhaps, we might worry about national security. Perhaps."

"You'll regret this," the man said.

"So, perhaps, will you," Takamura told him. He gestured for the third ranger. They stepped away, and Takamura asked him about the others.

He shook his head. "They'll be impossible to track in this weather. The swamp is a tough place to find people, anyway. It's very easy to get lost in there, especially when it's foggy like this. We'll have to wait for daylight."

Takamura checked his watch in the dying light of the burning cabin. He nodded. "Two hours," he said. "Then we start."

48

The Alakai Swamp fed into the Wai'ale'ale caldera. The swamp was a soggy depression running some fifteen kilometers diagonally across the top of the island. In places it was only a couple of kilometers wide. The volcanic rock underneath is impermeable, and the tremendous rainfall there collects in this natural basin. The crater itself, at the southeast corner, is the wettest spot on earth, averaging 465 inches of rain per year.

It is a maze, the Alakai Swamp, a random collection of bogs and points, spits of relatively dry land interspersed by waist-deep mud, graceless ponds, twisted, distorted vegetation, trees growing dwarfed, stunted and gray. Water collected in pools reflects the leaden sky, sometimes merges with the sky when the cloud closes in, as it has this night.

Only the hardiest of the ancient Hawaiians ventured here, and then only to collect plants or perform religious ceremonies; they never stayed. The swamp is inhospitable, wretched, wet, hauntingly beautiful, rich in steamy life adapted to this unspeakable damp, its twiggy branches clutching at the clouds and a thick carpet of fern and bog plant concealing hidden pools.

The trails created by the park service are well marked for hikers, a series of poles stuck in the ground during World War II for military communications, or brightly colored brown and white pipe markers indicating relatively firm ground. Unfortunately, they are all invisible in the cloud and darkness of night. No one hikes the Alakai Swamp in this kind of weather, at this time of day, ever.

Even in the best of weather, during those rare intervals of sun and clear sky, daylight and good visibility, it is necessary to circle around pools of mud or water along the trail. In this darkness, though, Chazz and Patria must move by touch, with constant false steps and terrible caution. Progress is slow, yet behind him he feels pursuit, he senses Renfrew, and his nape stands up, panic clutches him more tenaciously than the mud. The only saving grace is the impossibility of this trail.

He thought in the hours since they fled they could not have covered much ground. Yet he wanted to put some distance between himself and the cabin. Their flight was random, and it was fortune that had led them here and not toward park headquarters, or down the cliffs. Chazz wanted to avoid the obvious directions, had known their route to the cabin, so had a general sense of which way to go. Hide out in the swamp, he thought. Take the difficult way, and perhaps Renfrew will not follow.

He could feel rather than see that the forest around them was thinning, flattening, disappearing. Patria clutched at his hand trailing behind him when he slipped in a bog. From time to time they could smell a sharp scent of anise from the mokihana tree.

Finally there was an imperceptible brightening of the thick fog around them, a lightening of the wind that had moaned through the night, and dim shadows appeared, the almost shapeless clutch of trees and ferns.

"We've got to stop soon." Chazz's breath was ragged with fatigue; they had been running on fear, and their reserves were gone. Finally he could see Patria's face, spattered with mud. Her clothes were soaked to the waist, her face pale and drawn. He tried smiling at her, and she tried smiling back. The effect of the two of them struggling to be cheerful was suddenly funny, and they began to laugh, a little hysterically. The laughter sounded loud and strange, and stopped as suddenly as it had begun.

They began to look for some sheltered high ground where

they could rest. Ragged clumps of cloud blew by, hiding, then suddenly releasing, the landscape. When they could see any distance, they saw only flat and level swamp. There was no sign of a trail, no sign of man's presence at all. It was a primordial chaotic world before them, made of water and demented life, fern gulches, dead branches and shrubs, twisting vines. The tallest trees, if they could be called that, grew no higher than Chazz's head and offered little shelter.

"Any idea where we are?" Patria asked.

"No," Chazz said.

He pointed. "Stay here a minute. That looks like a spot."

A small gulch of ferns backed against a relatively dry hummock. He pulled out the ferns and made a nest. "Come," he said. They settled as comfortably as possible in the driving mist and light rain. The storm was moving around them somewhere, but here, for now, was a moment of safety.

"As I see it," Chazz said, "we have to wait. We need sleep. By noon it might clear up enough to see where the sun is, or figure out directions. Then we need to find our way to high ground. This swamp is crisscrossed by trails. We ought to find one. Then we follow it. We get out of the swamp, find a road. Very simple."

"Yes," Patria said. "Very simple."

He felt worse after some sleep. Patria was shivering, drawn and sullen; and the cloud was as thick as ever. He took sight on the outline of a tree; they made their way to it, perhaps ten meters or so. It took ten minutes to get there. He tried to maintain the direction, find another landmark, struggle to it. Keep the heading, find another, go there. It was painfully slow, and he felt the thick clutch of despair drag at him; they were lost, their resources were depleted, Patria was shivering violently. They were suffering from exposure, and he knew they could not keep this up much longer. Yet he plowed on.

They stopped often to rest. The stops grew longer and more frequent. They were hungry and thirsty. Then they were no longer hungry, no longer thirsty. They were no longer cold and tired and dirty.

They were no longer moving.

It seemed like a long time in the dream before Chazz considered that the shouts he heard might be real, that the voice calling his name might belong to Cobb Takamura, that someone might be looking for them. He answered in the frail croak his voice had become; after that it took forever before anyone appeared. The fog had closed around them all in a fist of woolly indifference, and they dropped off at last into a long, slow spiraling descent into pleasant darkness where nothing mattered anymore.

Part III

PURGATORY

49

Too many dead, Takamura was thinking as he climbed the broad cement steps. Too many in the hospital. His head was down against the tangible wind whipping spray around the corner of the modern gray bulk of the building. Debris littered the empty streets. Too many disabled. He knew what he was up against now, and it wearied him, dragging him more than the relentless wind and damp.

The silence inside the hospital was startling. The lobby, a cavernous imitation-marble expanse, was cool with echoes. He felt an almost spiritual relief when the doors closed behind him.

"You'd think it would be busier here, with the storm," he said to the receptionist. She'd seen a lot of him the past few days, and nodded. He was making conversation.

"Try Emergency," she suggested. "They're busy."

"That's all right," Takamura said. "I'll take your word for it."

Despite the calm of the lobby, he had to wait for the elevator. A cardboard sign taped beside the door stated that the hospital had to go on and off emergency power and there might be delays at the elevator. If the matter is urgent, use the stairs.

The matter, Takamura thought, is urgent, and the stairs won't help. He was powerless to rush anything.

The elevator arrived at last. Two frowning doctors came out, gave him a nod and headed down the west wing toward pulmonary care. Takamura smiled thinly in the car, thinking this would be a busy time for pulmonary care. Pneumonia galloped in weather like this.

There was more activity on the fourth floor: patients on gurneys, nurses hurrying with trays, the general level of barely controlled crisis. Takamura saw Dr. Shih in conversation and moved toward her. She looked up when he appeared, tilted her head to one side questioningly.

He lifted his eyebrows in answer.

"Do you always answer a question with a question?" she snapped.

He nodded.

"I'm here because there is a shortage of doctors today. Two staff are down, one with a broken bone—a branch fell on him or something—the other has a something or other they thought I might be able to fix. I fixed his something or other, and now they want me to stay up here. I must say it's a change of pace for me, dealing with live people. I don't like it."

Takamura smiled. "I expect not," he said. "'Man is not incurably drowned—if he still knows he's all wet.'"

"Hah!" She snorted. "Charlie Chan again. Everybody on this island is all wet, let me tell you. When people are already dead, they stay that way. That's why I prefer pathology. Frankly, Lieutenant, clinical work scares me. I never liked losing patients. Your two friends are going to be all right. You can go see them."

"Thanks." He went on down the hall.

Chazz was sipping orange juice through a bent plastic straw. Somehow the sight of that big man holding the tiny plastic glass in his hand sipping delicately through a bent straw pleased Takamura.

"That's nice," he said.

"What's nice about it?" Chazz growled.

"You're sitting up. Almost."

"Yeah." Chazz paused. "She's going to be all right. They said Patria's all right."

Takamura nodded. "They were worried about exposure, dehydration, but she's tough."

Chazz nodded. He crumpled his plastic cup and tossed

it at the wastebasket across the room. It hit the rim, balanced for a moment, fell in.

"Good," Takamura approved.

"First one I've made. How long have I been here?"

"What do you remember?"

"There you go, answering a question with a—"

"Question. A habit. Police work, you know."

"Not much. We went into the swamp. I wanted to avoid the cliff. We went east, I think. It was dark and raining and very boggy. I didn't know where the hunter was, either. Renfrew. He's dangerous. Immediately dangerous, anyway. The others are more so in the long run. They've got to be stopped."

"Yes, that is our problem."

Chazz closed his eyes. "We were in the swamp at least one night and then a day, a dark one. We had no food. Plenty of water, but I didn't trust it."

"You were right," Takamura agreed. "Feral goats, pigs. It's bad, full of parasites."

Chazz nodded. "Before that, though, there was a fight. In the cabin. It burned. I broke someone's arm, the muscle builder. I shouldn't have broken his arm."

"No?"

"I should have protected him too. I wasn't good enough."

"You got away. He'll recover."

"That's all I remember. You found us."

"Park rangers. They're good at that sort of thing."

"Thanks."

"Anytime."

"I hope not."

Takamura watched Chazz in silence for a time, twisting the brim of his damp hat up and down in both hands. Finally Chazz said, "Something's bothering you."

Takamura said nothing.

"There's been another one?"

Takamura nodded.

"Who?"

"Collins. Navy, a lieutenant. No visible marks, a nasty expression. Neurologic."

Chazz nodded. "Their bugs are loose. He was there. They could have some kind of epidemic at the Naval Facility. Why haven't they notified you? The health people?"

Takamura shrugged. "He'd tried to walk into Kekaha. The driver of an emergency road vehicle found him. He wasn't dead yet. He said a name. Lolo."

"Brain? A code name?" Chazz asked.

Takamura shook his head. "I don't know. Sammy had met him at a bar. He'd talked about boats. Paint. He didn't make much sense, but Sammy called it in."

"Yeah, I know about the boats. Any way to check with the Navy?"

"The phones are down. Only very high priority messages can use the satellite link, and even then transmissions are unreliable. This is high priority, of course, but nothing's come in. This island is isolated, Chazz. This is the worst storm in many years. There's been a lot of damage. I almost didn't find out about Collins."

"Can I see Patria?" Chazz asked after a few minutes. There wasn't much he could do about the weather. It would pass by itself.

"I'll see if she's awake." Takamura went to the nurses' station to ask. When he came back, he was pushing a wheelchair. "Come on, Koenig, she'd like to see you."

"I don't need that," Chazz said, standing. His legs gave out and he toppled into the wheelchair.

On the way down the hall Chazz stopped the chair to look at Takamura. "I heard about Sammy. How is he?"

Takamura shook his head. "Not good, Chazz. Not good. It took too long to get him down. It took too damn long to get everyone down. They don't think he's going to make it."

50

Paul Ulana arrived at the hospital at dusk, driving a battered pickup well past its prime. The roads were closed to all except emergency traffic, yet the old man had no trouble getting through.

It was the third day of the waning storm. Debris littered downtown Lihue. Surf had breached the Nawiliwili harbor wall and washed away a park. Some resort areas lay in ruins, beaches gone, trees toppled, roads washed out.

He parked the truck and pulled an ancient cheap suitcase from the back. The wind lifted the case in his hand, tugging at it. Rain swept across his back as he limped up the stairs. He dripped on the floor in the sudden quiet, nodded at the receptionist, who smiled fleetingly and went back to her romance. Bruised old Hawaiian men were a common sight in this hospital, even during the storm, even at night, even carrying suitcases. Paul Ulana walked painfully to the elevators, waited patiently for the car to arrive, nodded to the doctor and two nurses who emerged, and rode in silence to the fourth floor, touching the raw scrape on his forehead. His knees ached, his ribs turned painfully when he breathed, yet he smiled pleasantly to all he met.

Unnoticed amid the orderly frenzy of medical activity just before bedtime, he sauntered down the hallway to West Four. In a waiting area he looked for a long moment out the windows at the night. Drops spattered the glass, and most of what he could see was a reflection of the room distorted by the drops as they rolled slantways down the glass, blown by the wind. Finally he shrugged and moved on down to 407. He pushed open the door and moved into the room. One shaded lamp beyond the bed cast a dim circle onto the floor, the wall beneath the window and half of a leatherette easy chair; the array of monitoring equipment on a trolley beeped and flickered in the rudimentary language of medical technology. It was, he thought, a different sort of magic, no more effective than his own. Perhaps less.

The figure lying on the bed was deep in coma. He could read that in the slow flicker on the oscilloscope screen, the monotonous drip of the IV, the languid spike of respiration, the nearly motionless sheet across the man's chest.

The old man murmured some words, in which his other name, the poison god Kalaipahoa, was clear. His eyes grew red in the shadowed light as he approached and saw the tiny frown of pain on Sammy Akeakamai's face, almost invisible amid the plump wrinkles of good humor. The old man moved the straight-backed metal chair beside the bed and sat cross-legged on the floor. Silently he set the suitcase beside him and bent to open it. It was filled with five-ply braided coconut-husk fiber called sennit. He took the bundle out and laid it to one side. A folded tapa cloth made from the inner bark of the tree called wauke, or paper mulberry, filled the rest of the case. The cloth was carefully decorated with a black and white pattern of chevrons of various sizes.

The old man set to work with the fiber, weaving an odd basket shape. From time to time he looked up at the monitors, but there was no change in the slow green pulse of the oscilloscope, the spike of respiration. The dim lamplight threw highlights off his hair as he bent to his work, glistened on the whites of his eyes when he looked up. His mustache was ghostly white.

Gradually the thing he was making took shape, a pinch-waisted barrel shape the size of a man's trunk. Row after row of sennit plaiting moved up to shoulders without arms, sloped in to a neck. It was after midnight when he began work on the head, an elongated grotesque with goggle eyes, small bumps for ears, a rudimentary nose, and a grimacing mouth filled with skull teeth. He attached the completed head to the neck and held the light object at arm's length to examine it.

Satisfied, he stood beside the bed for a long time, gazing down at Sammy's face. There had been no change in the expression, that subtle hint of pain. The arrow had done considerable damage to his right lung, two ribs and some major blood vessels. Prognosis was bad. Plastic tubes looped from the bandages over his chest to bottles on the rack beside the bed. One of the bottles bubbled with air from the pleural tears. Chest wounds of this kind were difficult to treat in the field, and usually fatal.

Kalaipahoa moved the metal chair back beside the bed, arranged carefully so that anyone entering the room would see the patient first, and then notice the objects he now set out. First the carefully folded tapa cloth, handmade and extremely valuable, for tapa represented hours of labor, pounding and working the bark until it was soft and felted. On this he set the monstrous human figure, facing the patient. He stood for a moment gazing at the two shapes, the man and his woven ghost, then he closed his case and eased out of the room. It was nearly two in the morning when he returned to the waiting area. The plastic-cushioned couches and chairs held a smattering of relatives of other storm victims. The old man settled himself onto one of the couches and almost immediately fell into a light sleep.

Three and a half hours later, hospital routine picked up. The breakfast trolley moved down the halls; medicines were delivered; the phone at the nurses' station began buzzing quietly. Outside, the wind had died down. No one paid any attention to another old Hawaiian man sleeping in the waiting room. Finally he sat up, stretched once, went down to the hospital cafeteria and ate breakfast, returned to the fourth floor and waited some more. Eventually, he knew, they would show up.

They did. The neat Japanese policeman with the porkpie hat appeared, carrying a leather bag slung over one shoulder. The old Hawaiian dozed in the waiting area, watching the lieutenant walk briskly down the hall. Minutes passed. He reappeared with Koenig and his wife, walking slowly. At the nurses' station they spoke for a few moments with the duty nurse. They went down the hall to 407. Kalaipahoa went after them. He knocked at the door.

"Come in." It was Takamura's voice.

He pushed open the door. They were standing by the bed. The woven figure sat on the chair; but now, in the gray daylight that filled the room, the figure did not look so monstrous.

"Ah," Cobb Takamura said. "Mr. Ulana. What the hell happened to you?"

"A slight fall, Lieutenant. Nothing serious. How are you?"

To Chazz the exchange had an unreal quality, beside the bed where Sammy lay dying, but Takamura was introducing them as if this were the street on an ordinary day. "You've met Mrs. Koenig already, I believe. This is Dr. Koenig—Paul Ulana, Sammy's uncle. Is this your work, Mr. Ulana?"

He indicated the torso on the chair.

Paul nodded. "It's an 'aha fiber casket, Lieutenant. *Ka'ai*. For his bones. He is royalty, you know, an ancient *alii* family. If he dies, he will need this."

Takamura nodded. "Of course. If he dies. If he does not die, he will thank you for your concern." There was no irony in his tone. "So far, The Kukui Nut is holding his own."

Ulana nodded. "I'll come back later." He paused. "I believe the storm may be soon over."

"Yes," Takamura said. "May be."

"Nice to have met you, Dr. Koenig, and your wife, of course. We had a very interesting talk. It was a pleasure being her informant, as I believe it's called." He smiled affably as he spoke, and Chazz, watching his face closely, heard words that did not seem to match the movement of his mouth: Renfrew. Beware, he seemed to say.

But he was saying good-bye, moving toward the door, and Chazz wasn't sure he'd really heard. A face swam in his mind, though. Bound in camouflage. Chazz nodded and the old man left the room.

Chazz looked at Takamura, but he was standing by the bed looking down at his partner. He did not appear to have heard what Kalaipahoa had said, but Patria looked at the departing figure thoughtfully.

The *ka'ai* on the chair seemed to be grinning.

51

"He is," Takamura said softly, looking down at Sammy's face framed by the pillow, at the frown of pain, "The Kukui Nut. Also known as the candle nut. Children would take the midrib of a coconut leaf and string the kernels of the kukui nut on them. They were burned for light. The kukui nut burns well, not long but bright and clear; the children would keep them strung and lit. That is children's work in the world, I suppose, to keep the light alive. I hope he will not need that thing." He nodded toward the casket on the chair.

The wind was brisk with ragged clouds, palm fronds turning end over end across the parking lot. They said nothing, each absorbed in thought.

Later, on the way to the laboratory, Patria whispered to Chazz: "Something's wrong. What's bothering you?"

He shook his head. "The man in the cabin. I broke his arm."

She stared. "He would have killed us."

"Doesn't matter."

"Don't be too hard on yourself, Chazz. You protected us. The first ethical order is to protect yourself, isn't it?"

He nodded.

While Takamura drove carefully around the eucalyptus debris that littered the road, Chazz asked about Paul Ulana.

"You'd have to ask The Kukui Nut about him."

"I mean, what does he do? Besides helping Dewilliter find lobelioids and making straw coffins?"

Takamura looked at him sharply. "Retired, I believe. Why?"

Chazz shrugged. "Don't know. I suspect everything."

"Well, consider this. All the victims apparently worked at the sugar mill near Koloa at one time or another. Except Collins, of course."

"I'll consider it."

They waited in the quiet of the Douglass Research Center for the computer search to end. "Here it is," Chazz said. As lists scrolled up the screen, the computer beeped softly, indicating a match. Numbers flashed: $2.3*10^7$ kb 712 bp match, Sample 1 Sample 4, another beep, Sample 3, Sample 7, Sample 10, Sample 14— The numbers shifted and rippled, lining the samples up in columns, all $2.3*10^7$ kb 712 bp match. A yellow line divided the screen in half, and the color image of a sequence of DNA appeared, bases twisting in colors around the helix. The sequence was coiled upon itself, the helix itself twined into a helix, the ends unraveled slightly to label 3′ and 5′ ends.

"Mitochondria again," Chazz murmured.

"What does it mean?" Takamura asked.

"It means that every one of the victims has an identical sequence in the mitochondrial DNA at a location 2.3 times ten to the fourth kilobases in from the 3-prime end, where, see here, there is a homologous site, this 59.283 kilobase-pair sequence. The computer's run through all the samples looking for matches. I didn't really expect any this good, but this is what Strachey and I were doing all night. A hunch. It is very odd for people to have identical sequences this long. It ties them all together. See, the controls don't have this sequence at all."

"What does it mean?" Takamura asked again.

"I think it means they had something in common, something genetic, a gene plus, perhaps, a viral intrusion of some kind. Something inherited from the mother, plus something else. They were targets for an intruder."

"I don't get that either," Patria said. "An intruder?"

Chazz leaned back in his chair and crossed his hands behind his neck, partly to stretch and partly to think. Finally he straightened up.

"Imagine a secret agent, a spy. To do his job he needs to get into the host country, the host culture; once there he needs to look and act like a native. It's just as important for that culture to have ways of recognizing impostors or invaders, of telling *them* from *us*. Living beings do this by labeling their own DNA with a chemical marker that says this molecule belongs. Foreigners are destroyed, attacked and broken apart by enzymes; natives are left alone. For a secret agent—a virus, say—to survive, it must be disguised as a native, have the proper chemical marker. He must wear the right clothes, speak the right language, know the right cues, gestures, responses and so forth."

Chazz tapped the screen where the DNA sequence slowly rotated, displaying its structure. "There's the spy. Part of it, anyway."

Takamura and Patria leaned forward to look at the screen, frowns of puzzlement on their faces. "How do you know?" Patria asked.

"The odds against a sequence this length matching at this location between two human genotypes are astronomical. Lots of sequences will match, of course; genes are genes, after all. Or recognition sites. But they are very, very rarely in precisely the same location. Yet all the victims had this match. That could mean that the victims were invaded, a fragment of foreign genetic material insinuated itself into the host DNA and became indistinguishable from the host. The perfect secret agent."

"Go on."

"The viroid, a fragment of RNA, perhaps, looks for a common sequence. A marker, say the genetic code for blue eyes—I'm drastically oversimplifying, of course. It snips the DNA and inserts itself there. Presto, a new gene has appeared."

"A disease?" Takamura suggested.

"Maybe. Some cancers work that way. But where does it come from, and what does this particular sequence do?

What does this foreign gene express—what protein does it encode—and when? The secret agent must get in, then he must get rid of the evidence of how he got in. In other words, he must cover his tracks. We don't really know, but from what Freeman said to me, the bugs they are working on at PACMAN have gotten loose and mutated. In itself, that's extremely unlikely. Very puzzling. There should be evidence of how this sequence got established in its host, and there was none, no evidence that Dr. Shih could find, none that Strachey or I could find. That's suspicious. And second, of course, the spy has a mission. In this case, though, the mission is to kill the host organism. The question is how. We should run this program on Collins, too, but I'd bet the results will be the same."

"No bet," Takamura answered. "Pray continue."

"We had a common theme for the victims, a sugar mill."

"Except Collins," Patria said.

"Except Collins," Chazz assented. "Shelving Collins for now, when did the victims work there? Why, if this is intentional, did someone test this substance on them? It's almost like a shotgun experiment—blast it at the population and see what happens. We have some effects similar to slow virus; that would mean this thing got out a long time ago, before we had recombinant technology. Not likely, but a possible biological warfare agent. Now, though, what does this genetic material do? What does it code for? I don't know. Is it a group of dangerous and very unscrupulous people who can call on the resources of the U. S. Government and the cloak of national security to hide the effects of a long-term and very dangerous project? Or a small group of sloppy biochemists who got careless? They've killed, kidnapped and threatened; they're desperate. They got Strachey transferred back to Atlanta. They've blocked our appeals for help, I'm pretty sure. Even for sloppy biochemistry, that seems excessive. And it takes clout and people willing to kill. I don't like that."

Takamura put on his hat very precisely. "I don't like it, either. I'm a policeman. The law has been broken, national security or not. 'Man who fights law always loses; same as grasshopper is always wrong in argument with chicken.'"

"That makes us the chicken." Chazz smiled. "And I hope you're right. I can't help remembering Robert Oppenheimer's remark after the first atomic explosion: 'Physicists have known sin; and this is a knowledge which they cannot lose.' Recombinant DNA is the same kind of double-edged sword as splitting the atom. It can do a great deal of good, but it could as easily be used to kill."

"Like magic," Patria said. She touched the bandage on her forearm.

"I don't believe in magic. But, yes," Chazz answered. "I suppose like magic, too." He paused and looked out the window. The sky was dark and gray, though the wind and rain had stopped. Palm fronds littered the ground, and the gardening crews were out, beginning the cleanup.

"Sometimes," Chazz went on, "I think the world's aware of itself; that we are its consciousness, its awareness. The world is beginning to attend to its own internal workings, to monitor and control. The world now has remote sensing satellites; satellite communications weave an electronic network around the world, a halo or aura of meaningful information. The planet itself has its physical processes too, of course: volcanic, meteorological, chemical, tides and currents. We are the intelligence informing it all, struggling to understand our own nature as a planet. That's the purpose of life: to increase in complexity until it begins to know itself. We will not survive unless we understand, and soon, that we are the mind, and the planet is the body. It is a great responsibility."

"Perhaps," Patria said with a smile, "you're not such a materialist after all."

"Thanks. And from that distant but vital perspective, this project is a life-threatening virus in the body of the world, a disease of the brain, an error in the code, a misread enzyme. It must be corrected, of course. We have to be the body's defenses and eject the invader." He looked at Takamura. "It must be purged."

52

"Come on," Takamura said, pushing his chair back. "I'll drive you back to your condo. Someone'll bring your van over later. Meantime you have Patria's rental, don't you?"

He drove slowly through the litter. Broken cane had blown across the road, and the air was thick with sugar scent. In front of the complex, he parked the car and got out. As Patria walked away, Takamura took Chazz's arm.

Takamura looked sheepish. "You will be glad to know you are no longer a suspect," he said.

Chazz stared. "A sus— Well, I'll be damned, of course. And the Subaru, I suppose that could have looked like a setup?"

Takamura was embarrassed. "Well, it did seem as if you arrived here just when all these things began to happen. And you were at a biological research center. 'Good fisherman, like clever merchant, knows lure of bright colors.' Kauai is a sleepy place, perfect for some unauthorized research, perhaps."

Chazz grinned. "Don't worry. There may be lots of bright colors here, but I didn't come to buy, or to bite."

"Then maybe 'Each man think own cuckoos better than next man's nightingales.' Professional jealousy is a powerful motive sometimes. But not in your case, Dr. Koenig. I apologize for suspecting."

"You were doing your job, that's all. I should have thought of it myself. I hope Sammy makes it, Cobb."

Takamura nodded.

He got back in the car and drove away.

Patria was waiting by the pool. "A real mess," she said.

"Yes," he said, not knowing whether she meant the storm damage, the deaths on the island or their relationship.

"What did Takamura want?" she asked, not looking at him.

"He wanted to apologize."

"Ah. So do I."

"What?"

"This is hard, Chazz. Don't make it more difficult. I'm sorry."

"What for?"

"I don't know. For not being honest. For leaving you. For coming back when I knew you wanted a family and I didn't. For making love with you under false pretenses. For being unfaithful."

He stared at the back of her head. A soft gray light shimmered on her hair. He realized she was shaking.

"Don't," he said at last. "Don't say anything."

"No," she said. Her voice was strained. "You saved my life. I owe you."

They sat by the desolate pool; its surface reflected nothing; only the dull, flat leaves of blown palms drifted aimlessly there. Later she said, "It was good, the other night, after I got here. I had forgotten how good it could be with us. Perhaps I have too much ambition."

"Never mind," he said. "Perhaps I don't have enough."

"Something happened up there, though. In the swamp."

"I know."

"I think it was something good."

"Perhaps."

"Then why do I feel so awful?"

"Come on," he said, standing. He offered his hand. She took it, and they went inside.

He tried to arouse her then, to touch her in the secret places he thought he knew. But she lay cold and numb beside him, staring up without moving, lost in some Alakai of her own where the ground pulled down her feet and kept her from moving toward him.

Finally he moved back and gazed at her in the twilight. She looked at him then, started to speak, to apologize once more, but he stopped her. Instead he touched her body where the bruises showed; he traced the edges of the bandage on her forearm; then he kissed the soft dark places. When he said, "I didn't mean to bring you into this," she put her finger against his lips. "You came for me up there," she said. "That's what mattered, that you came for me." She was crying. That was when he discovered that he was, too.

Then they slept as if drugged while night fell on the island. She awoke in the dark, and from his breathing knew he was awake. "Who's doing this?" she asked, partly of her dream.

He said, "I'm afraid I know," and she didn't ask again. They got up, both naked and frankly admiring of each other's shapes, and rummaged in the refrigerator. They sat cross-legged on the living room carpet with a towel between them covered with crackers and sliced mangoes and papaya, a bowl with tuna salad thick with mayonnaise and black pepper. They ate with their fingers until their mouths and hands were greasy with juices and sauce. He reached out and dabbed her lips with mayonnaise, and she pushed a slice of mango into his mouth, squeezing juice down his chin.

So he leaned forward to clean her lips and chin with his tongue, and soon they were lying together on the carpet. Their need rose together and they satisfied it together.

This time it was short and fierce and there was no river, no languid drift, only the sharp earth smells of the two of them lost in the gray filtered moonlight after the storm, with a wind blowing intermittently. He approached her as if she were no longer water flowing together, but was instead a fire burning somewhere deep in the forest, and she approached him the same way; and though this time there were two of them and not one, as before, it was the sweeter because the pain was so clear. It seemed they had never made love before, that all their years of marriage had been a charade of intimacy, a show they watched between school and lab and field trip; or that it had been something they did to each other, a ritual greeting without substance.

This time, though, it was something they did for each other, a dance of mutual give and take. When he approached, she moved back accepting; and when she moved against him, he listened with his body, then answered; they spoke together with fingertips and tongues, with flames that merged without consuming. When she soared, he gripped her fiercely, soothing against the intensity of her pleasure, and when his turn came and all his muscles were tight before release, her fingertips fluttered over his flesh so sparks flew into the darkness, twirled and winked out.

They awoke much later, still on the floor. He leaned on one elbow to watch her breathe, so naked and vulnerable and open in the shadowed light, her breast rising and falling with each breath, and he thought that this was all there was in the world that mattered; that tomorrow would certainly be soon enough to think of the sugar mill and viroids, of what might have been done in a laboratory not far from here that should never have been done. Tomorrow would be time enough to face those things. For now, this was all there was.

"What are you thinking?" she asked.

"You are very beautiful," he said. "Breathing. That's all. Come to bed."

Standing, she hugged him, hiding her face against his shoulder. "It worked, you know," she said. He could hear the undertone of humor in her whisper.

"What worked?" he asked.

"The spell. I had the kahuna put a spell on you. A love charm. For us."

"Yes," he said, pulling the sheet up over them and cradling her against his side. "It worked." After a pause he added softly, "Be careful what you see."

She murmured something as she put her head against his shoulder and slept.

53

Renfrew plunged the mud-clotted blade of his shovel into the cleared spot. The soaked soil turned with a wet sucking sound.

Beside him on the ground was a package tied up in thick black plastic. Overhead the clouds moved lazily, as if satisfied at the extent of the damage their storm had done. Leaves and branches covered the dirt road, hid the deep ruts and pooled water where already the mosquito larvae were quick in the thin gruel of the roadway.

Renfrew was preparing for burial.

He was taking this simple precaution; the failure of his plan was going to cause difficulties downstream. He'd managed Collins, but he smelled trouble. The Koenig matter had not gone well, and Renfrew had been involved in enough covert operations to know who the fall guy was when things went wrong.

So Renfrew was now preparing for his own CYA operation. CYA meant Cover Your Ass. Team A cover, Team B run, Team B cover, Team A run. Problem was, Renfrew was both teams.

That was okay with Renfrew. He was used to running. He was used to cover, too.

But this was not just defensive. Renfrew wanted revenge.

Water welled up in the bottom of the hole, reflecting his head haloed in cloud. He had turned the bill of his hat around backwards, and his eyes glittered darkly in the water. He unrolled a sheet of the plastic and lined the hole. Then he gently placed the package inside and folded the excess over the top. It was only money.

Then he removed the doll from his pocket; this was his insurance. He would turn the weapons of kahuna on the kahuna; who knew, maybe it worked. If the old man believed in that nonsense, it just might kill him. This was the way of the world. Renfrew must prove what he had learned, and there was only one adversary worth proving it to, only one person at the heart of this power: his master.

He would honor his master by killing him.

So he performed the rituals; he sent the prayer of darkness to pull away the old man's mana. It shouldn't matter whether he believed in it himself, he thought. It was important that he do the rituals, that's all. He had to convince the old man that he had done them, that the curse was in effect. He was going to apply the suggestion when he saw the old man. He knew how to do that. And he *would* see the old man, he was sure of that.

The doll lay on the dirt; an invisible thread of smoke rose from it; the feathers curled, shriveled, burned with a tiny flame. The shell face blackened, the wooden body charred. The doll died.

Renfrew buried it.

"You will burn, old man, and then you will choke." He threw dirt into the hole. It was fitting to bury the poison god with the money the Navy had paid him.

He liked the sound of the heavy wet dirt striking the plastic; he liked they way it was soon muffled as it fell. In moments he was patting the top of the mound with the flat of his spade. He tossed some storm debris on top, scattered it around.

He sat down on the wall. Just a few tens of meters to the north, the ruts in the road dwindled to nothing, and the road itself was overgrown, though it could still be walked. He wondered where it led. From the maps, there should be some kind of structures a few miles that way.

The spindly trunks of the head-high shrub blocked the view in every direction. It was an utterly private place here despite the mess of footprints in the mud.

The flattened toad bodies annoyed him, and he kept his new Thinsulate Campo Guide boots off the road.

When he stood on the wall, a clear view of Koenig's condominium presented itself. He'd spent time nearby watching the fat cop watch Koenig's place. Now the fat cop was dead, most likely.

He had shot the cop. A second failure. How could Renfrew know? It was dark, the man had a gun. Renfrew responded instinctively. How had this happened? How had the mission gone wrong? The poisons were one thing; they were discreet. He was protected. The arrow was something else. It would point straight to him.

The tops of the windows and the door in the west corner apartment were visible over the gently swaying branches of this weird shrub. He could see the big palms in the courtyard: one was leaning precariously. He doubted the others would survive.

He'd been thinking. Digging in the thick clay, turning the lumps, burying the doll, he'd been thinking. The police knew who he was now. His name was out. Renfrew. Koenig had eluded him. Renfrew had pushed the plan, the kidnapping, and the plan had failed. Koenig had escaped, Koenig had started the fire. Koenig had driven Renfrew from the cabin. Renfrew had shot Sammy Akeakamai because of Koenig.

Therefore Koenig was the primary danger now. He was an affront to Renfrew's professionalism and a threat to his safety. It was not only a matter of honor: it was business.

Renfrew's position was not good.

First, he had shot a police officer. Renfrew himself was now quarry, the hunted, not the hunter. The police would be after him.

Renfrew could handle that. But Kalaipahoa would be after him now, as well. He wasn't going to let himself be prayed to death without a fight. Renfrew thought he was stronger, but the old man was good. He had needed time to think this out.

And, finally, now he was a liability to the very mission for which he had killed, which would mean his employers were probably after him as well.

So Renfrew was under pressure; his time was running out. Operations like this had time constraints. Either they were successfully concluded or you cut your losses and got out. It was clear, when all those cops showed up at the cabin, that time was extremely limited and success unlikely. When he loosed his arrow at the fat cop, the time nearly ran out.

Renfrew didn't panic. He had slipped into the wilderness and vanished. He was still gone. Renfrew knew how to survive. He had been trained as a survivor, and he'd learned from Kalaipahoa. He could live on this island unnoticed, for years if need be. But that was not a first-choice option. Renfrew planned to cut his losses.

To do that, he needed Koenig. Because, when this operation ended, Renfrew planned to be on whatever transportation went out.

That was good. Renfrew jumped down. The toad bodies yielded unnoticed under his camouflaged boots.

Renfrew slung his bow over his shoulder, folded his spade and hitched it to his pack. Then he trotted north, up the old weed-choked road, away from the highway, toward whatever the old buildings might be. He needed to do something unexpected, something strange and dangerous. He needed to strike and then escape. The road was there. This was as good a time as any to find out where it led.

54

The man in camouflage fatigues haunted Chazz. The arrow in Sammy Akeakamai haunted him.

Renfrew.

Takamura was examining his hat intensely.

"What are you thinking?" Chazz asked.

"I'm thinking, 'Talk will not cook rice.' What is the connection among the victims? Why were they stricken? I'm thinking that the poet William Blake has said that the tigers of wrath are wiser than the horses of instruction."

"Don't forget the German proverb," Patria put in. "Anger without power is folly." She smiled at Chazz. "There is a certain kind of culture."

Takamura was attentive. "What do you mean?"

"A culture of ghosts. Ghosts of fear, remorse, anger. We know this culture; it hides inside our own, pretending it's ours, disguised as ours. But it is not ours, because it's ruled by ghosts: dead fears, old angers, vague, displaced remorse. Guilt."

"About whom are you speaking?"

Chazz was smiling. He'd seen Patria tease with her words before. She did it with students. She used cryptic, potent words: anger, guilt, remorse. He loved it about her, this mischievous methodology.

"Faith," she continued, not answering Takamura's question. "Conviction. Righteousness. Holy Writ. Zeal. People with a mission. Dewilliter, for example. He's a believer. His faith will make him strong because it gives him meaning. But meaning isn't enough: he needs a place, a niche, recognition. He needs to know he is noticed. So he provides drama too. Oracular pronouncements. 'A Sense of Foreboding,' he said. He knew something was about to happen, and he had to let someone else know he knew. The way he slipped out Lolo."

"Where does the faith come in, if he knew? If he had certain knowledge, he didn't need faith."

"Oh, yes. He needed faith. He needed it very much. He needed to believe it was right. People were dying. The cause must be just."

"What's the cause?" Chazz snapped. His own anger was a dry stick breaking in his voice. "Faster boats for the Navy?"

"No. Fear. Fear drives faith. People fall easily into the sleep of ghosts. We all do." She shook her head. "Then the killing starts. Nazis, Communists, patriots. Why do you study aikido, Chazz? Because you want a better ethic. It's why you went to Asilomar, why you argued for sensible constraints. You argue now in favor of honoring the ban on recombinant DNA in weapons research. The ghost-driven would argue against constraints. Out of fear."

"These people are making boats go faster. That's not a weapon, as far as I know."

"Quite a few people have died. Violently, without judgment or mercy. That's a weapon."

"It could have been an accident," Chazz suggested without conviction.

She shrugged. "It could have been. That's not really the point. The point, and by now they are quite literally impaled upon it, is that they are capable of doing it, of killing all those people. They're willing to do it. Remember what you quoted at me not so long ago. Robert Oppenheimer. 'The physicists have known sin.' The problem most of us have dealing with these hidden cultures within cultures is that we are the ones who know sin. It limits us. They work under no such handicap."

Takamura put on his hat. "They have power," he said. "The United States Navy." He shrugged. "The FBI was unavailable; the Centers for Disease Control recalled their man. At least one of the bodies was KGB. Was he killed? Was he looking into this for the Soviets? Is CIA involved too? Who would know? How could we tell?"

"We could turn it over to the Feds. Call the senators, the congressmen, tell them what's happening. We could get out. We're not responsible for this, you know," Chazz said.

"My friend is dying in the hospital," Takamura reminded him gently. "We have no allies. Who would believe us? We don't know our enemy's face. We don't know what they're up to or why they're doing it. We only know they must be stopped. My peace has been disturbed, Chazz. The public trust violated. We are here. I am here. So I will stop them. I'd like your help. At the moment, for instance, I only know who two of them are, and I'm going to have to let them go."

Patria cried out "What?" but Chazz nodded.

"I think that's a good idea," he said. "Patria, if what you say is right, then Freeman and Dewilliter really don't know what they're doing. Only an idiot would trust Dewilliter with the truth. They are not idiots."

"No. They're not idiots. They're a conspiracy, a culture within our culture. They look like us, they talk like us. They're not spies, not foreigners. They have our best interests at heart. They're sincere. They believe. But they are driven by ghosts, Chazz. They're afraid, and that makes them dangerous."

"They're a virus, then," Chazz said. "Something invaded the people who died. Something got into them and pretended it was part of them, and then it did something that killed them. Every victim has a long stretch of identical DNA. That stretch codes for something."

"Perhaps we'd better find out what," Takamura suggested.

"Perhaps we'd better," Chazz agreed.

"What about this sugar mill? It must be nearby," Patria said.

"Yes," Takamura said. "We'll have to go there eventually."

"And we have a more urgent possibility," Chazz said. "There's a well-equipped biological laboratory on this island: this place, the Douglass Research Center. Dewilliter was there. Dr. Morgan ought to know what his research facility is being used for." Chazz stood and stretched.

"Yes, he should," Takamura agreed. "He ought to be told, if he doesn't know already."

Chazz nodded. "Yes, he might know already," he said, but he was thinking about Renfrew.

55

Morgan had gone to the lower palm gardens. They commandeered a Scout and drove the three miles down the dirt road. He was in the grove on his hands and knees.

When he saw them coming, he stood slowly. He wore large leather pads strapped to his knees and very muddy gloves. He gestured a pair of clippers at the grove. "Lots of damage," he said. "Some of the exotics were crushed."

Chazz introduced Patria and Takamura. "I believe," Dr. Morgan said, squinting skyward, "that there might be sun. Perhaps we will see the end of the wet for a while." He led them all to a gazebo with benches.

"Now," he said, settling in.

Chazz watched Morgan closely while Takamura asked questions. "What do you know about Freddie Dewilliter?"

Morgan frowned. "Dewilliter? Lobelioids? Youngish man with rimless glasses? He works with plant viroids."

"Do you know his work?" Takamura asked.

"I really can't say that I do. He came from Johns Hopkins. He's been here almost a year. You know, it's funny."

"What's that?"

"I hardly know the man. Been here almost a year; he came at the end of the spring semester last year, the beginning of the summer. Yes, summer. Highly recommended."

The palms were full of birds: cardinals, mynas, a thrush that warbled liquidly. Chazz listened. A varied and rich song drifted among the palms. The sun was coming out.

"You're listening to the shama," Morgan said. "From Malaysia. And over there, see, the red-crested cardinal, from Brazil; there the northern cardinal, the red one. The myna was brought to the islands from India in 1865. Nowhere can you see a bird native to the islands."

But then, he went on, nothing is really native to the islands. Everything came here from somewhere else, seeds and insects borne on the air or water, birds strayed from migratory paths, people and pigs from Polynesia, goats from Europe. "Life," Dr. Morgan said, "is tenacious. It likes to spread."

"Who recommended Dewilliter?" Takamura asked.

"Oh, I am sorry. I do go on sometimes. An enthusiast, you see. Birds, gardening. I believe Ben Silver said he was a graduate student of his some years ago."

"And Dr. Silver? How long has he been here?"

"Oh, goodness, quite some time now." Morgan pushed his palms down on his leather knee pads and straightened his arms in a gesture that lifted his shoulders. "Let me think, now. He and Andrea came out here three, no, four years ago, for a few months. He dropped in one day, I recall, just after that shipment of seedlings from Java—some of them were in very bad shape and didn't survive—and asked about the facilities. Quite a delightful man, Ben Silver, delightful to talk with, a very knowledgeable man. Quite remarkable. You were a student of his also, weren't you, Dr. Koenig?"

"Yes," Chazz said. "You're right, he's a gifted scientist." He looked at Takamura. His expression was bleak.

"Indeed," Morgan went on. "Very precise. Careful attention to detail, but with leaps of intuition. He would have made an extraordinary gardener if he'd wanted."

"Yes," Takamura said. "He came for a visit, then, is that right? He didn't stay?"

"No." Morgan's head came back down. "No, he didn't stay then. We corresponded over the next few months. I'd say he's been here three years now, though. Why?"

"Dr. Morgan, there's been some unpleasantness lately."

"You're telling me! The storm did untold damage. I'll have crews out for weeks assessing it all."

"That's not really what I meant," Takamura said gently. "Dewilliter, and very likely Dr. Silver, have been possibly engaged in some research that is . . . suspect."

Morgan put up his hands in shock. "Oh, no, surely not! I can't believe that! I can't imagine such a thing. No, Dr. Silver has impeccable credentials. He is a personal friend, Lieutenant. And Dewilliter, he studies diseases of the lobelioid family. Surely there is nothing suspect about such things."

"'Humbly suggest not to judge wine by barrel it is in,'" Takamura quoted.

"What *are* you suggesting?" Dr. Morgan's chin trembled.

"Where was Dr. Silver before he came here, Dr. Morgan?"

"San Diego, why? I really must insist that you tell me what you're after. Ben is my friend as well as a colleague."

"I'm afraid I can't tell you much about it just now," Takamura said. "I hope we're wrong. Perhaps we are. You've been very helpful. Thank you." He shook Morgan's hand. Morgan, still seated, looked uncertain.

"What did you think?" he asked Chazz as they wound up the dirt road to the Center.

"He's a good gardener and a nice person. He doesn't know anything. This place is a convenient cover for certain Navy researches into a bacterium. Except it isn't behaving like a bacterium. Has Dr. Shih tried to culture the tissue samples?"

Takamura shook his head. "I don't know. You'd have to ask her."

"Good. Let's do that, shall we?"

They called from Chazz's office. She had.

"Nothing you wouldn't expect," she said. "A perfectly ordinary zoo of bugs. Normal strains. I thought of that long ago, Dr. Koenig. Long ago. Strachey and I went through the catalogues."

"Could I get some tissue samples?" Chazz asked.

"Come and get 'em."

The clouds were gone. Sun dazzled the lush landscape, the greens as dense and rich as the blue of the sky. A rainbow splashed across the Hoary Head; almost gaudy. As they drove past the gatehouse, Chazz thought of the surfer. His replacement was wearing a T-shirt that said, "Just Another Shitty Day in Paradise."

56

"Power is still out all over the island. The south side's in shambles. At this point it's the only damn thing going for us."

Commander James Goode was angry. "I don't know what we're going to do when the mess is cleared up. They have that lamebrain Dewilliter and Ward Freeman under arrest, for Christ sake!"

"Freeman only knows about Cetus. He can't let anything out." Dr. Silver's long fingers stirred restlessly despite his reassuring words. "As for Dewilliter, he's a zealot. That does make him dangerous, of course: careless and rather stupid. But he doesn't know much, either. As for Collins—"

"Collins is dead," Goode snapped.

"As for Collins," Silver repeated, "he knew nothing. Transferring him was a mistake. Using *Lolo* was an even worse mistake. Still, the same cover will work. The bugs got out; they mutated; they are no longer viable. The situation is under control. They haven't uncovered the sugar mill yet, either. They're still at least two levels away from the truth. That should hold them until this is over with."

Goode paced. He paused by the window and spread the slats of his Levolor blind. There was nothing to see out there but the aftermath of elemental chaos, torn vegetation, debris, fragments of cloud-scud in the blue sky. "We're out of touch," he muttered. He turned back to the room, dropping the slat.

"So are they," Silver observed. He twined his fingers together and stretched them with a crack.

"Then it's a stalemate," Goode said. "For now. Dewilliter wasn't quite good enough. *You* needed Koenig. I knew it wouldn't work, kidnapping his wife."

"It was Renfrew's plan," the other said. "It was worth a try. Appeal to his patriotism."

"Koenig was at Asilomar. He was in favor of restrictions. You told me that yourself."

"That would have worked in our favor, Jim. He has credibility. Just in case. I knew Koenig well; he was my student. He was a good student, singleminded and tenacious. Now he's gotten stale. This could have been a challenge for him, you know. He could have gone for it."

"At this point we don't need credibility, we need containment. Besides, he emphasized the Biological Weapons Convention; he's written letters requesting a more specific ban on the use of recombinant DNA for biological warfare. We would be in violation of the Convention."

"This is not designed for biological warfare, Jim. This is deterrent. I don't think the Convention would hold up in this case."

"We don't want to test that, do we? In court, in front of the world?"

"Of course not. But we could; that's all I'm saying. We could. Besides, we all know we have no choice in the matter. We were forced into it. The Soviets are doing it. According to the 1984 Pentagon report on Soviet military power, they are making an effort to use rDNA for biological warfare."

"Hah! The report referred to 'apparent effort.'"

Silver cracked his knuckles again. "We have Dmitrov's paper, Jim. That's why we're doing this. There are at least seven BW installations in the Soviet Union; can we doubt they are using rDNA in those installations?"

"All right." Goode placed his palms on the empty surface of his desk and leaned on them. "I pushed it because we had proof the other side's not only technically in violation, they may well be ahead of us. If they could develop this thing before we do, we can forget nuclear deterrent. We can forget national defense. We can forget our entire mission! Damn it, Ben, we can forget everything; we might as well lie down and surrender right now. That way we might, at least, survive. I for one don't care for that option."

A sudden heavy gust of wind shook the window behind him, a last breath of the dying storm.

"I don't care for it either, Jim. God knows, I don't care for it. My grandfather fled Russia under the Tsars; the tyranny of the Bolsheviks is no improvement. And that KGB agent delivered proof—"

"He was killed in a freak accident, Ben. Now I don't know if it *was* an accident. Was he really a double agent? Naval Intelligence can't tell us, it seems. He was on the SAFE list as a suspected Soviet agent. Why did he bring us that second paper? Was he really feeding us a valuable document or was he snooping around us? Or perhaps he was planting a little disinformation?"

It was Silver's turn to look away. "Military intelligence is not my field, Jim."

"There are those who say it's a contradiction in terms, military intelligence. Sometimes I wonder. I suppose it doesn't matter whom he worked for. The fact is, this project is vital, and we had to do it the way we did. You know how things are in Washington. The difficulties were political, not moral. CIA wants it, NSA wants it and doesn't want CIA to have it. Army wanted it because they already have a Chemical-Biological-Radiological infrastructure at the Fort Detrick infectious disease containment lab. DARPA wanted control, but we'd have a bunch of civilians and liberal universities involved then; that would be unacceptable. Then people at NIMH said it was illegal and nobody should do it. As far as I know, they're all working on it, anyway. I would if I worked for them. But I'm in the Navy, so the Office of Naval Research is doing it. We found it. We started the work. We funded it. We did it without Congress; we did it, and even the Joint Chiefs don't know about it. Hell, hardly anybody in ONR knows."

Goode sat down behind his desk with a sigh. He wiped his hand across a forehead damp despite the air conditioning. "Hell, if we hadn't found the *Valiant*, we'd have gotten nowhere. And now security has been breached. We've gone public, and that could be disastrous."

Silver frowned. "Recriminations are useless at this point. We both know we're doing the right thing. Besides, we have a more immediate problem, Jim: Takamura and Koenig. And Koenig's wife. We're obviously not going to convince the three of them that this is merely an escaped bug for long. They may believe that now, but they can add it up. And they're filled with moral outrage. That's a dangerous substance, Jim, moral outrage."

"There're only three of them. We have resources. We have her tissue samples; the lab is working up her genotype now. We've got Koenig's, as well. If necessary we can apply pressure. Or they can die of it."

"I wouldn't like that, Jim. We're killing too many people. Koenig is a prominent scientist. So's his wife, for that matter. A bunch of Hawaiian derelicts might go unnoticed, victims of poverty and malnutrition, perhaps, susceptible to a mutated virus now under control. But the Koenigs, no, I think that's a bad idea. But they *are* going to figure this out sooner or later. Probably sooner. I'm not sure we could get at them, anyway. After all, you said Renfrew barely made it. He took out Collins, of course, but it's going to be difficult getting at the rest of them."

Goode was pacing again. "It's worse than that," he said softly.

"What do you mean?"

"Renfrew shot a cop." Goode pushed a sheet of paper across his desk. "Here's a hospital report. It's sketchy: the phones went out in the middle. But we got this much. The three of them were taken to the hospital. No firm report on their condition. Everyone but Takamura seems to be out of it, for a while anyway, but we don't really know. They could be out of the hospital by now. Since Renfrew shot the cop, though, Takamura is going to be very persistent, and he has the Koenigs on his side."

Goode slapped the desktop with his palm. It made an explosive sound. "The whole situation is too dangerous, Ben. We're so close, so very close. We could walk into the President's office within a month and present him with the complete plan already in place. We'd have a tool for national defense, a deterrent that would be absolutely foolproof, relatively safe and basically free. It would be a Navy project! We're so damn close. We had to test. I almost wish we hadn't. But it was necessary."

Silver nodded. "We needed the tests, of course. We picked the subjects very carefully. Everything worked according to plan. A couple of things got a little out of control; that's to be expected. All we have to do is bring events back under control and we'll be back on track. That means *convincing* Koenig and Takamura. Killing them is a last resort, Jim. A last resort. I suppose we'd better prepare for it, just in case, but I'd be very reluctant to follow through. But pulling all their support out was not adequate to persuade them."

Goode sighed. "Then we'd better finish preparing for the Koenigs. Just in case, as you say. If you can think of a way to convince them, so much the better. And we'd better do something about Renfrew. His methods have been . . . excessive."

"I'll go to the lab; there's a lot to do yet. You handle the Naval Intelligence. And I'll let you know if I think of anything. I think we need to push up the schedule. We can still beat them if we hurry."

57

Takamura dozed. His eyelids drooped, and his chin dipped low enough to show Dewilliter the bald spot on the crown of his head.

He was looking down at his fingers curled in his lap, thumb tips together, fingers overlapped, so his hands made a circle. He was meditating. Dewilliter twitched uneasily.

The table between them was empty, a green, institutional surface devoid of data. The walls were equally blank, equally green. The only relief from this emptiness was the door, and the mirror opposite it. But the mirror was behind Dewilliter, and he couldn't turn around. The hidden fluorescents which cast a sickly pall over the room tinted the detective's bald spot an unhealthy purple. Dewilliter twitched.

Takamura did not move; his breathing was undetectable.

There was no clock, and they had taken Dewilliter's watch. He was restless and impatient, and now, without a watch or clock, he fretted. Takamura watched him surreptitiously. He was counting seconds; he was planning what to say; then he was realizing he hadn't been asked anything. Time acquired a liquid quality for Dewilliter, viscous and slick. Takamura said nothing.

Dewilliter counted seconds. He wondered what Takamura was thinking. Then he wondered if Takamura was thinking. Then he said, "You can't do this." There was no reply. "You can't do this," he repeated, louder. Takamura's eyes lifted to his. This appalling serenity was infuriating; Dewilliter said: "I won't stand for it."

Takamura's eyes told him nothing. They were, Dewilliter thought, empty and alien. Damn his eyes, he thought.

"You can't do this," he said again. "The Project is secret. There are important people behind this. Very important. You don't know what you're doing."

Takamura gazed at him in silence.

"You don't understand," Dewilliter said; his voice was a sullen whine. "I haven't done anything wrong. I work for the government. I didn't know what they were doing in that cabin. They took me there. I knew Koenig. I didn't know that was his wife. I never met her. Freeman said go to the cabin, so I went. He said I'd be needed. What did they need me there for?"

"I don't know," Takamura said quietly. "What did they need you for?" He seemed indifferent.

"They needed me!" Dewilliter insisted. "They still need me!"

"That's not what Freeman says," Takamura told him.

"Oh? What does Freeman say? Tell me that. What does he say? Does he say they don't need me? Is that what he says? God damn him, he doesn't know. Hell, he's working on Cetus. I haven't finished with the vector. He doesn't . . . oh, no. They need me," he finished abruptly.

Takamura shrugged slightly. "Perhaps." The word said, no, they don't need *you*.

Dewilliter fidgeted. He took off his rimless glasses and wiped the lenses on his shirt. He put them back on and pushed his shirt into his trousers again. He started to speak, then stopped. In the end he said nothing.

Takamura's eyes drooped again. When he spoke, his tone was sympathetic.

"Of course we know the project is important," he said. "The vector–"

"Yes," Dewilliter interrupted eagerly. "The vector. It'll work, it does work. The stability, though, we had problems with stability. The strain–either it kept mutating or it wasn't viable; it died out. So small, you see? They couldn't stop it. I fixed it, though. Me, I fixed it. I don't care what Freeman says. They need me. Ben told me."

"Yes." Takamura nodded sympathetically. "Ben was right, I'm sure."

Dewilliter's head bobbed. "Yes. Just ask Ben."

Takamura nodded. "Certainly. I'm letting you go. Perhaps you can convince Koenig."

"What?" Dewilliter barked. "Convince him? They overrate Koenig. They don't need him. I can do it. Maybe they thought if I was at the cabin he'd want to join, hah?"

"Maybe they thought Koenig could help with the stability problem," Takamura said. He made a small gesture, a tap at his right temple.

Dewilliter said, "Too right. He's a liberal. You understand that, you're a policeman. You understand the importance of stability. Of course, I mean the stability of the vector—but the people involved, they have to be stable, too. Koenig isn't stable, is he?"

The door opened behind Takamura, and an officer came in, followed by Ward Freeman.

"Ah," Takamura said, standing. "Mr. Freeman, so good to see you. We're releasing you and Dr. Dewilliter."

Freeman stared at Dewilliter. "Oh?" he said.

Dewilliter showed his teeth. "Don't worry, Ward. Everything's under control. In a week it won't matter, anyway."

Takamura smiled thinly.

Freeman looked at Dewilliter in disgust. "You're a fool," he said. He turned to Takamura. "He's a technician. I assure you of one thing, though: this entire situation has been blown all out of proportion. Really. It's completely under control by now."

"Is it so?" Takamura said politely. "Well, of course, when the police uncover murder, they must investigate, despite what others who work in government might say. You understand that, of course, Mr. Freeman. Several people have died, as a result of your experiments, apparently. A man with a bow and arrow shot one of my men, too. That disturbs me."

Freeman shifted. "That was a mistake, I assure you. I don't know where that man came from, really."

"I know you're lying," Takamura said gently. "Or a fool. But I can't hold you any longer. Lawyers have been making noise for your release. You're required to remain on the island, though."

"Of course," Freeman said. He waited until Dewilliter had preceded him out the door. Dewilliter did not look at him; his triumph was gone. Freeman followed him out. Takamura nodded at the officer waiting by the door.

"Check them out, would you? They're free to go."

He called Chazz at the Douglass Research Center. The sun was shining brightly. Temperatures returned to seasonal norm. Takamura would not be fooled by that, though. When Chazz came on the line, Takamura said, " 'Tongue often hang man quicker than rope.' "

"Come on over," Chazz said. "I've got something to show you."

58

The screen was tinted yellow. Chazz made an adjustment, and a square of ordinary black and white television picture opened in the center, framed by the yellow tint. He moved the controls and the image swam to the side, the black and white window moving over alien terrain: spheres and elongated cell structures, tangled sheets of whitish cobweb, vacuoles, snakes of chromosome.

The scene floated above a long cell, found a shoot, moved outward. The shoot turned left, and Chazz drove the view in that direction. Then he stopped.

"There," he said. "It looks like we're moving over the sample, but of course it's really the other way around, the sample is moving under the scanning beam. That little place there is what we're after. Nerve cell. This is the wall." He tapped the screen with a finger. "Something is invading the host—the victims. How's it getting into the body, how does it insinuate itself into the host's DNA, and what does it do once it is there? I think we have the answer to the last question right here."

He tapped an indentation in the cell wall. "This is a receptor site, a synaptic junction. A neurotransmitter called acetylcholine should cross this gap and bind in there. You can see the way that the surface, which should be deeply pocked with niches like this, is flattened out. A protein is responsible for this, similar to the exotoxin from *Clostridium botulinum* spores."

"Sounds like botulism," Patria said.

"Right."

"That's a bacterium, right?"

He nodded. "Gram positive, easily identified rods. No signs of them in the victims. That doesn't necessarily mean there's no toxin present. One ounce of the botulism toxin would be enough to kill the entire population of the United States. It doesn't take much to kill one person, and that makes it very hard to find."

"Surely there are tests," Takamura said.

"Certainly." Chazz was sweeping across the cellular landscape once again. "Dr. Shih ran them. Negative. Results were negative. But a toxin could break down and disappear. Look." He pointed out another spot.

"Looks the same."

He flipped a switch, and the image acquired depth. He switched off the yellow filter and began to bleed in colors. "Computer-generated," he said. The receptor site jumped forward. The image moved, exploring. Chazz moved the image up a stalk-shaped structure to small round bodies. "Vesicles. They produce the acetylcholine. If it's blocked, the transmitter builds up inside the cell. Muscles don't get the message to move. The result is considerable pain. It could explain their expressions. Note the distorted shape of the nerve ending here. The toxin enters the cell and binds to the inner surface of the nerve membrane. No messages get out."

There was silence. Such a tiny place to go wrong, such a subtle perversion of the complex processes that made life possible. Patria thought of cultural diseases, also subtle, difficult to notice. The wrong kind of repression, a small misdirection of energy, and you could have National Socialism or organized crime. This was smaller. Much smaller. Yet this was no product of evolution: humans had willed it.

Takamura stood up. In the darkness of the microscope room, he was a dim shape outlined in red moving in shadows. "We have a week or less. Then something is going to happen."

Chazz creaked his chair as he sat back, lifting his hands off the controls. "How do you mean?" His voice was tight in the darkness.

"Something Dewilliter said. 'In a week it won't matter.' I don't know what he meant; it was a slip. I almost failed to notice it."

"You didn't fail."

Chazz could almost hear the tight smile in Takamura's voice. "No, but he thinks I did."

"That could mean . . ." Patria stopped.

"Yes?" Takamura spoke politely.

"This is deliberate. They're not just making boats go faster."

"They are making people go slower. They're killing. But why would the Navy want to kill people?" Chazz was thinking of something else, his voice dreamy.

"Assassination? That's not their job. Their job is boats and missiles and submarines." Patria could hear the concern in Takamura's tone. Such a tiny thing, this bug.

"What's happening in a week?"

"Yes," Takamura said. "My thoughts exactly."

"We need to pay some visits, Lieutenant. As you said, talk will not cook rice."

Amber lights flicked on, replacing the red, and Chazz prepared another sample. The specimen chamber was vacuum sealed. A small airlock in front cycled the sample out.

While he worked, Patria spoke thoughtfully. "Everyone worked at the sugar mill except Collins. So some infection—a slow virus, you said—got to them at the mill. Years later, they began to die. Someone discovered the disease and thought it could be used. Someone at PACMAN, where Collins was stationed, say. Others, here at DRC, got involved. Collins was accidentally infected, and dies quite soon. The bug has mutated; it now acts quickly. A cover-up begins."

"That fits some of the facts," Takamura agreed. "Not all of them, but some. Enough for now, perhaps."

"The cover-up involved kidnapping and murder," Chazz said. "They tried to get me involved. Perhaps to help unravel the genetic background of this bug. But how does it relate to a bug that makes boats go faster? Unless they are involved in rDNA research of what used to be called a 'purely defensive nature.'"

"What does that mean, exactly?" Patria asked.

"Supposedly it means researching methods of detecting and defending against things like nerve gases and Lassa fever. In reality it means manufacturing variants on such things in order to understand them. Unfortunately, it also makes them available to those who think we should develop such weapons. It's particularly insidious because it is very difficult to detect, research is cheap and easily hidden; and even with treaties there is no safe way to detect development and stockpiling of such agents."

"I don't like it."

"Neither do I."

Chazz had another specimen platform about the size of a half-dollar ready. He cycled it through the airlock. The lights went off. The image began to swim across the small screen. Colors filled in the shapes, vivid greens, yellows, reds. The plain they flew over was littered with debris that looked like tumbled rock. A chain appeared, as if dropped on the ground. The magnification jumped toward the chain, a vivid purple on a gray-green ground. It had red and yellow highlights.

"Imagine something, though," Chazz said in the darkness. "Not a disease like Lassa fever or tularemia—things which are, adequately or not, covered by the Biological and Toxin Weapons Convention. Imagine instead a piece of RNA, a messenger version of DNA. Like Dewilliter's spindle viroids, for instance. It enters a cell. It has certain senses, this messenger, certain, well, talents. It can sense things, recognize them; and when it does, it can make something, and it can make the thing it made do something. It can recognize a place on this chain of DNA lying on the ground here. It produces an enzyme that will break this chain. It can then manufacture from materials at hand, from locally available precursors, a sequence of DNA that will fit into the broken chain. Then it will encourage this piece of DNA it has made in its own image to take its place in the chain, restick the broken ends. Now imagine that the messenger, having done its job in silence and secrecy, dissolves, falls apart into its own components, which become locally available precursors once more. Poof, it's gone. It has, in effect, committed suicide. But something new has appeared in the host DNA."

"Okay," Takamura said.

"Now imagine that this new sequence is some kind of time bomb, or perhaps it's remotely triggered. Something must happen, some event, and the bomb goes off. It is, let us assume, a gene for the production of a protein. It will code for the protein, and when the conditions tell it to, bingo, a botulism-like toxin is produced. The toxin rapidly and efficiently kills the host by blocking the transmission of acetylcholine. The toxin is small and very powerful; it too disappears when it has finished its job."

"I've imagined it," Takamura said. "I think we are in a lot of trouble."

59

In the scrub wasteland the heat was intense, windless. A line of perspiration had formed across Renfrew's brow. It started to drip, and he drew the back of his hand across it to clear his vision. The entrance of the Douglass Research Center was visible from here.

Renfrew was waiting.

He had withdrawn from the dirt road to his camp. He'd explored the area, knew the dirt roads, the cattle trails and goat tracks and cane roads in the scrub. He knew how often they were used and by whom; he knew who was likely to wander by, and when.

Only one highway separated Koenig's apartment from the DRC. It was a nearly ideal situation for the hunter. Only if they went somewhere else, to Lihue or Koke'e, say, would he be out of luck, confined as he was to moving on foot. Even then, they would always return to one of these two places.

The door opened. Renfrew raised his binoculars. Koenig, his wife, and the cop came out.

They drove off in the cop car. Renfrew could run back to Koenig's apartment in less time than it took them to drive. He headed back into the scrub.

There was no trail, and he had to pause from time to time to sight on Wai'ale'ale to the north and the Hoary Head to the southeast, but he made good time. When he came to the trail which led him to an old cane road, he turned right. Five hundred meters farther, he came to the Koloa Road.

A road crew worked on a tree fallen across the road, filling the air with fragrant eucalyptus scent and the sound of McCullough saws. Fallen branches and sawdust littered the area. Renfrew paused at the edge of the scrub, uncertain, but the quarry was driving back and he should be there first.

He moved down the road, away from the crew.

It took him an extra ten minutes to get across. His clothes were drenched and the bugs had begun to bite by the time he found himself standing on the stone wall again. Somehow the discomfort gave Renfrew an obscure satisfaction.

The car was already parked beside the condo. No one was in sight. Renfrew jumped down onto the dirt road. Most of the flattened toads had dried up, leaving leathery shapes on the dirt. The dirt was already dry, too, despite the recent heavy rains. Only a few pools of standing water, places where the four-wheel-drive ruts were particularly deep, caught the harsh sun. The surface of the mud had solidified and cracked; but underneath, it was still wet enough to leave three sets of prints, headed north, on the dirt road.

Two men and a woman had walked here recently. Renfew couldn't walk on the road without leaving his own track, so he was forced to move parallel, through the scrub.

He noticed the sound first, strange, inarticulate barks, deep, muffled speech made up almost entirely of vowels booming out into the baffling brush. Shrill whistles, clipped metallic noises at irregular intervals. Rumbles. Gruesome indecipherable chewing. Gulps.

As he got closer, the sounds separated, became more distinct.

"Whittaker. Front office." The voice was bass, distorted. A cane truck rumbled out of sight somewhere. A shrill whistle blew again, followed by the sound of a truck backing up, warning with a monotonous beep-beep-beep.

The cane factory rose above the tops of the scrub, stacks and roofs, the long open-sided sheds, finally the road itself. Renfrew stopped up at the edge of the scrub and examined the mill. Loudspeakers mounted on the walls of the main building blared nearly incomprehensible messages. The Koenigs and Takamura were just climbing the short flight of wooden steps to the main office. Renfrew watched as they vanished inside and the screen door slammed shut behind them. Why were Koenig and the cop visiting a sugar mill?

He settled down to watch.

"Hey! Hey, you!"

Renfrew looked around to see who the man was shouting at. The confusing cacophony from the public address system drowned out the speaker.

He was shouting at Renfrew!

Without a pause Renfrew uncoiled to his feet and melted back into the scrub. There was a cattle trail a few yards away, and the man, already suspicious, was on top of Renfrew before he could get away.

Renfrew turned. The man was slightly overweight; a gap of belly exposed between his dirty T-shirt and green pants. "Hey," the man shouted, moving toward Renfrew. "What the hell are you doing here? This is company property."

"Sorry," Renfrew said. His hand rested on the hilt of his bayonet. He realized he was not an ordinary sight, dressed in now filthy fatigues, binoculars and canteen, hunting bow and muddy guide boots. "I didn't know."

"Like hell, buddy. There's no hunting down here. What the hell are you doing? Planning to steal something, were you? I think you'd better come into the office."

"Listen, really," Renfrew said, unsnapping the leather strap across the hilt of his bayonet with one finger while he waved the other hand in the air. "I didn't know."

"You were casing the place," the fat man said. "Come on."

Renfrew slipped the knife out in one fluid motion and slashed across the exposed inches of sweat-grimed belly. The man jumped back as a red mouth opened in the skin, yawned widely and began to weep bright blood. He fell back, his scream lost in the pounding inarticulate sounds of the loud-speaker. His hands clasped across the open wound in his gut as Renfrew melted into the scrub and was gone.

The front of his green pants were soaked a wet chocolate by the time he crashed through the screen door into the front office. Patria caught him as he fell. Behind Takamura the manager of the mill said "Jesus Christ" very softly.

60

Patria lowered the man to floor. "Get me a towel," she barked without looking around. "And some tape, if you've got it."

The manager muttered, "I've never seen anything like this before. Never."

"Just get tape," she ordered. The manager vanished into the back.

"Emergency vehicle will be here in twenty minutes," Takamura said, putting down the phone. The man on the floor had fainted and was unavailable for questioning.

"He'll be all right," Patria assured him. "It's a good thing he's fat; that saved his life." She tucked the last of the white adipose tissue back into the wound and closed it up. The manager handed her a towel, and she folded it over the wound. Methodically she taped it to his belly. "This was done with a sharp knife. Look how clean the edges are. That'll help save him. I've seen wounds made with Stone Age weapons."

"Renfrew," Chazz said.

"Eh?" Takamura and Patria looked at him.

"Renfrew. The fellow in fatigues up in Koke'e. With the bow and arrow. It's him, I'm sure. He's following us."

Over the odd sounds of the mill they could hear the siren screaming. Once it had vanished back down the dirt road, bearing the wounded man, they went back inside. The manager was shifting uneasily.

"I don't like it," he said. "You've got to stop him. He's out there in the brush; somebody could hide out there for years, you know."

"Please don't worry," Takamura said. "We will catch him. We have good reason. He shot my partner. Now, about these people, Mr. Hodgkin. They were all associated with the mill, is that correct?"

Hodgkin shook his head. "We had a man named Cameron here. He was younger, though, and he left the island. The kid, Delarota, it was his father worked here. The others, yeah, they were here. Hall worked here years ago, I remember, but only for a short time. I think he used drugs. A bad worker. Wyman was here later, stayed, oh I suppose about a year."

"Damn." Takamura frowned.

"It's what I thought," Chazz said.

"How do you mean?" Takamura looked at him sharply.

"This mill is not the connection. You had to check it out, of course, but this isn't it, unfortunately."

"Oh. Why unfortunate?"

Chazz shook his head, and Takamura turned to Hodgkin. "I seem to be forgetful these days," he said. "Please forgive me, Mr. Hodgkin. Thank you so much for your invaluable help. We needn't delay your work any longer. Shall we go?" he said to Chazz and Patria.

They walked back up the dirt road. There were no tracks in the mud, but Takamura kept his gun loose in its holster, and the two men walked on either side of Patria. When they got back to Kapuna Road and were walking toward the condo, Takamura repeated his question. "Why unfortunate, Chazz?"

"Because," Chazz said, "that fact increases the probability that I'm right, and that is unfortunate."

"Would you care to share it with us?" Patria always needled Chazz when he grew reticent. It was his lecturing mode; she thought it was merely withholding.

"The connection among the victims is not that they were all associated with this mill at the same time. They weren't."

"Wait," Patria said. "The connection is a common ancestry. They all have Hawaiian blood. Right? The old woman, Freddie Delarota, Robert Hall, even that diver, Wyman, all of them had Hawaiian ancestry."

"Yes," Chazz said.

"Collins? The Canadian girl?" Takamura asked gently.

"The Canadian girl was murdered, throat cut. Collins could be part Hawaiian, or it could have been something else he died of, or they poisoned him."

Patria said, "This is some kind of racist proposal."

"Yes, it looks that way. Project Cetus is a cover. Oh, it's real, all right, I'm sure of that. Freeman believed in it, Collins had seen it. They are making boats go faster."

"I think the Navy likes to call them ships," Takamura said with a smile.

"Ships, then. I'd be willing to bet that, inside the Navy lab, though, there is another group, probably smaller, a conspiracy working on a biological weapon. And that they are nearly finished with it. That's what worries me."

"Meaning?"

Patria said, "Meaning that he doesn't know what the weapon is, but it has something to do with a common genotype of some sort. They could design something that would go after ethnic genotypes."

"Right," Chazz agreed. "It's worse than that, though. It couldn't work. Not anymore. There's been too much mixing. I doubt if there's a single population in the world today that doesn't share genes. I don't think it could be fine-tuned precisely enough. That's what scares me. Human subgroups may have complex families of genes that could help identify them, but it'd be extremely difficult to find them precisely . . . Unless . . ."

"Unless?"

"Unless the mitochondria is important after all."

Billy was cleaning the pool. He waved cheerfully and shook his head as the three walked past. The pool was a mess. One of the trees was almost down; the other two were leaning precariously; the surface of the pool was still so covered with palm fronds it was difficult to see the water.

"Gotta clean up, Dr. K. Never any end to it."

Chazz nodded. "Never any end."

Later they sat in the living room and watched the darkness gather. No one moved for a long time. The gecko chirped in the rafters. Mynas hopped on the lawn. Chazz stared out at the scrub and thought of Renfrew hiding somewhere. Never any end.

"We're going to have to move," Chazz said finally.

"Mm." Takamura didn't seem interested.

"Thinking about Sammy?"

"Mm."

"How is he?"

Takamura stirred in the twilight. "Holding his own. Barely. Lung punctured, just missed the aorta, two ribs. He'll be lucky if he lives. Very lucky. Longer he lives, though, the better his chances. They say. I miss him. There's something else."

"What's that?"

"He's Hawaiian. If what you think is true, he'll be a prime target. Ground zero, I think they call it."

"That's nuclear weapons," Patria said.

Takamura shrugged, almost invisible in the darkness.

"He'll live," Chazz said gently. "I know it."

"Sure."

Chazz repeated what he'd said before. "Something keeps nagging at me, Cobb. Something about the kahuna at the Russian fort . . . Going after Hawaiians doesn't make sense. What would be the point? We've got to do something. We have to make a move."

"Any ideas?"

"We've got to take a look."

61

Silver worried at the ridge of bone just under his temple with a lean finger. His tiny office was just big enough for a small workbench and the chair in which he was sitting, rubbing that small spot beside his temple. Goode hung in the doorway watching him with annoyance.

"What's wrong?" he asked finally.

Silver looked up, saw his own hand hovering near his head and put it abruptly on the workbench.

"Come on, Ben. You do that when something's bothering you."

"We're rushing it," he said slowly. "It's not ready, not yet. With the vector the way it is, deploying it is risky. The last batch mutated again."

"What are the numbers?" Goode asked.

"Fifty-five percent."

"Better than fifty-fifty," Goode said. "It'll have to do. We're out of time."

"We're setting national policy, Jim! We don't have the authority! If we had ninety percent certainty. Even eighty . . ."

Goode examined the ceiling as if examining architectural details of interest. Involuntarily, Ben looked there too. Acoustical tile.

"Ben," Goode began, still gazing upward, "we're not setting national policy, and you know it. We're creating a situation in which national policy can be implemented in a certain way, or not. We're providing the chief executive with an option, a good one, that's all. The decision isn't ours to make. We don't have to make the choice. They gave Truman the atomic bomb; they didn't use it, he did. This is the same thing. Believe me." He looked at Silver then. "Believe me," he repeated.

Their eyes locked, motionless. Very slowly, hesitantly, Silver's index finger rose again to his temple and he began to rub.

"Everything's set," Goode said softly. "Don't worry. Just finish what's begun."

Silver nodded without looking up. The officer withdrew. After a few moments Silver left the room. At a pressure-sealed door he opened a clothing cabinet. He slipped a paper cap over his head, a mask over his nose and mouth. He gowned, slipped off his shoes and put on paper slippers. A frame offered him rubber gloves. He pressed a coded sequence into the lock beside the door, which sighed open. He entered a small chamber. Pressurized air showered over him. The next door closed behind him, and his ears popped as the pressure equalized. He keyed in another sequence into another electronic lock, and the inner door opened slowly.

The room beyond was large, cool and scrupulously clean. The hidden lights had an orange tint; the benches along the walls were surfaced with a white slick plastic laminate; even the walls seemed to repel dirt. A breeze flowed through the room, maintaining laminar flow over the workbenches. Silver knew that the space above and around the room itself was packed with equipment, pipes and ducts, cables, wiring, filter after filter. Air flowing out was sterilized with heat, ultraviolet radiation and a set of electric grids that killed any organism that may have evaded the earlier precautions. This was a P4 containment facility, with the finest, most advanced and sophisticated kinds of physical barriers to anything, living or dead, larger than .05 microns in diameter either entering or leaving the room.

He still did not feel safe, even here. No one could feel safe in this environment.

Yet the risks were not so great, nor the precauations here so elaborate, as the room beyond it: P5. Pressure suits, impermeable membranes and special atmosphere were used in there. He could work on materials in the P5 room from here using a series of glove boxes along the walls, or he could, if necessary, put on a pressure suit and go into the P5 room itself.

Incubators, centrifuges and refrigerators lined the walls beyond the glove boxes. Flasks inside them contained extraordinarily virulent life, microbes or viruses that waited; that divided and ate and waited to kill. It was a seething veneer of life which barely concealed the skull of death.

Silver did not like it. Two people had gotten careless in this laboratory over the past three years. Their bodies had been incinerated for seventy-two hours in the furnace set into the far wall rather than allow an opportunity for what their bodies had taken in to escape outside. The ashes had been subjected to another set of decontamination processes, the same ultraviolet radiation, but more intense and longer-lasting, the same filtering processes, acid baths, alkaline baths and final neutralization baths. The remains had been ground or dried to dust, heated again, sterilized utterly, buried.

Such procedures were expensive. The budget for this project was nonexistent. It was large and could not possibly have been concealed. Which was why the *Valiant* had been such an essential part of the plan, why that man Wyman had to die. Fortunately, he had also been a suitable subject for the Lolo Project.

But there were international laws, national laws, hell, even local laws against what went on in this laboratory. There were treaties that had been sacred for eighty years or more. Governments would fall if word of this project got out. People would die if the bugs got out, a very large number of people.

People, Silver thought—as the door sighed shut behind him and latched with a small but heavy sound—would die anyway. Some people already had.

That was the business of this laboratory; that was his business. He knew how important it was, how essential. What they did here would, after next week, prevent World War III. So he went to work.

A refrigerated cabinet was filled with small vials labeled with codes and names. Here were samples from everyone at the Pacific Missile Approach Network, samples that had once been blood but now were minute amounts of viscous fluid: mitochondrial DNA. A twisted double chain almost six feet long when unraveled, but so thin it would not be visible except under the scanning beam of the electron microscope; a strip of computer tape with the physical, mental and emotional identity of a human being. Somewhere on that molecule might be the information on a man's general character, the age at which his toenails would begin to yellow, his hair fall out, his eyesight fail.

Ben Silver's vial was in there. So was Jim Goode's, and Charles Koenig's. The new one was labeled Patria Koenig.

So much genetic variety! Silver looked at the ranks of bottles sadly. It was too bad that all these people didn't have more in common, that they didn't share his ideals and concerns as well as his genotype. Diversity had made his job extremely difficult, but in the end he had found the common thread and the vulnerable point that thread would lead to. He could plant the deadly seeds in those bottles at that point. He could pull the thread that tied them all together. He could do what was necessary; he could make them dance or sing or die.

He went to work.

62

Renfrew crossed the spine of the island, moving as swiftly as he could beneath the power lines. There was a dirt service trail under the wires, and as often as it was safe he stayed on it. Initially his one desire was to put distance between himself and the Koloa Mill. From time to time he took to nearly invisible trails he knew about, but the service road was faster, and Renfrew was in a hurry.

It was not a great distance, as the rare Hawaiian crow called 'alala flew, but the ascent was rugged; the road twisted, badly maintained, difficult and wet.

At times he skirted the housing developments at Kawaihau; the road climbed the steep slopes of ridges, followed their spines northeast through rain forest, descended into narrow valleys thick with ferns. At one time he walked for three hours through a wild bamboo forest where the trees were thirty or forty feet tall and darkness settled around him. The trees cracked and barked in the dim light with a sound like gunshots from different directions. The trunks were sometimes six inches in diameter, bare to great heights, then thickly branched, so the leaves brushed against one another in continuous whispering. The trail under here was extremely wet and slow, and mosquitoes filled the air, hung in a cloud around him and covered him with bites. Despite the mud he daubed on the exposed skin of his face and hands, they managed to get through. Finally he forced himself to stop slapping at them and settled into a jogging rhythm where nothing existed but the suck and pull of the trail at his feet.

He rejoined the power lines after a time, moving parallel to the north coast of the island, passing within a few hundred yards of the shack where the old lady had lived. He had to ford the river there, holding his bow above his head. He kept moving.

It took him two days. He arrived at the Ke'e Beach at the head of the Na Pali Coast Trail. Even at this time of year all the campsites were taken, and hikers trudged west along the eleven-mile trail to Kalalau Beach. There was, Renfrew knew, a trail crew cabin halfway in at Hanakoa where he could stay the night. Just another hiker.

It was raining again. Drops fell on the broad, notched leaves of the ti, dripped down their graceful stems. Kukui, koa and hala trees crowded the edge of the trail. He ran in the rain.

He found some mountain apples, called ohia ai, and paused to eat the crisp white meat. Later he found guava and mango.

It was dusk by the time he got to Hanakoa. There were three people in the cabin, two wispy-bearded boys and a girl changing her shirt. She had a narrow face and large breasts. Renfrew gave her an intense look. She turned toward him as she slipped on a dry tank top in the gloom of the cabin.

The two boys were preoccupied with their bedding. One of them turned just as she was rolling the tight top over her breasts, saw Renfrew staring, and growled at him. "What're you looking at, pal?"

Renfrew glanced at him casually. He reached back slowly and unslung his bow case, placing it between his feet on the plywood floor. He removed his pistol belt with his bayonet and canteen slung on it. He placed them on the floor as well without taking his eyes from the boy's.

The boy looked away. "Come on, Swett," he said to his companion. Swett looked up in surprise. It took him a few moments to read the situation. Renfrew, out of the corner of his eye, watched understanding dawn. Swett didn't say a word, but began in silence to roll his sleeping bag up again.

"You coming, Dora?" the first boy asked the girl. She didn't even look at him, but occupied herself with putting down her own bedding. Swett left the cabin without looking back.

The other boy paused at the doorway to glare at Dora. She did not appear to notice. She was sitting cross-legged against the wall, her pale thighs below her shorts gleaming in the darkness. She was opening a can of peaches with a Swiss Army knife. She didn't change expression when the boy turned and vanished into the twilight outside.

Renfrew ignored her. He opened his own pack, pulled out some of the fruit he'd picked, and some dried meat. He chewed thoughtfully in complete silence. It was as if there was no one else in the cabin with him. The windows had plywood shutters, closed now to keep out the insects, and the darkness was complete by the time he finished eating. He put away his food by touch.

"You a hunter?" the girl asked in the dark.

Renfrew grunted. He moved his pack under his head for a pillow, curled into a half-fetal position and dropped asleep in moments. Sometime in the middle of the night she came to him like a moth to flame. He made love to her with a silent ferocity that made her cry out through teeth gritted in pleasure. Afterward he fell asleep instantly.

Later in the darkness he awoke with the sense there was someone else in the hut. Fully awake at last, he saw the red-glinting eyes of the kahuna Kalaipahoa. A faint glow clung around his mustache and hair. The figure, seated cross-legged, stared at Renfrew in the dark.

"I warned you," Kalaipahoa said in a low voice.

Renfrew tried to move, but could not. He sat paralyzed for hours.

In the morning the hut was empty.

It was noon when he reached the Kalalau Beach, a long, gentle curve of white sand. Rain was intermittent, alternating with harsh sun in the open. The fragrance of beach naupaka was so intense it was almost nauseating. Renfrew jogged doggedly down the beach to the end. There was a volcanic spur into the water. The only way around it was to swim. He sealed his bow case and plunged in. The waves were enormous in the winter season, the currents treacherous; it took Renfrew forty-five minutes to make it around the point to the small beach. He ran, dripping, down the middle of the lava tube in the running water. On the other side he continued without pause to the secret trail of the ancient *alii*.

Two hours later he was inside the Koke'e Park. Whenever he sighted people, he hid. At night he camped again. Next morning he moved through dense mist to the Coast Guard lookout. From there he moved down the west side of the Waimea Canyon, descended Kahelu Ridge into a westward-running ravine toward the desert. He came across a family of feral goats, killed a kid with one arrow, butchered, cooked and ate some of it, leaving the rest to the birds.

It was late afternoon when he reached the desert. There was little cover, and he had to negotiate the barbed-wire fences of cattle ranches. He'd left the rain behind him in the mountains, and his shoes and legs were white with the dust that puffed up at every step. The heat was intense, and he was forced to wipe off his face every few minutes.

He waited in scrub at the edge of the Naval Facility. The Cyclone fence was topped with barbed wire. The tall confusion of radio masts cluttered the horizon in two places. Otherwise there was nothing to see from here. He waited.

Toward six, a twin-engined Navy plane banked in from the south and landed at the airstrip out of sight. Even the sound of engines died away once it had dipped below the low hills.

He waited.

Finally it was dark. He slipped across the Mana Road to the Cyclone fence. Renfrew had decided who his employers were.

63

"It's not the Hawaiian genotype," Chazz announced. "It's not Hawaiians at all."

"I thought that was what they all had in common." Patria chewed a fingernail, looked at it thoughtfully, then folded her hands in her lap.

"That's what I thought. But consider. Where did we first see the kahuna, and, I think now, Renfrew?"

"The Russian fort. Oh, no."

"That's the common genotype sequence. It's so obvious I missed it. Cobb, look. In 1817 quite a few Russians lived on this island. They would have descendants here. All the victims have Hawaiian blood, true. But I would bet they also have Russian ancestors. Female ancestors. Robert Hall, hm? His real name was Luria, a Russian name. Was his mother Russian? And didn't you say something about Sally Cameron's mother being Russian? Someone did some geneological homework. Then, somehow, they got cell samples from the chosen victims . . ."

"Kalaipahoa! I did a ritual with him. He took a bit of my skin." Patria looked at the scraped patch on her arm. "They could have my cells by now."

"Paul Ulana works for the Navy? I find that hard to believe," Takamura put in. "Sammy's uncle."

"I don't think he would give it to them deliberately," Patria suggested. "It's a common practice for a kahuna to take bits of flesh for healing purposes. That man Renfrew could have known about it. I'd bet now he was studying kahuna."

"At the Fort! Of course. Renfrew was learning that day. Calling sharks. It means they might have my cells too," Chazz said grimly. "That's what they were doing in the condo, disguised as the phone company . . . my comb, brush, any number of samples left around. It's even easier to do with individual genotypes. Match any long random stretch. We're on the list."

"This is incredible," Takamura said. "It sounds like voodoo. How could it work?"

"Think about the mole," Chazz said. "He sits there waiting. He's one of us, does what we do, but he's burrowed in, waiting. Then something happens. A signal is given. He is activated."

"Activated?" Takamura asked politely.

Chazz nodded. "Activated. He does a job, performs some function. Something uncharacteristic, something that doesn't belong, that isn't what he does when he's one of us. He spies, he steals, he makes a phone call, he meets someone he doesn't know in a park. Of course, the parks are usually in England. The English are better at this sort of thing."

"Ah," Takamura said. "You're joking. You have been reading fiction."

Again Chazz nodded. "This is not fiction, though, and we're not talking about human beings. We're talking about a nucleic-acid molecule. Ordinarily . . ." He leaned back and orated. "Ordinarily DNA is highly redundant. A long stretch would have many repetitions, start and stop signals, recognition sites and so on. Nature can be quite profligate with it; after all, it is a skinny little molecule and a lot can fit in a small space. Repetition pays off. Redundancy. Important for critters that don't like to change much. We like to have human beings for children, not lizards or lambs.

"But nature can be economical, too. The genetic code is made up of words. The words have three 'letters,' codons. Three bases to a codon. A series of exchanges go on; the message is read, translated, sent; proteins are made. Imagine you want to compress a message, pack it into a smaller space. You can overlap words. Start at a letter, read a word. Later, start at letter number two, and read a word. Change the frame, and it's a different word. Very economical. Each pass through the message could work like that, if the encoder was very clever. It would then all depend on where you started reading what the message was. A viroid does this. It makes DNA that fits into the host's DNA. A new gene, or series of genes, is there waiting. A mole, you see. An intruder. Waiting."

He paused. Behind him, out the window, the forest was splashed with light and dark. The patches moved like disease across the island's skin.

"The mole is a potential, waiting for a signal. If the signal comes, the gene produces a botulism protein or some kind of fast kuru. Something that interferes with nerve cells, produces the effects we saw. If the signal isn't sent, no harm is done."

It was raining on the side of Wai'ale'ale, a dense gray cloud trailing veils of heavy rain behind it. The rain fell into sunlight. A rainbow sat in there, distant and small and pure.

"Like us. Waiting," Patria said softly.

Chazz shifted in his chair. "What time did you tell him to be here?" he asked Takamura. It was the third time he'd asked.

Takamura smiled. "Nine. He'll be here, don't worry."

"Okay, I won't worry." Chazz worried.

"The victims didn't wait. Renfrew, or someone else, got to them and they died. There was no signal sent." Patria's hands were folded in her lap, but her fine knuckles were yellowish in the fading twilight.

"Two possibilities," Chazz said. "One, they weren't ready with the two-part procedure and wanted to test the second stage alone; or, two, they administered the mole and its signal at the same time. It doesn't matter. It must be a two-step process. If it isn't, we'll have the end of the world. I don't think these people are that stupid."

"Is it possible?" Patria asked. "Is it really possible to do something like this?"

"Once someone has thought of it and is determined to try it, it's possible. A lot of work, a considerable investment in resources, but possible. This is not a terrorist group tailoring an antibiotic-resistant typhus. That would be cheap to do, but in the end relatively easy to handle. This involved a lot of research. A lot. You would think someone in Congress or in some other oversight committee would have found it in the budget."

"The *Valiant*," Patria suggested. "She was full of platinum. It would explain why they killed Wyman. He had the propeller in his garage. He was close to finding the wreck. This group had been removing the platinum, using it to fund the research. No concealed budget."

"I expect you're right," Takamura said. "But of course it's against international law, every treaty, common decency. The Biological Weapons Convention expressly prohibits the use of recombinant DNA for biological warfare. Unfortunately, if I understand you correctly, it does not prohibit research for so-called 'defensive purposes.'"

Chazz nodded. "The problem is, it's a damned sly idea. A potential. Infect the other side. Tell them about it and force capitulation. Perhaps a little demonstration; a minority group, perhaps. It would be like the atomic bomb. There was a debate whether to explode it over the ocean, just a demonstration of its power. They decided it was more effective to use it on people. That's the way they think. Or publish enough of the data to convince their scientists it's there. Tell them what to look for in the genotype. A lethal remote-controlled bomb that would kill only the enemy. Find a sequence of genes common to them all, or most of them, and have your viroid insert itself there. (And I'd bet now it's Dewilliter's spindle viroid that's the backbone, the vector.) Then, if someone doesn't have the recognition sequence, the viroid does not insert itself and disappears. You've got to admire them. It's very clever. I hope it isn't Ben Silver. He's a good man, a good scientist. The best, in fact. That's what makes him so likely for this. If anyone could do it, he could. Damn."

The rain had swept past, and the rainbow faded into the gloom. Chazz got up to turn on the lights, and the landscape disappeared into darkness.

He sat down heavily again. "They were testing the goddamned thing. On Wyman, and Cameron, that junkie. On the kids. Testing it on human beings. It kills fast and very unpleasantly. The ritual mutilations were probably Renfrew's embellishments. They were testing several ways of administering it. Aerosols, injections. Viral material would be absorbed quickly into the mucosa, the lungs. They could doctor cigarettes. The girl smoked. It could recognize a tissue, a cell type. Migrate there. They could make it sexually transmissible. They could do any damned thing. Not easy, but possible. They could make it any length, make it as specific or general as they wanted. It could be tailored for one individual or a nationality. That would be sloppy, of course. Trying to make it work only on Russians. Others might die. There would be casualties on our side. 'Acceptable' casualties, presumably. Christ."

In the silence that followed his outburst, there was a soft knock at the door.

Takamura got up. "That'll be him."

Chazz nodded. He said to Patria, "You know what you have to do?"

"Of course," she snapped, then softened. "Yes, I know. Don't worry."

"Good." Chazz stood as Shinawa Hiroshi, *Shihan*, master teacher, eighth-degree black belt in aikido, holder of advanced ranks in a number of other ancient arts from ninja-jutsu to flower arranging, entered the room. The older man smiled. "Are you ready to die?" he asked, and Chazz, palms together, bowed.

"Let's go," Takamura said. He smiled. "We'll go to their nest. After all, 'Birds never divide worm until safe in nest.' "

Chazz shook his head as he snapped off the lights. They all left together. Outside, the darkness was complete.

64

Dr. Benjamin Silver leaned back wearily and ran his fingers through his thin hair.

He sighed, then slid a transparent sheet of film into the viewer. Horizontal smudges marched in lines from top to bottom. His computer screen read them out, labeled them automatically, matched them with others in computer memory. A few seconds later a soft bell chimed and the words "match successful" appeared on the screen. Slavic genotyping was complete.

He moved more swiftly then, changing to mask and paper hat, gloves and paper shoes. Through the glove boxes into the P5 room he went to work preparing the cultures. Beyond the glove boxes inside the manufacturing facility, he could see a space-suited figure working amid the industrial 400-liter fermentation tanks and the maze of stainless steel pipes, pressure gauges, valves, fittings, coolant feeders. Lambda phages were carrying the viroid sequences to *E. coli*, inserting them into the bacteria where they swiftly merged with host DNA. The processes were monitored and controlled by computer through microsensors performing continuous chemical analyses on random samplings of protein synthesis.

Silver returned to the computer room. As the bacteria reproduced in the vats, their numbers ticking silently across the screens, he slept on a small cot near the door. An alarm awoke him when the first batch was nearly ready; he watched monitor screens attentively as the cultures reached peak concentration and went into the centrifuge. The paste was spun down and unwanted proteins removed by high-performance reverse-phase liquid chromatography, leaving a dense pack of viroid RNA ready for insertion into a viral aerosol, which on contact with the air would form rapidly dispersing droplets. This end result, prepared automatically by robot sequencers, contained the final vector, the spindle viroid backbone that would carry naked RNA viroid to the target hosts on the other side of the world.

Ben didn't hear the door behind him open, so intent was he on watching the screen. He jumped when the voice behind him said, "Quite a sight."

He turned. "Oh. Hello, Jim," he said to the white-suited figure who entered. "It is quite a sight, yes." Silver waved at the screen. "That's the first *Slavophilia* off the line. Once it's in place, we can hand the President a *fait accompli*. No more expensive nuclear missiles, Jim. We'll hold the key to the end of the Soviet Union. World peace is a real possibility."

"You've recovered from your attack of the doubts? Good, Ben. It's an extraordinary achievement, truly extraordinary. Almost unbelievable." They watched as another robot arm placed the Styrofoam top on the package and spray-sealed the carton. The conveyer belt moved another box into place.

"Perhaps," Silver said. "Perhaps."

"What do you mean, Ben?"

"I mean that it's still unstable. It needs fine-tuning. It might not be as discriminate as it should be."

"It's called *Lolo slavophilia* because it was designed to find the sequence which defines Slavic ethnic characteristics. Are you saying it might not do that, Ben?"

"No," Ben said slowly. "I'm saying it might do more than that. The local Russian vector worked, but there the vector was controlled. We tailored the bugs for specific targets. We applied it carefully. We had individual genotyping to work with, to assure the match. It won't work that way in Moscow. Within hours it'll be over a considerable part of the Soviet Union. Within weeks, it'll be all over the world. It should be designed for full Slavic ancestry. That's fifteen percent of the Soviet Union."

"A crucial fifteen percent, Ben. The ruling elite."

"I have Slavic blood, Jim. My grandparents were from Leningrad. We used my genotype to find the recognition site. I'm an American now. I don't want Americans to die."

"Ben. Please. In six months, the vector will degrade. It won't be viable any longer. Meantime, it's been as carefully designed as we could make it for full Slavic genotypes. Don't worry. By the time any of the viroid could blow back into this country, it'll be harmless."

"I know. I just don't like rushing it." He turned to look at the monitor of the P5 lab. The LED over the airlock doors into the room indicated negative pressure, integrity preserved. Condition normal.

There was a loading bay at the far end of NBL-212. In a short time Styrofoam containers would emerge from P5 into the loading bay, each container roughly a foot on a side containing a tiny vial of colorless fluid. The containers were sealed. A television monitor showed the assembly line where the first container was waiting. A robot arm moved out of view, returned holding the vial, placed it inside.

The space-suited figure turned at the airlock and waved at the camera. Then it cycled through and vanished from view.

"I brought you a sandwich," Goode said. He put a plastic package down, and Silver smiled his thanks. Goode went on. "We're not out of the woods. Koenig and that Jap are still out there. Dewilliter and Freeman are out of custody, but we can't use them anymore."

"I know. That's one reason I'm worried about the vector. Dewilliter did a lot of the work on it. He knew the structure."

"It was almost done, anyway, Ben. You finished."

Silver nodded. "You know," he said. "When I was in the Soviet Union and I learned what they were up to, I didn't believe it. If Dmitrov hadn't given me that classified paper by mistake, we'd never have known. The only advantage we have in all of it is that the difficulties for *them* are far greater. This is the melting pot, after all. The genetic mix is too heterogeneous."

Jim Goode smiled. "It's a great achievement, what we've done."

"I'm still worried. It's unstable, but you're right. It has to go as is. How're the deployment plans going?"

Commander Goode looked surprised. "Don't worry, a nuclear sub is coming on a goodwill visit to the islands. Its orders will take it to the Aleutians. From there we have routine reconnaissance flights. It's a simple aerosol. Meteorology has it doped out. Dispersal patterns, prevailing winds, current weather—that sort of thing. Of course they won't know what it's for, but it'll fall all around the Moscow area. If it enters a non-Slavic host, it will dissolve harmlessly. If it finds the target, it'll insinuate itself. A time bomb. From there they infect others. Computer simulation suggests the ten vials dispersed upwind of Moscow will have spread throughout most populated areas of the Soviet Union within six months. After that, if we release the trigger, their losses would be unacceptable. Sixty-seven percent, minimum. Technocrats, scientists, bureaucrats. Since they've done the same basic work, all we'd have to do is show them what we've done, and they'll knuckle under. We could even let them save face, give them some of the credit for universal peace. We can afford it."

"The President does not care for the Soviet Union. Is he likely to let them save face?"

Jim shrugged. "That's his worry, of course. I'd recommend it. If we back them into too small a corner, they might do something desperate. First-strike or some such. Even the President wouldn't want that. No, he may not like it, but he'll let them have some credit. A diplomatic breakthrough. It's a fail-safe plan, Ben. We should get the Nobel Prize. Too bad no one will ever know."

"Yes," Ben Silver said. "Too bad."

"Well." Jim stretched. "Big Fish will be here at 0400. We should have everything ready to load by then." He gestured at the screen. The sixth package was just rolling out of sight. "After that, it'll be five days. Then everything will be in place. Nothing to worry about."

"Nothing to worry about," Silver repeated. He finished his sandwich and headed to the airlock, where he began to put on his pressure suit. He was thoughtful as he cycled through the airlock.

65

Patria Koenig feared violence, though she had confronted it often in the field. Primitive societies tended to ritualize their violence more than technological cultures. Bows and arrows, spears and stone knives were commonplace in her work. So were chants and spells, poisons and magic, innuendo and ostracism, violence physical and psychological, emotional and spiritual.

The methodology of control was on her mind, the techniques of coercion and fear, dominance and submission. Who did what and how. Most violence, she thought, was bluff and threat. Killing someone was violent, of course, but ultimately self-defeating. Dead people were slow to follow orders. Killing was useless as a method of control, except by example: the threat of the same violence to another.

Chazz said that to attack is to reveal in yourself a weakness. Lift your arm to strike, and you leave exposed ribs, vulnerable belly. She hoped it was true.

The bushes on either side of the path were heavy with blossoms. She paused to inhale the frangipani fragrance. Stars were thick in the sky, dripping as generously with light as the flowers were with scent. There was no moon tonight, not yet. There were no clouds, nor threat of rain.

The front door was ajar, spilling light into the darkness.

She looked around, but the dark night was still. Jupiter was high and bright. The larger universe moved on.

She conceded submission was not a good response to violence. It bred contempt, resentment, anger, more violence.

To be a victim meant, in part at least, attracting attack. Show muggers a film of people walking, and they will agree on which ones are the potential victims: the haphazard, the unwary, the distracted, the timid, the fearful. The easy marks.

Bluff and counterbluff. Puff up the fur, inflate the throat, raise the hackles, be bigger, growl deeper, bark louder.

She stood a moment, poised on the walk, steps slowed beside the frangipani. On the dimly-lit surface of the lawns she could see toads hopping clumsily, snapping mosquitoes from the air. She could hear their awkward plopping in the undergrowth.

Her steps crunched on the gravel walk. A blare of radio music spilled from the doorway, faded away, shut off. She pushed the door open.

"Dr. Silver?" she called urgently. "Hello. Anybody home?"

Andrea Silver appeared from the rear of the house, brushing her gray hair with the back of her hand. She wore a large yellow-and-red plaid apron and carried a wooden spoon. "What is it?"

"Oh, thank God. Is Dr. Silver here? I'm sorry, I'm Patria Koenig. They sent me . . . thank God you're here. There's an emergency at the lab, people hurt. I've got to find Dr. Silver. Is he here?"

"Why, no. No, he isn't. Oh, dear. What's happened?"

"There's no time, no time. We have to contact him right away. My husband . . . Dr. Morgan . . . the others. Horrible."

Andrea put down her spoon on an end table. It held a telephone. "Wait here. Please. I'll call him right away. He's at . . . I'll call him. Please, just wait." She hurried into the back. Patria waited. When she heard Andrea pick up the phone, she lifted the handset in front of her, placed the microphone of her minirecorder against it and pressed RECORD. She could hear the tones spill onto the tape.

"Ben's at the Naval Facility," Andrea began, "He'll . . . Oh!" The living room was empty.

The man in the car had a device. "It's quick and dirty, but it works. There was no time for a tap." He played the tape and read out the numbers on the small LED screen. Then he put in a radio call. He started driving very fast with one hand.

The dash clock indicated 10:38. "Come on, come on," he murmured. "We don't have much time."

They were already passing Sinner's Head when the call came back. "Write it down," he said abruptly. Patria nodded, and scribbled the directions as they crackled over the radio.

"Good!" They cornered through Kekaha on two wheels. "Now the map."

She unfolded the map of the Pacific Missile Approach Network. "Where'd you get this?" It was extremely detailed.

"Emergency services." He shrugged. "Just in case. They might have a fire someday. Besides, Hawaiian Bell installed most of their equipment. We owe Lieutenant Takamura a favor or two." His teeth showed in the dash light.

"It's classified." She gestured at the red warning.

He shrugged again but said nothing. The car slowed as they approached a curve, spun suddenly to the left.

The dirt road, barely a road at all, headed toward the beach. Around here roads like this always went to the beach.

The car stopped at the edge of the surf. The waves were high, broad swells that broke on the steep shelf just offshore. They seemed to be very far apart, deep lulls between them. A black object bobbed in a trough. "There they are," he said. "Good luck."

By the time she reached the sand, the car was gone. The Zodiac rode a wave in, and Chazz, a vague shape in black, climbed out. Takamura was behind him. The old man was invisible, hunched beside the motor. A pencil-thin flashlight beam stabbed at the map in Patria's hands. She pushed her scrawled notes up beside it.

"Here," she said, moving her finger in from the numbers along the edge. "And here." She found the second coordinate and fixed the U-shaped building. "NBL-212." She and Chazz memorized landmarks, directions.

"Good," Chazz said, folding the map. "NBL—Navy Biological Laboratory? There's a lot of activity around here. Cobb's goddamn fish detector has been clanging all night." He helped her into the Zodiac.

66

Along the shore by the facility, they had to stay just beyond the break line, wallowing low in the troughs.

"There," Takamura hissed. The Zodiac curved slowly in toward the promontory. Waves were crashing on the rock with sullen booms muffled by kelp. It was too dark to find a landing place. Chazz looked at Takamura, who nodded. A pencil beam leaped out, showed a circle of rock, wandered along the high-tide line. Chazz gestured, and the Zodiac edged along the breakers toward a dark patch concealed by rockfall. The combers rolled smoothly from south to north, breaking off the end of the promontory, trailing out to sea. Spray hid the stars.

Shinawa said nothing. The rock wall fell back, revealing a cave of collapsed cliff face, no good. The boat moved on, pushed by the nearly silent electric motor. The thin beam danced across the black-wet volcanic tuff. Spindrift glowed ghostlike. At last the beam stopped. Chazz glanced back and Shinawa nodded. They rose on the crest and rode the wave in, gravel and sand grating under the rubber hull. The silence between waves was abrupt and short-lived.

Patria read the compass in the pencil light. Then she led the way northeast, into the facility, and the sound of the surf faded behind them.

Low scrub grew on the dunes behind the rock promontory. From the top they could see parts of the facility spread out before them: roads with sparse traffic, control towers, a forest of radio masts, satellite and tracking dishes, radar dome, the empty twin lines of runway lights. Scattered groups of two-story beige wooden barracks. Takamura guessed that the distant building under construction, with a web of naked scaffolding over a visibly ornamental facade pocked with dark, empty window sockets, was the Officers' Club. Shinawa moved ahead, vanished from sight below the edge of the dune. Takamura's watch read 11:52.

They could hear the distant whine of truck engines, muffled loudspeakers. An abbreviated *whoop* of a siren, cut short. Chazz and Patria had the map spread on the sand. They traced their location. Chazz drew a line with his finger to NBL-212. It crossed two roads and at least one fence. Shinawa reappeared, holding something.

Chazz gave him a quizzical look. Shinawa smiled, turning it over, a small black plastic case with two leads. "Ultrasonic detector," he whispered, pointing.

"Go off?" Takamura asked.

Shinawa grinned, shook his head. "No. Ninja walk is very quiet," he said. "Besides, I completed the circuit. No problem. Gadgets, pah." He tossed the box down the dune. It made a sound like a small rodent scrambling on the sand. Someday a sailor on a walk would find it.

He led the way, showing them how to move, an irregular motion, sometimes swift and tripping, sometimes slow and bent crabwise down the dune. He showed them where the detector line was, his completed circuit. They stepped over it.

"They'll have infrared, too," Chazz said. Shinawa shrugged, sure. But the dunes were still heated from the day, radiating like crazy into the cooler night sky. No one would bother to watch: a waste of time. They were just part of the cooling earth, vague shapes dancing in pale heat haze.

The first road was empty. They crossed, single file, swathed in black, invisible.

Around a low rise a group of floodlit garage buildings appeared, surrounded by Cyclone fence. Not on the map. The yard was filled with parked dark blue vehicles, sedans, pickups, panel trucks. There were two identical Subaru Brats parked at the end. "Damn," Chazz murmured, backing up. "They moved the motor pool."

Shinawa put a hand on his shoulder, melted into shadows and was gone.

He was back in minutes, shaking his head. They retreated, moved off east. This meant an extra fence. They could hear the current-click in it, electrified.

"How do we get through?" Patria asked.

Shinawa was unwrapping the black material of his *obi*, his wide cloth belt. He wrapped the wire, found a stick and propped two strands apart. "The way you make love to a porcupine. Very carefully," he whispered, showing her how. One hand through the gap found the ground. Bent over, supporting himself on both sides, his leg went through, then the other hand, the other leg. The current hummed and clicked. He stood on the other side. She reached through, and he guided her hand to the ground, a clear space. She made it. Takamura made it.

Chazz was big. He used his face wrapping to cover the bottom wire, squeezed himself through. Sparks jumped blue in the dark, but he made it. Carefully they let the wires relax, unwrapped them and moved on. It was 0014 hours, Tuesday.

There was a roar, a sweep of light, and they flattened into shadows in the desert. A Navy Grumman went overhead at fifty feet, climbing. They were a hundred meters from the end of the runway, faces in the dirt. The plane circled, headed southeast toward Oahu. Shinawa led them on.

"Halt," snapped a voice to their left. "Who goes there?" They stopped.

A figure stood fifteen meters away with a rifle leveled at them. They stopped, the four of them, and turned to face him. His face was hidden in shadow, but the weapon was visible.

"Very good, sailor," Chazz said genially. "Your partner wasn't this alert. Very good."

"What's the password?" the sailor demanded. His voice betrayed him, though. He'd always feared this would happen when he was on guard duty. Intruders. He had to run through the Identify-Friend-or-Foe procedures, a process he found, in peacetime at least, embarrassing even to contemplate. Yet here they were. "What's the password?" he demanded again.

The rifle did not waver. Chazz had doubts it was loaded, but they had to assume it was. After all, Silver had been warned: Andrea had called him at the lab. By now he would suspect the emergency was a deception, and that Koenig was involved, but he could not know for sure. Hawaiian Bell had ensured that the lines were temporarily out to the Douglass Research Center.

They would all be jumpy.

"Password?" Chazz asked. His voice indicated a frown. "Jesus Christ, didn't they tell you?" He was moving toward the sailor. His hand moved, and the rifle barrel followed it. Shinawa vanished.

"Tell me what?" The guard's voice was suspicious.

"About the password," Chazz said. He had moved to the side a little. The rifle tracked him, but the others were out of the line of fire. Takamura was relaxed. Patria stood stiffly. She thought she would be no good in a fight.

"What about the password?"

"I can't believe this," Chazz said. "Nothing ever gets done right. Nobody told you?" He was incredulous. "If you want something done right, you have to do it yourself, eh?"

The rifle was still aimed at Chazz, though. "Don't come any closer." The sailor's voice shook.

"Sure," Chazz said, gliding swiftly in beside the rifle barrel, turning his hips as he did. The guard's finger snapped back and the rifle went off. His bullet spanged into the dirt and whined away into the darkness, trailing orange sparks. Chazz twisted his hips back into the guard, bringing the heel of his left hand up into the guard's face, a fake *atemi* to the chin. Surprised, the man jerked his head back. Chazz had reached up behind him with his other hand. He casually took a few fingers full of hair at the sailor's nape and eased him back over his hip onto the ground. Chazz had his hand on his throat.

"You should be more careful," Chazz suggested to the wide eyes. "Someone could get hurt. I can't believe they didn't tell you about the password." He tied the sailor up with nylon cord looped at his belt. He cut the sleeve from the sailor's fatigues and gagged him with it. Chazz picked up the fallen rifle and melted into the darkness.

Shinawa nodded; he'd taken care of the other guard. Takamura came back up the road. He pointed. The second road was floodlit. Pickets were stationed along it every ten meters.

There was no way across. In the distance they could see the lab.

67

Renfrew had found himself a rating. The rating's nameplate said BRADLEY, N. R. in white letters. Bradley, N. R. was bleeding onto his Navy blue necktie at the moment, and his nameplate had lost one of its clips and hung at an angle. His eyes were wide and very frightened.

Renfrew held up the half-eaten sandwich. "Spoils of war," he said genially. He took a bite. It was Bradley's dinner. "Sorry about the cut," he murmured through a full mouth. "Excessive zeal, they used to call it. Come on, now, tell me the truth. You're Blue Team, right?" He wiped his mouth with the back of his hand and looked at Bradley.

Bradley, backed against the cement wall, shook his head vigorously, watching his captor. Drops of blood scattered in the narrow shaft of floodlight that fell across him. They looked black. The man must be a maniac. He was carrying the most complicated archery set Bradley had ever seen slung on his back. He was festooned with equipment. He had caught Bradley completely without warning, had the knife at his throat before he heard a sound. "I don't . . . I don't know what you're talking about."

Renfrew shook his own head sadly and took another enormous bite of Bradley's sandwich. He didn't really like liverwurst, but it was food. He hadn't had anything but fruit and dried goat for some time now. "Look," he said patiently, "I'm Red Team, see. War games. That's why I'm made up like this. Camouflage, you know. I was supposed to infiltrate, but this place is a Swiss cheese, for Chrissake. It was too easy. Almost as if you weren't even expecting me. But there must be a Blue Team. There's always a Blue Team."

Bradley shook his head. "No. No, I'm sure . . ."

Renfrew finished the sandwich and carefully folded the plastic wrapper into a tiny packet. "You know," he said as he put the small colorless object in a pocket, "you can kill somebody with a sandwich wrapper." His voice was dreamy. "This stuff is airtight and very flexible. Hell, it practically molds itself to the face. Suffocation. A nasty way to go."

He clucked his tongue. "Very nasty. It's pathetic, really. You Navy people are hopeless on land. You need the marines. Well, my orders are: first, plant an explosive device on the emergency generator at the motor pool. I already did that. It'll go off. No simulations on this mission. It's just a diversion, though. Second, take a prisoner. That's you. So, all I have to do now is take you, or someone else if you die or something, to the proper officer."

Bradley's knees felt weak with relief. "I'm a computer technician," he said.

Renfrew shook his head. "Great," he muttered. "Well," he said pleasantly, "there are really only one or two little obstacles to the completion of my mission, you understand."

Bradley nodded yes. He understood.

"Good," Renfrew agreed. "Very good. One of those insignificant obstacles is this little cut on your neck. It's not supposed to be there. Is it?"

"No," Bradley squeaked, "it's not."

"No." Renfrew shook his head. "I thought not. I don't really know what to do about that cut. If it's not supposed to be there, I mean. Now, as I look at it, there are two things possible." He held up the blade of his bayonet to illustrate his points. "One . . ." He waved the tip in the air. Bradley watched it intently as it dipped through the shaft of light. "One, you could say you cut yourself shaving." Renfrew nodded as if this were an appealing notion. "Of course, it is a bit long for a shaving cut, and a little deep unless you shave with a straight razor. They might not believe you. Gosh, you'd have to be awfully convincing."

He looked at Bradley, who said nothing.

Renfrew leaned back. "Two," he continued. "I could widen it a little. Deepen it, too. Then you'd bleed to death, sooner or later, depending on how the wound is adjusted. That would be unfortunate, and a lot of extra work for me, because I would have to dispose of your body. It wouldn't do to have the body found. You would go kind of AWOL, you see."

Bradley tried to shake his head, but failed. His voice didn't work either.

"All in all, I suppose, I lean in favor of option two, despite the extra work. What do you think?"

Bradley said nothing.

"Of course," Renfrew reflected, "you might be able to help me. Yes, I think there might be something you could do for me. That could make keeping you alive almost worthwhile. What do you say?"

Bradley nodded wildly.

"Good," Renfrew said. "We have a deal. Now here's my problem. My instructions are to find a specific man, an officer. That's okay, except I don't know his name. Red Team was not given the best of intelligence for this exercise. I can tell you what he looks like, though. I can tell you where he might be found—around some kind of biological facility, a lab or something. Of course, he might not, too. But if you can help me get to him—you see, we have to kind of sneak up on him—then perhaps we can find some way to convince them that really is a shaving cut, and not a nearly severed jugular. You'll have to be very clever, though. We're probably going to have to enter restricted areas and stuff like that." He frowned. He was still hunkered down near Bradley, but the point of his bayonet was resting very lightly on the cement ground. He twirled the blade a couple of times, watching the play of light on the vanadium steel.

He looked up, slid the bayonet into its sheath. "Red Team's mission is clear. We're testing security here at PACMAN. This is a serious test. A real test. Security's very lax, but that could be a trap. You're going to have to be very clever. Think of it as a patriotic duty, though. You'll be helping your country. That's a good thing, don't you think?"

Even before the full-alert sirens and searchlights came on, Bradley had agreed that it was a good thing.

68

PACMAN was on full alert. Sentries patrolling the road blocked access to NBL-212. The four black-clothed figures hunched in the drainage ditch watched as moving floodlights washed the scene in a high-contrast light, blackening the shadows in which they hid.

"They're worried. And they're about to move. Dewilliter was right." Takamura's whisper was a small scurrying in the darkness.

"Diversion," Shinawa suggested.

Takamura illuminated his watch: 0147. "Not much time."

Patria moved away toward an intersection thirty meters away, removing her black face muffler as she did. She stood, dressed in black, and jogged toward the nearest sentry. The others, crouched in the shadows, could not hear what she was saying, only the urgent rise and fall of her voice as she pointed away down the road. She could have been a security officer, dressed the way she was. The sentry held his rifle at port arms and jogged off the way she had indicated.

They rose up and moved swiftly through the gray area where the two floodlights almost overlapped. Patria was already in the scrub on the other side. Light sand and stone crunched underfoot.

"*Kunoichi*!" Shinawa hissed. "Female ninja. Good." He tapped her shoulder and they moved on toward the biology lab. To their right was the new Officers' Club.

Traffic began moving on the road behind them. A blue Jeep raced, trailing a plume of dust into the shafts of floodlight. The men in it were armed.

"We need the diversion." Shinawa motioned them down and melted into the bushes. While they were waiting, a patrol moved along the road, poking a light at the dark pools of shadow on either side. At least they didn't have dogs. Takamura, Chazz and Patria shrank back, wriggled silently under the bush. When the light probed toward them, they pushed their faces into the sand, showing only the black-draped tops of their heads, more shadow. The light passed on. They could hear the sentries talking curtly. Speculation about spies.

"Russians," one of them said, the one with the flash. Three rifle barrels followed the beam as it seeped into dappled spaces between branches. Long, irregular shadows fell across a well-watered lawn toward the empty Officers' Club. "I heard Russian spies. After the speed paint. Hell, they wouldn't want the fucking Ferret! The missile that never works!"

From this angle, the scaffolding at the east end of the Club could be seen laced against the dark sky, a silver, bottom-lit tracery. Suddenly a gout of orange flame erupted from the empty windows, capped by a thick, roiling coil of black smoke. Shouts scattered through the night, followed by the urgent rising *whoop*, *whoop*, *whoop* of the emergency siren. Somewhere in the building a bell began clanging. The scaffolding buckled and collapsed in a curiously lovely slow motion.

"There he is!" someone shouted, and a few shots—ridiculous pops amid the bedlam of noise—followed. Someone shouted,

"I'm hit." Not Shinawa, who reappeared on the road, walking calmly.

"Come," he hissed as he passed the bush, and the others scrambled out. They all removed their face wrappings and walked briskly toward the lab. The smell of smoke washed over them as fire equipment raced down the road.

A panel truck was parked at the back of NBL-212 by the loading dock. Harsh lights and a squad of armed sentries inside the parking area protected it. The drive and road were protected as well by a high Cyclone fence topped by barbed wire tilted outward. Shinawa shook his head as they walked past. The fence was connected to thick steel posts embedded in the corners of the building.

No one challenged them. The flames were visibly licking the facade, parts of which had already crumbled away, exposing the inner cinder-block construction behind veils of orange fire and gouts of smoke.

"How'd you do that so fast?" Chazz wanted to know. They were approaching the U-shaped front of the lab. One wing had an elaborate door with sentries. The other wing was blank. They passed the door and moved on into relative darkness.

"Ha," Shinawa laughed almost soundlessly. "Ninja tricks."

The building was more than one story high, but less than two. Chazz had laid out for them the probable structure, with the elaborate interstitial spaces needed for a P5 containment facility. "Assume they need P5," he'd said. "Assume what they're doing is very nasty. It's a safe assumption."

That meant an extra half-story of ceiling space for ducts, fans, pipes, filters. There would be a building within a building, which in turn would be within another: three layers of protection, each one isolated from the others. The third, inner nest would be the laboratory and manufacturing facilities themselves. Second layer would be P4 most likely. P1 would be the least secure. P5 was extraordinary, seldom used, even for those working with typhus or plague. P5 was mostly military, and Chazz was not certain what it might entail.

Interstitial was the vulnerable part of the facility. Ducts were needed to draw in the air necessary to maintain negative pressure in the lab, air that would be filtered both entering and leaving the building. The lab would not want to draw foreign organisms in from outside, and it certainly would not want to release anything to the outside.

At the east side a securely fenced area contained frost-covered liquid gas tanks, nitrogen, hydrogen, oxygen, hissing. Pumps whined and thumped softly. A forklift held an empty wooden pallet waist-high. There was no one around, and the area was poorly lit; Shinawa was over the fence in one effortless movement. He opened the gate from the inside and the others slipped in.

The sounds of pipe and pump covered their own. Leering shadows sprawled on the side of the building, mechanical ruled-edge shapes of pipe joint and pump housing. Sirens, bells, flame-crackle, chaotic shouts filled the night.

The forklift was near the wall. The piping entered the building low, offering no place to step. Even standing on the wooden pallet, the roof was fourteen feet away. Shinawa produced something from a hidden pocket, whirled and threw. A three-pronged hook sailed over the edge of the roof. Shinawa pulled gently back on the thin nylon rope, and the hooks held firm. There were knots in the rope, which he handed to Patria. She wedged her feet against the first knot and hauled herself up. Takamura and Chazz held the end of the rope for her.

Shinawa leaped lightly off the pallet and moved to the corner. He pressed his back into the corner, both palms against the two walls, and inched himself upward. Chazz watched him for a moment, shaking his head. The small old man was a wonder.

Patria vanished over the edge, and Takamura took the rope. Chazz started up behind him as the facade of the Officers' Club collapsed with a roar. Sparks spiraled into the sky, flickering in black smoke which obscured the stars.

69

Shinawa was waiting beside an aluminum intake vent. The sound of air sucked through the first array of physical filters was loud. Chazz set to work immediately while Patria held the pencil light.

"Arson," Takamura said softly, as though to himself. "Destruction of federal property. Assault, with and without deadly weapons. Criminal trespass. We could be in some trouble."

"Not to mention the hunter," Chazz said. A bolt fell into his waiting palm and he went to work on the next one. "After all, he works for these people. He's real trouble."

Takamura assented with a smile. "No shortage of trouble this trip."

"I just wish I knew where Renfrew was now," Chazz muttered. Without looking up from his work he laughed uneasily. "You once quoted your mentor Charlie Chan as saying, 'Trouble rain over many already wet.'"

"Sure," Takamura agreed. "He also said, 'Perfect case like donut—have hole.'"

"You think our case has a hole?" Chazz pried the metal mesh cover off the vent and set it to one side. A filter blocked further progress. "Damn," Chazz said. "They've added some refinements since I worked on design for these things." He started removing the clamps that held the filter in place. "Are you having doubts, Lieutenant?"

"I think of Renfrew, and Sammy Akeakamai with an aluminum arrow through him and doubts disappear,"

Takamura said. "I was just rolling over some of the laws we have trifled with."

The filter popped loose, and went to one side as well. The sound of rushing air diminished to a duller roar. "Think about the laws these people have messed with." He stood up and smiled. "Shall we?" He ushered Takamura and Shinawa to the vent. Patria took up her position. The orange flames leaped, lighting her smile. "You know how to whistle, don't you?" he asked Patria.

"Sure," she said, pulling the headset on. "Just put your lips together and blow." She tested her microphone, and the puff sounded in their ears.

"Ah," Takamura said. "*To Have and Have Not*. Lauren Bacall. You like old movies too." He turned and vanished inside.

"Just call us if there's any activity at the loading area. We've got to stop it. If they load it on a plane or submarine, or even on the truck, it'll be too late. We'd never prove a thing. This's gotta be stopped now."

"I'm not an idiot, Chazz. Just get going." She gave his bottom a smack.

He started to say something else, then tapped his earphone with his forefinger, entered the vent and vanished into utter black.

Despite his girth, he had to press his feet and palms against the metal sides as he slid down. He could hear, now he was inside, the rasps of Takamura and Shinawa breathing over the whine of moving air, yet he envied them their agility here. He did not like cramped spaces, nor the thought that he was going down a shaft that might not have an outlet, which would mean a difficult climb back up in this darkness, pursued by deadly bacteria.

His hands were sweat-slick already, and squeaked as he slid a few inches at a time. He had to press his feet out harder, and his thighs began to cramp.

"We're at the bottom," his earphone tweaked. "The duct turns west." Takamura's voice was a cobweb in the dark. Chazz could not see past his own bulk to the light they had until a tiny feeler of white twitched past him, catching the wall, the sleeve of his black jacket, his eye. "We've got you," Takamura said, and he felt hands on his ankles, easing him down.

The three of them crawled single file away from the right angle of the duct when Patria's voice came on the channel. "The loading bay door just opened," she said. "No one visible yet."

"Time check," Chazz muttered into his throat mike.

"Oh-two-thirty-six," she said after a brief pause. "There's a big fuss at the front, shouting. Shots too, I think. I'll go see what's up."

"Be careful," Chazz muttered. He could hear the fans, feel their vibration and the air moving faster. The rush of air wrapped them all in a cocoon of noise as it first tugged then pulled them along.

"Should be just before the next set of filtration," Chazz said. "Access to replace the grids. Electrostatic filters will be downstream of the fans, after the big stuff is removed."

The hatch was designed to be opened from the outside, of course. The three crouched in the duct staring as Takamura moved the pencil light around the outline. It was sealed tight.

Shinawa moved Takamura aside gently, produced a tool from one of his pockets and went to work. A line appeared along the edge of the hatch, grew longer, came to the corner, turned. Ten minutes later a large square of metal fell in. Shinawa caught it, and the light stabbed out into a low-ceilinged space filled with a complex of ducts, pipes wrapped in white insulation, electrical conduits and junction housings, X-shaped supports. They crawled out onto the joists.

Acoustical tiles lifted from the floor, pushed out by the air pressure below. Shinawa replaced the metal square he had cut out, and taped it. The panels fluttered back into place.

Cable trays, bolted to the joists and supports, ran in all directions. Pipes were carefully labeled: NITROGEN, OXYGEN, VACUUM, with arrows indicating the direction of flow. Chazz led the way.

"Ah," he breathed. "Look." He rapped the surface under

them with his knuckles. A dull metallic clank sounded. "Faraday cage. This is the P5, RF-shielded. The whole room will be contained inside a steel cage. If we get in there we'll be out of radio contact. It's like getting into a submarine." He pointed to the RF shielding clad around the conduit where it entered the steel room.

"Patria," he murmured into the throat mike.

"There's a battle at the front door. Someone's trying to get in, I think. Looks like he succeeded."

"Keep watching. We're going to be out of radio contact. There is a shielded room. If the truck gets loaded, drop the grenade."

"Don't worry," she said.

They moved on.

The labeling was clear on the thick electrical cable they found next. Chazz moved aside, and Takamura crawled forward. The device he had was small, just an oblong box with a clamp, which he slipped around the cable. When he turned it on, there was a brief hum, then the fans died.

"Induction. Power supply is off. The charge will last a half-hour. After that, the lights'll come back on. It better be all we need." His light found the round top of a hatch. "I wonder what that's doing here. It's a safety hatch. See, there're the filter boxes. For emergencies. This is an emergency."

They could hear the sound of the emergency generator whining up the scale then. Abruptly, and unexpectedly, the sound ran out of control for a moment, followed by a series of harsh metallic barks, and the emergency generator died.

"What the . . . Quick, help me get this open. The emergency generator shouldn't have died like that. Something's happened. We don't have much time at all now. Only the emergency batteries are supplying power, and they won't last long."

The three worked together at the hatch, spinning the wheel that opened it. This too had RF shielding around it. It opened out with a puff of air.

"I hope to hell this isn't contaminated," Chazz said as he dropped through a short tunnel to a floor below. The others followed.

They found themselves inside a small rectangular room lit dimly by red lamps. A few empty animal cages were heaped on the floor. A door at the far end was closed. When Takamura tried it, he found it was locked and immobile.

"Don't mess with it," Chazz said. "This is the cage sterilizer room. We might be able to get in through here. Understand, we're entering the lab backwards. The air will be blowing behind us, into the lab. Looks like they haven't used this autoclave in a long time."

It was the size of a restaurant dishwasher, large enough to hold the animal cages. The door was ajar, and Chazz squeezed himself inside. He crawled along the conveyer belt that ordinarily carried the cages through, when the back of his jacket caught on a spray nozzle. He couldn't move forward.

"I'm stuck." He felt Shinawa behind him, unhooking the snag; then he broke free. "Thanks."

The entry door was closed, but swung open when he pushed on it. "Christ, they've given up here. These doors should be sealed. Of course, the positive air flow would have kept it closed. Perhaps that's why they didn't notice. They finished with animal tests some time ago."

Ahead was a short corridor. The room to the left had a drain in the floor, and a furnace on the opposite wall. "Incinerator," Chazz said. "For dead animals. Or anything else that would burn." He led the way down the corridor. A sealed door closed off the only way out.

Chazz stood back, and Takamura went to work. The door swung open. The small room they were in contained racks of animal cages, all empty and clean. Chazz pointed, and they went through the room and out the opposite door into another short corridor. They turned right, and moved down to the end where an airlock door stopped them only for a moment. The door was open. Inside, a rack held a series of pressure suits: clear bubble helmets, heavy overalls, gloves, boots, air tanks.

"Find one that fits," Chazz said, searching through the series. He was locking on the helmet of the largest when the door they had entered started to swing shut.

70

Renfrew, with a small part of his mind, had heard the *crump* of the emergency generator going. He hadn't expected the front of the lab to be this heavily guarded, not by a long shot, and even though he had Bradley's help, it had not been easy getting in.

Bradley had done a creditable job. He'd led him to the biology lab, and discovered the present whereabouts of the man named John with the mustache. Unfortunately, Bradley was now dead, killed in the crossfire.

The guards were also dead, all three of them. Renfrew had seen to that. Well, Renfrew thought, almost dead. One's breathing still bubbled noisily through the gash in his throat.

With both the main and the emergency generators out, it was only a matter of pushing the heavy electronically locked front door aside to get in. None of the electronic security measures was effective without power. Renfrew moved into the building, his Jennings cocked and ready. Beyond the second door, the building was lit only by red emergency lighting. The sergeant at the desk was standing in three-quarter view, talking to someone inside the first office. He had his gun drawn, and Renfrew calculated his options in a fraction of a second before he shot him. The arrow made no sound, and the silencers on the bowstring did their work. The sergeant slumped softly. His .45 slid from limp fingers onto his desk before he tilted sideways and collapsed on the floor.

Renfrew had another arrow nocked and ready by the time

Commander Goode got to the corridor. Goode raised his hands.

"Don't shoot," he said softly. The Razorback broadhead arrow tip protruded from the sergeant's chest. A drop of blood fell from the tip onto Goode's spit-polished shoe. It looked black in the red emergency light. Goode moved his foot back. "You're Renfrew. What the hell are you doing? You're working for us."

Renfrew barked. It might have been a laugh. "Not anymore," he said. "Contract's canceled. It's the other way around now. You're working for me." He gestured slightly with the razor tip of his arrow. The light glanced blood red off the steel.

"I don't understand. All hell's breaking loose. Tonight is crucial. We need you."

Renfrew ignored him as he stepped over the body, touching the arrowhead to Goode's chest. On the way he picked up the .45 and slipped it into one of his patch pockets. "Let's go," he said.

Goode backed away, then turned and went down the corridor. Renfrew followed. "What do you want?" he asked without turning.

"I want the poison," Renfrew said. "Whatever it is."

"You're crazy." Goode stopped for a moment, but the tip prodded him into motion again.

"Depends on your point of view," Renfrew said. "That way."

They moved on to the P4 facility.

"We'll have to suit up," Goode said.

Renfrew shook his head. "Let's just get the vials," he said. "This is the end of your Project, anyway." He swung open the door.

The emergency lights were slowly dimming as the batteries drained. Renfrew looked through a thick glass window into the P5 lab, where a small group of space-suited figures tugged at the airlock door. He could hear systems shut down one by one, refrigeration units, fans, electric appliances he could not identify. They moved on.

"Where are they?" Renfrew hissed. Cautiously Goode led him into the lab.

The cabinet was dark and rapidly warming; the small vials looked black. Renfrew took them all, scooped them into his pouch pockets until they bulged. Goode stood with his back to the cabinet, hands down. "You're crazy," he said again.

"Move."

Goode moved. They were alongside the big window again when Renfrew noticed all the activity. The airlock door was open, and a group of suited figures was moving in while another group was trying to get out. Red-black shadows leaped on the vinyl walls.

"What the hell's going on?" Renfrew demanded.

Goode shrugged. "I don't know," he said.

"Something's going on in there. You're holding out on me, aren't you?" He tugged back on his arrow. The barbs gleamed.

"No. Wait. That's the lab. It's P5, you can't go in there."

"They've been making something, haven't they? Something with these bugs. There's more than just assassination, isn't there? You've got something really big here."

"No. It's not what you think, it's just not very reliable, really."

Renfrew shot him. The arrow penetrated just under Goode's right clavicle, the razor barbs slicing through the second and third ribs and the soft tissue between them as if they weren't there. The first audible sound was his scapula shattering. The barbs, still moving at close to 180 feet per second, carried Goode up slightly and backward against the vinyl and plaster wall, and sank into the soft substance before penetrating a fir stud. The arrow continued another four or five centimeters before it stopped, buried to the fletching in Goode's chest, the steel Wasp head embedded in the stud. Short of pulling the feathers through his scapula from the front, Commander Goode was effectively immobilized, standing on tiptoe. Blood oozed in thick pulsing gouts around the feathers, soaking his white uniform shirt.

"Christ," Goode said weakly. His left hand groped at the feathers protruding from his chest. It came away black with his own blood.

"That's for lying," Renfrew said cheerfully. "Like I told you, you're working for me now. I demand more loyalty than you did."

Goode said nothing. His eyes rolled up. He sagged against the arrow. Pain revived him, and he pushed himself up on his toes.

Renfrew had another arrow nocked. There were three left on his bow quiver. "Looks like I might have nicked an artery," he said. "That's too bad for you. Means you'll bleed to death rather slowly unless I get you down. You should keep your hands up, you see, especially when you're lying. I would have missed the artery if your hands had been higher. Well, can't be helped."

"Get me . . . down," Goode said. He was staring in disbelief at the black shining liquid on his hand.

"You didn't tell me about the lab here."

"National security," Goode wheezed. "I couldn't . . . It's . . . Soviet Union."

Renfrew stared at him. "You're going to off the Soviets? All of them?"

Goode tried to shake his head. He winced in pain. Waves of agony swept across his face. "No. I mean, not really."

"Son of a bitch," Renfrew said. One of the two suited figures in the P5 lab was gesturing urgently at him. Then the figure saw the intruders and turned away, talking urgently and in utter silence.

The lights flickered on, and the blood on Goode's shirt turned a wet, disturbing crimson.

71

Ben Silver was angry and frightened.

The conveyers and robot packaging equipment in the factory section had stopped. The red emergency lights were dim, and the white Styrofoam boxes were sitting on the belt, pushed up against one another. They were finished, packed and ready, bumped up against the door to the airlock, where they would have been sprayed with ethylene oxide and bathed in ultraviolet light. The liquid wastes would have gone down to the acid biowaste liquid sterilizers; the air itself would have gone through its own sequence of sterilization and filtration procedures.

But nothing was happening, and because the lab was isolated from the rest of the world, out of radio or telephone contact, communication could only take place through the plastic diaphragms set into the walls between P5 and P4. On the other side of the window Silver could see nothing in the blood-dim light.

Suddenly his positive pressure suit stiffened on him. That meant that pressure in the lab was rising and the suit's air system was trying to maintain positive pressure. The fans were down and airflow had been disrupted.

Fear told him that P5 lab integrity could go anytime. This could only mean sabotage, and that meant he needed help. He pushed the large red panic button set into the wall.

Help was slow in coming.

Instead, three new people had entered the lab. The tech was huddled against the far side of the autoclave, and Koenig was pressing him to the wall, demanding through his helmet audio system the location of the viroid.

"Koenig," Silver shouted, his puffy gloved hands out, "listen to me. This is critical. We're so close. You don't understand what you're doing."

Chazz saw his glance through the glass into the dim factory area. He saw the Styrofoam boxes. "Really?" he asked.

"What are you?" Silver said urgently. "Just another scientist. Ignored, undervalued. Give us this, people say. Give us a cure for cancer, unlimited power, perfect safety. They demand, don't they, Koenig? And we deliver, we scientists. We work. We work hard. Long tedious hours, days, years! And we deliver, we give them what they want. Or someone else does, and all our work is wasted. Look." He touched Chazz' sleeve with his fat air-filled gloved fingers. "You could share the credit. Come on our team. No more fear, no more carping and kowtowing to the Soviet Union. The President will honor you."

"The President?"

"Yes. This project is sanctioned from the top, Koenig. The very top. And the world will be grateful."

"Grateful."

"Disarmament. Total world disarmament. No more nuclear terror."

"We might keep a few of the bugs, though, mightn't we? Just in case?"

"I don't—" The lights flickered and came on. The air pressure changed again, releasing the clumsy puffiness of their suits, revealing the scene on the other side of the glass wall between P4 and P5. Silver gasped when he saw Jim Goode pinned to the wall and the camouflaged maniac with the bow.

Oddly, Chazz nodded as if he expected it. Renfrew, when the lights came on, moved out of sight, leaving Goode pinned. Chazz watched for a moment as Goode reached up and twisted the feathered end of the arrow in his left hand. Painfully, Goode seemed to be unscrewing the arrow shaft from the head buried in the wall. Chazz asked Silver about the trigger.

"Trigger?"

"The DNA inserts. Something has to switch on the gene. A trigger."

"It's a spindle virus mutation. You'll understand this. You're one of the few. You, and Jim. The trigger is easy. Cold virus. It's going in with some State Department people. They'd never know. The cold winters in Moscow. You don't understand, Koenig. The computer projections . . . six months puts us into fall. We can announce. There's no simple antitoxin; only two amino acids differ from standard botulism toxin, but the three-dimensional conformation—its shape—is different. Uninfected people—non-Slavs—they just get colds."

"And the test subjects, Dr. Silver. What about them? Cameron and Wyman, that couple by the Slide? No antitoxin for them either?"

Silver stared at him. "Are you serious? We had to test on humans. Who they were wasn't for me to decide, Chazz. Intelligence made the decision. Who the subjects were. That was a military decision. The stakes are so high."

"Ah." Renfrew, without a suit, had opened both airlock doors and was moving through the factory room toward the Styrofoam cases. Shinawa saw Chazz look, turned and opened the airlock door. Takamura shoved a wheeled steel table into the inner door. The pumps had started up again, but were not made to cope with this breach of containment.

"You can't do that!" Silver shouted at Renfrew. "This is a P5 facility."

"Project's over, Ben," Chazz said quietly. "The lab's closed." The outer door was open now. Air moved in eddies, not the smooth inward flow it had been before. The door at the end of the hall burst open, and six men ran through, finally responding to the alarm Silver had set off. The *whoop-whoop* of klaxons came from the P4 area now that the isolation had been broken.

"Halt!" One of the men waved his .45 at them. Koenig, Shinawa and Takamura drew back behind the airlock door as a bullet whined off the steel. Chazz waved, and they moved back through the first airlock door. The group charged through as Chazz pushed the steel table, which shot out into the lab and collided with Silver. He fell backward to the floor, hit his helmet hard on the vinyl. It starred with cracks. At close quarters the fight was a melee without form. Guns were useless. None of the intruders were wearing their suits, which allowed them far more maneuverability. Yet Shinawa moved with small fluid grace despite his bulky garments, twisting aside as the men charged, turning slightly away when a blow was directed at his helmet. No-neck, his arm in a cast, and the other man whirled, their charge taking them past the three in the airlock. By then Chazz and Takamura were out the second airlock door. Shinawa hurried through, and they swung the door closed. It clicked home, temporarily locking the group, along with Silver and the technician, inside. Chazz threw his helmet aside.

"Renfrew," he shouted, pointing. They climbed out of their suits and moved down a corridor parallel to the factory. Air was rushing past them now, and a rotating emergency flasher threw red shadows down the hallway. They entered a now useless second airlock into the factory and ran past the stainless steel fermentation vats toward the conveyer. Renfrew looked up, saw them coming, whirled, drew and loosed an arrow so swiftly that Chazz had no time to react.

The shaft buried itself in the door. Renfrew settled, drew and aimed carefully the second time. Chazz and Takamura moved behind the stainless steel vats.

Shinawa, however, stood still in *hanmi*, the triangular aikido stance, knees flexed, weight forward, hands relaxed. Chazz couldn't see the arrow move, but Shinawa's hand twitched and the arrow clattered to the floor, deflected. Renfrew had strung another by now. Chazz moved behind the vats toward Renfrew. The archer heard and, undecided, started to swing his bow toward Chazz.

"Stop," a stern voice called from behind Renfrew who, startled, loosed his arrow before it was fully drawn. It skittered across the smooth floor harmlessly, lost in the dimness under the fermentation tanks. He detached his last arrow, loaded as he swung around.

Silence fell like a guillotine blade.

Kalaipahoa stood in the doorway beside the loading bay which led outside. He held a wooden staff taller than he topped with a spray of colored feathers. He held the staff toward Renfrew and spoke in an eerie chant: "*Make emoole, naha ke kua, eu ka ilo, Popopo a helelei, kau make, e Kane.*"

Renfrew crouched, cowering back. "You," he hissed. "You should be dead. No! No curse, old man. I did you! Damn you!"

He drew back the string. The silencers fluttered in the wind of the string's snap, but they did their job: the only sound was the slap of the arrow when it hit the old kahuna's larynx.

Ulana toppled back through the open doorway into the night. Renfrew threw his bow aside. He slashed open one of the Styrofoam packages, seized the small glass vial inside and started toward the door. A figure loomed up over Kalaipahoa's body, holding a gun. Patria. Renfrew, unarmed now except for his knife, turned back. He ran to the side, away from Chazz and the others, toward a side door leading to the P4 section of the lab, where the corridor ran along the length of the Cetus project labs. Commander Goode was in one of those rooms.

Silver was crawling along the floor, blinded by the shattered faceplate of his helmet. The technician was collapsed against the wall under the observation window.

Chazz ran at an angle to cut off Renfrew's escape. Renfrew saw he wouldn't make it, so he threw the vial, which shattered on the floor in front of Silver. Renfrew drew his bayonet. Chazz slowed and circled. The knife point followed him. Renfrew slashed at him, and Chazz jumped back. The knife followed, nicking the front of Chazz's black jacket.

"You must be ready to die," said a voice, and Chazz never knew whether Shinawa actually said it then or he only remembered the words. Fear vanished, though. He stopped backing up and waited. Renfrew crouched, stepped forward and slashed again. This time, instead of jumping back, Chazz took one small step back; the knife grazed his shirt, and Renfrew, angered by this second failure, reversed the knife and slashed again.

Instead of stepping back, though, Chazz stepped forward, inside the arc of Renfrew's slash. He pivoted with it. Renfrew's knife arm continued, this time harmlessly in front of

Chazz, who gently blocked with his inside forearm while guiding the hand holding the knife around and up, spinning his own body down on top of Renfrew's shoulder as he did. Renfrew staggered off balance, tried to correct, lost control. Chazz now had the blade pointing straight up, and was driving his own shoulder down. They spiraled together to the floor. Chazz leaned forward as he twisted Renfrew's hand and wrist, and the knife fell.

The glass from P5 shattered, and a heavy stainless steel table came through, the same one they had used earlier to wedge the airlock open. John and No-neck started through. Chazz scurried back as a pistol fired. Ricochets clattered and pinged through the vats. Somewhere a steam pipe burst.

Renfrew leaped up and dashed toward the corridor again. Chazz saw he had another Styrofoam container, but couldn't move directly. He crawled back along the line of vats, eyes on Renfrew's feet.

There was a strange whirring sound. Even Renfrew's steps seemed to hesitate a moment at the sound. No-neck screamed.

He was clutching at a metal object embedded in his chest, a *shuriken*, a small disk-shaped star with razor barbs on it. Shinawa was just spinning the second one toward John.

"Stops but doesn't kill," Shinawa had told them earlier. "They are small, but they do hurt."

Renfrew's hesitation was over. He threw open the door to the corridor and dashed in. Chazz had jumped to his feet and was ten meters behind him.

He went through the door in time to see Commander Goode—a bunch of feathers protruding from his chest, the now tipless shaft of Renfrew's arrow emerging from his back, soaked with blood—apply a pressurized inoculation gun to Renfrew's shoulder.

There was a brief hissing sound and Goode slumped to the floor, dropping the gun. He was bathed in his own blood, ebbing weakly. Renfrew staggered back against the opposite wall, staring at his shoulder.

There was nothing to see. But Renfrew's face said he knew.

"He's killed me," Renfrew said wonderingly. Sweat popped out on his forehead, streaking his camouflage paint.

Chazz, kneeling by Goode, looked up. "The viroids will be replicating, a generation every few minutes. Growth is exponential. That's the stuff you've been hitting people with. The couple by the Slide, Sally Cameron, Collins. The toxin is deadly."

"Shut up," Renfrew said dully. "I did my job." He looked at Chazz then and smiled. "I buried the money. I cursed it, too. I knew this would happen. I knew."

His eyes rolled back in his head. His breathing became labored. He seemed to have trouble swallowing. The perspiration had broken out all over his body, now soaking his clothing. The paint ran in streaks down his cheeks.

His back arched. "I can't see." He was trying to shout, but his voice was strangled. He slumped to the floor. "I can't see," he repeated weakly. His breathing rasped a few times. Then he smiled.

Goode's eyes were closed, but he asked in a quiet, surprisingly calm voice, "Did he die?"

"Yes," Chazz said.

Goode nodded. His hand was still clutched around the empty vial with Renfrew's name on it.

"Come on," Takamura said behind Chazz. "It's over."

"What did the old man say?"

"The kahuna curse? Something about 'Let his be a speedy death.'"

"Looks like it worked." Chazz stood up. "You dumped the stuff?"

"We got it all. Except that one." He pointed at the shattered vial. Silver was gone. Shinawa and Patria were using a hose on the small pool of fluid. The stain on the floor washed toward a drain, dissolving, gone. The fragments of the vial swept away before the jet of water also vanished. The acid baths below would kill anything left alive.

"If Silver did his job properly, it should be harmless. There are no Russians around here, anyway. Let's go."

"Right. The truck is outside." Takamura grinned. "We do still have to escape, but as the great detective says, 'Justice can be brought to dead men.' Perhaps we can call on Dr. Silver later on."

Chazz nodded. "Okay. By the way, didn't the great detective also say, 'Good idea not to accept gold medal until race is done'?"

72

Sammy Akeakamai smiled weakly. "Hi, boss," he said.

"Kukui Nut. You decided to stay with us."

"Yes, boss. High-poi diet. I dreamed of ancestors and *ka'ai*. My bones in the woven casket."

"Kalaipahoa made it for you. He's using it now."

"I'm sad, boss. He was a great kahuna, my uncle."

"Yes, he was, Sammy. A great kahuna. We suspected him, but he was a good man."

Sammy closed his eyes. "He made me *ka'ai*, boss. That was good. Respect."

Takamura smiled. "You're a philosopher, Kukui Nut."

"Sure, boss," he said without opening his eyes.

The nurse touched Takamura's arm, and he went out. Chazz raised his eyebrows, questioning. "He'll be all right," Takamura said.

Dr. Shih was sitting in the gardens with Patria, discussing Han Dynasty burial practices. Chazz waited for a pause before he asked, "What about Ben?"

Dr. Shih tilted her head. "No." Her voice was dry and brittle. "I'm sorry. I'm told the bullet went at an angle through the palatine bone, the sphenoid process and exited the left parietal. There was considerable damage to the brain tissue. Frankly, it's a wonder his body is still alive. It won't be for long. A .45 does considerable damage when fired through the roof of the mouth. Why did he do it?"

"He'd put a lot into the project," Chazz said. "His reputation, his life's work, were at stake. More than that, he had Slavic blood. I never knew that. His grandparents were from Russia. He'd crawled through the vector. He'd been infected, undoubtedly. I think he knew he might die of it anyway, especially if the vector was still unstable."

"It's all over, then," Patria said.

"Maybe," Chazz agreed. "But I don't think we'll ever know for sure. They couldn't have mounted a project of this size locally. They had to get rid of the platinum. They had to build the lab. That meant they had to have some backing in Washington, in the Navy, in the Pentagon, the White House. I've read statements of the President's; he believes the Russians are developing similar biological weapons. He's asked for appropriations to do the same. Congress has turned them down, but presidents before now have been known to have a secret task force to do this sort of thing. I'd guess someone on the White House staff planted information, probably in Russia itself, that the Soviets were working on a viroid like this. Silver made several trips to the Soviet Union. A double agent of some sort could have handed it to him. The President could have wanted some zealot inside the scientific community to work on it. We'll never find out, and could never prove it anyway."

"That could mean there's another task force somewhere else, trying to develop it too," Takamura said.

"Yes. I don't think it's likely, but it certainly is possible," Chazz admitted. "It's hard to keep a project like this secret, though."

"Do you mean the other side probably isn't developing a weapon like this?" Patria asked.

"It would be extremely difficult for the Soviet Union to do. There are no pure American ethnic strains of any size. And even the Slavic vector had to be awfully complex and the viroid code extremely intricate. Overlapping is good, but there is too little redundancy. A slight mutation would have destroyed its effectiveness." He shrugged. "We'll never know if it would have worked. It all went down the drain. It might have worked as planned. The chances were better than fifty-fifty." After a pause he continued. "If it could be done once, it could be done again."

Patria shuddered despite the sun. "I hope not," she said.

The newspaper headlines noted a local bow hunter had gone on a killing spree at the PACMAN Naval Facility, and had set a fire that destroyed the Officers' Club and part of a laboratory. There had been fatalities, including the head of the laboratory, Lieutenant Commander James Goode, who had heroically given his own life killing the madman. Because of the disturbance and fire, a goodwill visit by the nuclear submarine *Fortune* had been cancelled.

In an unrelated incident, a biologist from the Douglass Research Center had been seriously injured by a self-inflicted gunshot wound and was not expected to live. The police said he apparently was despondent over ill health.

Takamura shook his head and turned the paper over. "I trust my statistics will return to a more normal level now. This is a quiet island."

"What about those other two, Dewilliter and Freeman?" Patria asked.

"We don't have anything on them, not really. Besides, the Navy doesn't want any more publicity." Chazz smiled thinly. "I suspect Dewilliter is going to become intensely interested in lobelioids again. They didn't really know what the project was doing, anyway. Dewilliter was working on the vector for Silver, but he knew only the spindle viroid part of it."

Kids ran by in dappled sunlight. Plumeria scented the air.

"Shinawa says you learned well," Takamura told Chazz. "He'd like you to take his class while he goes on vacation. His flower arranging master is going to be in Honolulu, he says. He is going there to study. He says the problem with Hawaii is that it has too much. It is difficult to develop simplicity."

Chazz grunted but said nothing.

"'End of journey bring sadness,'" Takamura said.

"Don't kid me," Chazz said. "You're glad it's over."

"Yes."

"What about Renfrew's money, the stuff he buried?" Patria asked.

Chazz shrugged. "I'm sure he did a good job. He probably did curse it well, too. He was very good at what he did. I doubt anyone'll find it. How about you? What are your plans now?" Chazz did not look at her.

Patria smiled. "I finished my fieldwork in Yucatan. I suppose I could stay here for a while." Her voice softened with silvery laughter. "Perhaps children . . . I've ignored their role in culture before. Perhaps even having a child or two—though certainly no more than that, and purely for the sake of science, you understand—wouldn't be a bad idea. Sort of see the problem from the inside, as it were. Besides, I've gotten interested in kahuna healing, too." She touched the sore spot on her arm. "Do you think I could find another kahuna?"

"We can ask The Kukui Nut," Takamura said. "He would know, if anyone would."

She nodded. "How about you, Chazz?" she asked without looking at him. "What are you going to do now?"

"Well," he said, and he looked at her now, "I suppose I might teach Shinawa's aikido class while he's on vacation. And in the meantime, maybe I can develop a taste for nice quiet lab work again. I could do with a little less excitement. Especially if you're going to stay on, Pat, I'd like to experience a little boredom for a change. How about you, Cobb? This was supposed to be a boring island, I heard."

"It is true," Takamura said. "This is a very boring place. We like it that way. So to pep it up a little, the two of you are invited for some of Mrs. Takamura's famous tempura tonight. It's about time, I think. After all, 'Man who sits by side of road sees world pass by.'"

"What does that mean?" Patria asked Chazz.

"Beats me," he said.